Bible
.now

by
Rhona Davies

Illustrated by
Gerald Rogers

CONTENTS

CHAPTER 1

THE PROLOGUE

IN THE BEGINNING THERE WAS NOTHING. IT WAS DARK AND EMPTY AND SHAPELESS.

'Let there be light!' God said. As soon as he had said the words, light came into existence. God saw that the light was good. God divided the

---

As he said the words, light came into existence.

---

light, so that there was day and there was night.

God made the sky and separated it from the waters below.

God brought the waters together into seas and created dry land.

'Let the land produce plants and trees full of seeds and fruits,' God said. Then all varieties of green and leafy vegetation filled the land, from tall redwood trees to fruit trees bearing olives and oranges, acorns and chestnuts. God saw that all he had made was good.

'Let there be lights in the sky for the night and the day,' God said. 'Let them mark times and seasons, days, months and years.' So the golden sun became the light that shone in the day and the silvery moon the light that beamed in the night sky. God also filled the darkness with stars, and saw that all he had made was good.

'Let the waters be filled with creatures that swim and the skies with every kind of winged creature. Let them multiply and increase in number.' Then every kind of fish and sea creature swam and splashed in the seas and the air above became filled with colour and shape and sound. There were dolphins and sea horses, eagles, owls, robins and wrens, buzzing bees and beautiful butterflies.

'Let there be all sorts of creatures to move on the land,' God said. So there were sheep and goats, elephants and giraffe, lions, tigers and graceful gazelles.

God looked at everything that he had made and saw that it was good.

Then God made man and woman. He put them in charge of his creation, to care for it and cultivate it for

He put them in charge of his creation.

food. God loved the people he had made and he saw that everything he had made was very good. Then God rested.

God gave the first people a beautiful garden to live in. It was full of plants and trees with fruit that was good to eat. The garden was watered by a river that ran through it and Adam and Eve tended the garden and worked in it together.

Adam and Eve were good company for each other. They shared the work and they lived happily together. Adam gave names to all the creatures that God had made.

God told them that they could eat anything except the fruit of one tree in the middle of the garden, the tree of the knowledge of good and evil.

One of the creatures in the garden was a snake.

He came to Eve and tempted her. 'Did God really tell you not to eat

Did God really tell you not to eat from any of the trees in the garden?

from any of the trees in the garden?' he asked.

'God told us we can eat from every tree, except the tree in the middle of the garden,' said Eve. 'If we eat from that tree, we will die.'

'You will not die…' said the snake. 'God does not want you to eat from that tree because if you do, you will know good and evil just as God does.'

Eve looked at the tree. She saw how lovely its fruit looked; she wondered what it tasted like. And Eve thought about what the snake had said. She took some of the fruit and tasted it. Then she gave it to Adam and he tasted it too.

As soon as they had eaten, Adam and Eve knew what they had done. They realised why God had told them not to eat the fruit. They had disobeyed God and now it was too late to put things right. They felt guilty and ashamed. Then Adam and Eve heard God coming into the garden to talk with his friends. They did not go to meet him – instead they hid behind the trees.

'Where are you?' God called out to Adam.

'I was afraid, so I hid,' replied Adam.

'Have you then eaten from the tree of the knowledge of good and evil?' God asked.

'It wasn't me,' said Adam. 'The woman gave me the fruit, and I ate it.'

'What have you done?' God asked Eve.

'It wasn't my fault,' said Eve. 'The snake tricked me and I ate the fruit.'

God was very sad. He had trusted his friends. Now their relationship was spoiled. He turned to the snake and told him that he would crawl on his belly from that time on. He turned to Eve and told her that she would have pain as she gave birth to her children. He told Adam that his work would be hard as thorns and thistles would choke the plants he grew.

Then God banished Adam and Eve from the garden he had given them. They had chosen to disobey him. They now knew the difference between what was right and what was wrong. They would know suffering and death.

Adam and Eve missed being God's friends but after a while Eve gave birth to her first child, a little boy. They called him Cain. When Eve had a second son, they called him Abel.

They now knew the difference between what was right and what was wrong.

Both boys grew up to be farmers. They knew how much they depended on God to give them sun and rain for the harvests and to help their animals give birth to healthy lambs and kids. Cain planted seeds and grew crops while Abel looked after the sheep and goats.

One day, Cain brought some of his crops as a gift to God, to thank him for the harvest. Abel also brought a gift of the first of his new-born lambs.

God saw not only the gift that was brought but the motives of the two brothers. He knew that Abel had brought his gift out of faith, because he loved God and knew that all good things came from him. God also knew that Cain had brought his gift because he thought he had to, because his brother had, not because he cared much about God. God was pleased with Abel, but he was disappointed with Cain. And Cain knew it.

Cain was jealous.

'Why are you angry, Cain?' asked God. 'Do what is right and you will be accepted like your brother. But beware of your bad temper or it may destroy you.'

Cain knew that God was right. But he wouldn't listen. He could think of nothing except taking revenge on his brother.

Beware of your bad temper or it may destroy you.

Cain asked Abel to go out into the field with him; he planned to wait for the right moment – and kill him there and then.

When it was all over, God asked Cain where his brother was.

'How should I know?' lied Cain. 'Is it my job to look after him?'

But God knew what had happened. 'I warned you about your anger,' said God. 'Now your brother's death will always be on your conscience. You will know what it is to feel guilty and ashamed for this terrible thing you've done.'

But God was good to Adam and Eve. He gave them another son, Seth, because Cain had killed his brother, and then other sons and daughters.

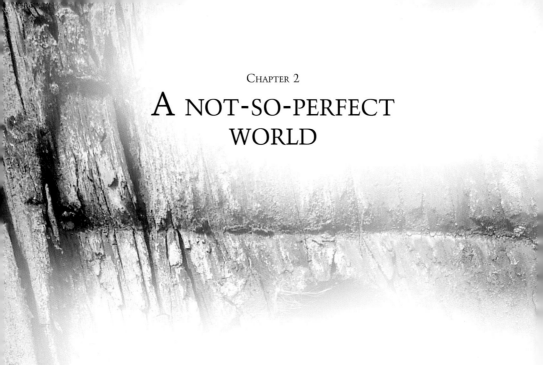

CHAPTER 2

A NOT-SO-PERFECT WORLD

MANY YEARS PASSED. THE LAND BECAME FULL OF PEOPLE. BUT FEW OF THEM REMEMBERED WHO HAD MADE THEM. FEW KNEW WHO GOD WAS. THEY DID AS THEY PLEASED. THEY WERE SELFISH AND UNKIND. THEY TOOK WHAT THEY WANTED FROM OTHERS. THEY SPOILED THE WORLD THAT GOD HAD MADE AND THOUGHT ONLY OF THEMSELVES.

God saw that the world had become an evil place, full of greed, hatred and violence. It was no longer the good place he had made. He decided to wash it clean and start all over again.

There was one man left who remembered who God was. His name was Noah. Noah had a wife and three grown-up sons, Shem, Ham and Japheth.

I am going to put a stop to all the evil there is in the world.

'Noah!' God said one day. 'I am going to put a stop to all the evil there is in the world. It can't go on any longer. There will be a terrible flood so that everything you can see will be washed away. I want you to build an ark – a huge boat that will float on the flood waters. I will tell you exactly how to build it so that you and your family and two of every kind of creature will be safe when the waters flood the land.'

God told Noah how to build the ark. He told him how long it was to be, how many decks it should have, and where to put the door. God told Noah to coat the ark with pitch to keep the water out, and to fill it with enough food for all the animals who would need to be kept inside it.

Noah set about cutting down trees to make the timber to build the ark. He began to make the huge boat miles from any sea. It took him many years of his life; and the people around him watched and pointed at him and thought that he was mad.

When the ark was finished and ready to be used, God told Noah to collect two of every kind of living creature; but seven pairs of every kind of bird and animal that would be used for sacrifice. The animals came to Noah as if they already knew what God had planned, and Noah took them all on board the ark. Then God shut the door.

Outside the rain began to fall. The rain fell steadily in large wet drops until the streams and rivers were full and burst their banks; the rain fell until underground springs broke through the earth; the rain fell until no dry land could be seen anywhere around.

Everything that had lived upon the earth was destroyed by the flood. But the ark that God had told Noah to build floated on the waters. God kept Noah, his family and all the animals safe inside the ark.

Noah, his wife, his three sons and their wives, worked to care for the animals, day after day. Weeks passed, and still the rain fell down.

There was nothing to see for miles around except water.

Then one day it was quiet. The rain had stopped. The ark floated

---

There was nothing to see for miles around except water.

---

gently on the floodwaters.

Slowly, very slowly, the water began to go down until the ark rested on the Ararat mountains. As the weeks passed, the tops of the mountains became visible.

Then Noah took hold of a raven and set it free. The bird stretched its wings and flew, but there was nowhere for it to land. It flew back and forth until there was food for it to find on the earth.

Noah waited a little longer then he sent out a dove to see if it could find any dry land. But water

still covered the ground. The dove returned to the ark.

After seven days, Noah sent out the dove again. This time the bird returned with an olive leaf.

Another seven days passed, and Noah sent out the dove out for the third time. When the bird did not return, Noah knew that it had found somewhere to rest. But Noah still waited. He would not leave the ark until God told him that the time was right.

Then they came out, Noah, his family and all the creatures that had been kept safe.

Noah watched as all the animals went to find their homes on the earth. Then he built an altar and sacrificed some of the birds he had brought with him for that purpose. Noah thanked God for keeping them all safe.

'I will never destroy all the earth with water again,' promised God. 'I have put a rainbow in the sky, as a sign of my promise.'

It was time to start again. Noah's sons had children of their own. Their families went on to have families too, and soon people spread out again across the land. One of Ham's descendants was Nimrod. He was a mighty hunter and founded the city of Nineveh.

'I will never destroy all the earth with water again,' promised God.

At that time everyone spoke the same language. They started to build not with stones, but with bricks baked in the hot sun. First they built cities; then one group of people decided to build a tower. The tower reached high into the sky so that everyone would know how great they were.

God saw the people as they were building the tower. He saw that once more they thought they were great and powerful and did not need him. God saw that they were proud and soon would be just like the people who had lived before the flood.

So God caused their language to be confused so they couldn't understand each other. The tower was abandoned and the people began to make new groups of people who shared the same language. The groups of people moved to different parts of the earth so that they lived with those who spoke their own language.

CHAPTER 3
THE FAITH PEOPLE

ONE OF SHEM'S DESCENDANTS WAS CALLED TERAH. TERAH HAD THREE SONS CALLED ABRAM, NAHOR AND HARAN. TERAH DID NOT WORSHIP GOD, BUT LIKE THE PEOPLE AROUND HIM, WORSHIPPED A MOON-GOD.

Terah's son Nahor married Milcah and gave Terah grandchildren.

Abram married Sarai, but though they wanted a family very much, they did not have any children of their own. They looked after their nephew, Lot, whose father, Haran, had died.

The whole family lived in Ur of the Chaldeans – a very prosperous city – until one day, Terah decided to move away.

Nahor and his family decided to stay behind in Ur, but Terah took Abram and Sarai, and his grandson, Lot. They planned to travel to the land of Canaan, but on the way they stopped and made their home in a place called Haran. Terah never left there. He died many years later, having never reached Canaan.

God knew Abram. God had chosen Abram even before his father moved to Haran. God had spoken to Abram while he still lived in Ur. God wanted to take him to Canaan, the land where he would set his people apart from other nations, and make from them a people who loved him and knew how to live the way God intended all people to live.

'It's time to leave this place,' God had said to Abram. 'I will show you where you must go. I am going to make your family into a great nation.'

Now that Terah was dead, Abram

I am going to make your family into a great nation.

---

had no reason to stay in Haran. He did as God had planned. He packed up his tents and other possessions, prepared his servants, and took with him his wife, Sarai, and his nephew Lot.

Abram's people were nomadic: they travelled together through the land, pitching their tents and moving on. So they made their way to Canaan. Then God spoke to Abram again.

'Here it is,' said God. 'This is the land I have promised to give to you and your children. It's a good place to make your home.'

Abram built an altar, a custom borrowed from all the people at that time. He thanked God for bringing them there. Abram believed everything that God had promised him, even though there were other people already living in Canaan – and some of them were not very friendly.

Abram and Lot farmed in the same part of Canaan. As time passed it became clear that there was not room for Abram and Lot to keep their many sheep and goats, oxen and camels in the same place. They each had many tents and servants. Both men were rich; they had many possessions. But the land did not have enough water for them all to enjoy and the servants started to quarrel.

It made sense for them to choose different parts of the land in which to make their home.

'Let's not argue,' said Abram to Lot. 'We have this whole land to choose from. You decide where you want to live, and I will take my family somewhere else.'

Lot looked about him. He saw that the plain before him was green and fertile. There was plenty of water. It would be a good place to live.

'I will live in the Jordan valley,' Lot said. 'I will make my home there.'

So the men parted. Lot left Abram and pitched his tents close to the city of Sodom.

'I have not forgotten my promise,' said God to Abram when Lot had gone. 'This land is yours. You will have so many descendants that

---

This land is yours. You will have so many descendants that no one will be able to count them.

---

no one will be able to count them. They will be as many as the grains of dust that fly in the wind. Explore the land that I have given you and enjoy it.'

So Abram moved his tents near the great trees of Mamre at Hebron. He built an altar there and thanked God for all he had given him. He had enough to eat and drink and took pleasure in his daily life... But there was something missing. God had promised Abram descendants. He was aware that he and Sarai were no longer young people – and they still had no child. He wondered how God could fulfil his promise.

God knew what Abram was thinking; he knew what he wanted.

'Don't be afraid, Abram,' said God. 'Trust me, and I will take care of you. I will be everything you need.'

Abram trusted God. He told God about what was worrying him.

'Oh, Lord,' said Abram, 'how can you reward me, and make my descendants great, when Sarai and I have no children? My servant, Eliezer, will inherit everything I have.'

'No, Abram,' said God. 'You will have a son of your own, a child who is yours in every way. Eliezer will not need to inherit from you. Look up into the night sky. Count the stars! Trust me. That's how many descendants you will have!'

Abram looked up. The night sky was alight with stars that no one could number. Abram smiled. He believed what God had told him. He knew that one day he would have as many descendants as that.

God gave him a vision of what the future would hold.

At sunset, Abram fell into a deep sleep. He dreamed, and as he dreamed, God gave him a vision of what the future would hold.

'You will have many descendants, Abram, but their future will not always be easy. There will be a time when they will live as strangers in a foreign land. They will be made slaves and be treated badly for 400 years. But the nation who enslaves them will regret treating them badly and I will make sure that they leave that country with great riches. One day they will return here to this land, and it will all belong to them. And you, Abram, you will live to a good old age, and die peacefully. All this will come true in due course.'

Abram and Sarai lived for ten years in Canaan. Sarai knew about God's promise, but she had still had no children and she was not as patient as Abram. She longed to hold a baby in her arms. She knew there was a way it could happen. There was an ancient custom which would allow her to give Abram a child. It meant letting Abram take her Egyptian servant, Hagar, to be his wife too. So Sarai told Abram her plan.

'Take my servant as your wife too. Perhaps she will bear a son that we can love in our old age.'

Abram did not know if this was part of God's plan. But he wanted Sarai to be happy. Abram took Hagar as his wife. Before long Hagar was pregnant. But as soon as she knew that she was expecting Abram's child, her manner towards Sarai changed. She did not want to be treated as a servant any more. She made Sarai feel unimportant because she could not have children. She was not very kind…

Sarai was very unhappy. So she blamed Abram.

'This is your fault!' She complained unfairly to her husband. 'Hagar despises me. What shall I do now?'

Abram tried not to get angry.

'Hagar is your servant,' he replied. 'Do whatever you think is best.'

So Sarai started to nag Hagar. She made her work harder and said unkind things. Then Hagar became so unhappy that she ran away.

After she had been gone a while, Hagar stopped by a spring in the desert. She rested and drank some water there. Then a very strange thing happened. Hagar saw an angel. The angel asked her where she had

come from and where she was going. But as soon as Hagar said she had run away from Sarai, the angel told her the best thing she could do was to return.

'God has seen how sad you are, Hagar, but you must trust him. Soon you will have a baby son and he will be very special. Give him the name Ishmael. You will be proud of

Hagar was amazed. 'Now I know that God sees everything!' she said.

your son and he will give you many descendants.'

Hagar was amazed. 'Now I know that God sees everything!' she said.

Hagar decided to return to Sarai. Some time later, she gave birth to Abram's son and called him Ishmael.

Ishmael grew up to be a strong child and he made Abram happy. But when he was thirteen years old, God spoke again to Abram.

'I have not forgotten my promise,' he said. 'And as a sign that you and your family belong to me, I want you to be circumcised and to circumcise all the men in your family, including the servants. I will give you new names. From now on you will be called Abraham and Sarah, and by this time next year, Sarah will have a son of her own. He will be called Isaac.'

Abraham did not doubt the wisdom of what God had asked him to do. He and all the men among them were circumcised, just as God had said. They were his special people.

Some time later, as Abraham was resting outside his tent when the sun was at its hottest, he saw three strangers approaching. Abraham got up and greeted them. He invited them to rest in the shade under the trees and made them welcome.

'Make yourself at home. Sit down and rest out of this heat!' Abraham said to them. 'I'll bring you water to wash your feet. And I'm sure you'd like something to eat?'

The men smiled and accepted Abraham's invitation. He went and chose the best calf to be prepared and cooked for his visitors. They rested while the food was cooking and later ate the meal while Abraham stood apart in case he could get anything for them. But Abraham did not expect their next question.

'Where is your wife, Sarah?' they asked him.

Up until then, Abraham had not known who the strangers were. But now he understood that he was standing in God's presence. The men already knew his wife's name though he had not mentioned her.

'She is there, inside the tent,' he replied.

'By this time next year, Sarah will have a baby son,' God said.

The men could not see Sarah, but she was listening to everything they said. She looked at her wrinkled skin and bent fingers, then she laughed to herself.

'As if I could have a baby at my age!' she thought.

But God knew what she was thinking.

'Do you think anything is too hard for God?' he said. 'Wait and see: you will be nursing your baby son when I come here again.'

Then God prepared to leave Abraham. He had come with another purpose.

Do you think anything is too hard for God?

'The people living in Sodom and Gomorrah have done some terrible things,' God told Abraham. 'Everyone talks about it. I plan to visit them to see if what I hear is true. If it is, the city must be destroyed.'

Abraham looked down towards Sodom and thought about the people who lived in the city. His nephew, Lot, and his family still lived there.

'What if you find fifty good men living there?' Abraham asked God.

'Surely you won't destroy the city then.'

'No,' replied God. 'If I find fifty good men, it will be saved.'

'What if you find forty-five good men?' asked Abraham.

'Then I won't destroy the city,' replied God.

'Forty?' Abraham pleaded.

'I won't destroy the city,' said God.

Abraham took a deep breath. 'Don't be angry with me,' he said. 'But what if you find thirty good men?'

'I will spare the city,' promised God.

Once more Abraham spoke for the people who lived there. 'Twenty?'

God promised to spare the people of Sodom.

'What if you find just ten good men in the whole of the city?' asked Abraham. 'Will you still destroy it?'

'For the sake of ten good men, I will not destroy it,' said God finally.

Abraham was content that God would be just.

Lot was sitting in the gateway to the city of Sodom when two strangers arrived. God had sent angels to see what was happening there. The angels looked like ordinary men. Lot did not know who they were. He stood up to greet them and offered them hospitality in his home as Abraham had done earlier in the day.

'What if you find just ten good men in the whole of the city?' asked Abraham. 'Will you still destroy it?'

'Thank you, but we can stay the night in the city square,' they answered.

Lot was anxious. He was concerned for their safety.

'Please!' he insisted. 'Come and stay in my house and eat with my family. You will be more comfortable.'

The angels finally agreed and went to Lot's home. He started to prepare a meal for them.

Outside the house, a crowd was gathering. There were sounds of raised voices. The people of Sodom knew that Lot had invited strangers to his home. Then fists thumped on the door. Voices, growing louder, demanded that Lot send the men out.

'We know you have two young men staying with you,' someone shouted. 'Can't we meet them too?'

The voices were threatening.
'Come on, Lot - hand them over!'

Eventually Lot went outside and tried to calm the crowd.

'These men are my guests,' he said. 'They are under my protection. I won't let you hurt them!'

But the crowd did not like Lot's answer. They were used to getting what they wanted. The men became fierce and violent.

'You're not one of us,' they shouted to Lot. 'Send them out! And don't think it matters to us if you die first!'

The two angels pulled Lot inside the door and closed it firmly. Then they struck the men outside with blindness. Now they had some time to escape the angry crowd. People stumbled about outside in confusion, while the angels warned Lot to leave immediately.

'Go quickly!' the angels said. 'Take your wife and children and any other family you have and go! We are here to bring judgement against the evil in this city. It will be destroyed by morning – along with anyone who is still here.'

Lot did not hesitate. He went to the two men promised in marriage

The city will be destroyed by morning – along with anyone who is still here.

to his daughters and tried to warn them – but they laughed at him. They would not go.

So the angels led Lot, his wife and daughters to the edge of the city.

'Now – run as if your life depended on it,' ordered the angels. 'Don't stop till you reach the mountains. And don't look back!'

But Lot was afraid that they could not run that far quickly enough.

'Please – can we just get to Zoar? It's not so far!'

The angels agreed that they would be safe enough there. So Lot and his small family ran through the night. The sun had risen by the time they reached Zoar.

Then burning rain fell from the sky. The cities of Sodom and Gomorrah were buried under it. The towns were completely destroyed.

Lot and his daughters sheltered in Zoar, grateful that they were alive.

Then burning rain fell from the sky. The cities of Sodom and Gomorrah were buried under it.

But Lot's wife had forgotten the angels' warning. She could not resist stopping to look back at what had happened. She was turned into a pillar of salt.

When Abraham awoke that morning he looked down at the plain. All he could see was dense smoke. Then he knew what God already knew – that there had been fewer than ten good people left in the city of Sodom. And God had not let those few good people die.

Some months later, Abraham found Sarah smiling to herself. Eventually she told him why.

'I'm pregnant!' she laughed. It was a miracle.

Sarah gave birth to her baby son and they called him Isaac. Sarah could barely put him down.

'Who would believe that we would have a son in our old age?' said Sarah, as she nursed her little son.

God had kept his promise and Sarah was happy at last. But as Isaac grew from a baby into a little boy, Ishmael, Hagar's son, teased him. Sarah did not like it. Before long she had convinced herself that Ishmael would steal her son's inheritance.

'I want you to make Hagar and her son leave,' she said to Abraham. 'It will not be good for Isaac if they stay here with us.'

But Ishmael was also Abraham's son. He could not drive him away.

'Do what Sarah asks, Abraham,' God said to him. 'I'll take care of Hagar and her son. But it is through Isaac that you will be blessed and your family will grow.'

So Abraham gave Hagar food and water and said goodbye to them both. Hagar began her journey into the desert.

After a while their water ran out. Hagar and Ishmael walked as far as they could but Hagar became convinced that they were both going to die. She sat Ishmael in the shade of some bushes and then left him alone because she couldn't watch him suffer. Ishmael began to weep. And God heard his weeping. Then an angel spoke to Hagar.

'Don't be frightened,' he said. 'God knows you; he knows everything about you. He will not let you die of thirst here in the desert. Take Ishmael with you and go on together. The time will come when he will live to see his descendants.'

Don't be frightened. God knows you; he knows everything about you.

Then Hagar saw that there was a well that she hadn't seen before. She could draw water! She filled her water-skin and went to Ishmael to give him a drink. When they were both refreshed, they carried on through the desert. God kept his promise. Ishmael became a skilled archer and later married an Egyptian woman.

Meanwhile Isaac grew into a strong young boy. Abraham loved his son. God had given him everything he wanted. So he was alarmed when he heard God speak to him one day.

'Abraham! I want you to take Isaac with you to a mountain in Moriah. I want you to give your precious son to me as a sacrifice.'

Abraham was stunned. His heart pounded. But God had always been faithful to him. He had kept his promises. How could he deny him now?

Abraham cut wood for a fire and took Isaac and some servants with him on the three-day walk into the mountains. Isaac alone went with him for the last part of the journey.

'Father,' asked Isaac after they had walked for a while in silence. 'We have brought wood for the sacrifice, but where is the lamb?'

'God will provide a lamb,' said Abraham sadly.

Abraham laid the wood on the stones for the altar. Then he tied his son's hands and placed him on the wood. With a heavy heart, he lifted the knife to sacrifice his son.

'Stop!' It was God's voice from heaven. 'Put down the knife. Release your son! You have shown me how much you love me. You were willing

Put down the knife. Release your son!

to do anything I asked. I will bless you, Abraham. You will have as many descendants as there are stars in the sky and you will have them through Isaac!'

Then Abraham saw a ram caught in a bush. He could give something to God as a sacrifice but his son was safe.

Isaac grew up and his parents grew older still. When Sarah died, Abraham became anxious that his son should have a wife. He wanted to see his grandchildren before he died. Abraham asked his servant to go on a journey to find him someone to love.

'Find a good wife for Isaac,' said Abraham. 'I want him to marry a woman from our own people.'

So the servant took ten camels and expensive gifts and travelled back across the desert to the village where Abraham's brother lived, far from Canaan.

The servant reached the well just as the sun was setting. He made his camels kneel down as the women were coming from their homes to draw water.

'Lord God of Abraham,' he prayed, 'be kind to us today. Help me find the wife you have chosen for Isaac. May she be the first girl who offers to draw water for me and all my camels.'

Before he had finished praying, Abraham's great niece, Rebekah, came to draw water. Abraham's servant saw the beautiful young woman coming towards him.

'Will you get a drink of water for me?' he asked her.

Rebekah not only gave him water but she offered to water his ten camels. The servant watched as she went back to the well and filled her water jar again and again and again.

'She will be a good wife for Isaac,' the servant thought.

Abraham's servant asked Rebekah who she was and whether her family could offer him somewhere to sleep that night. When Rebekah told him, the servant was sure that God had answered his prayer – this was the woman Isaac should marry.

Rebekah accepted his gifts of a golden nose ring and two bracelets and rushed home to tell her family about the stranger by the well. Her brother Laban came to greet him and invited him back to their home.

The servant was sure that God had answered his prayer.

Servants came to feed the camels and a meal was prepared for him. But the servant would not eat until he had explained why he was there.

He told them about Abraham's wish to find a wife for his son from his own people. He told them about what he had prayed and the way that God had answered that prayer by sending Rebekah.

Then the family were happy. They knew that this must be what God

wanted. They asked Rebekah if she was happy to go back to meet Isaac. The servant brought to them the gifts he had with him and the next day he left with Rebekah to return to Canaan.

Isaac had been waiting. He saw them as they drew nearer and went out to meet them. When he heard the story of how Rebekah had watered the camels, he was happy. He and Rebekah were married and Isaac loved her.

CHAPTER 4

BLESSINGS, DREAMS AND VISIONS

ISAAC WANTED VERY MUCH TO GIVE GRANDCHILDREN TO HIS FATHER, ABRAHAM. BUT YEARS WENT BY AND NO CHILDREN CAME. ISAAC PRAYED FOR A FAMILY — HE WANTED GOD TO BLESS HIM JUST AS MUCH AS ABRAHAM HAD BEFORE HIM. WHEN GOD ANSWERED HIS PRAYERS, HE FOUND THAT REBEKAH WAS EXPECTING NOT ONE BUT TWO BABIES. REBEKAH WOULD HAVE TWINS.

God told Rebekah that the two children would be rivals and would each start a separate nation — but the older child would serve the younger.

Two baby boys were born within

> ## The two children would be rivals and would each start a separate nation.

minutes of each other. The first was covered in red hair; they called him Esau. The second child was born holding on to his brother's heel; they named him Jacob.

Isaac and Rebekah loved their

two little boys – but they were very different in character from each other. Esau grew up to be a skilled hunter and liked the outdoor life. He was his father's favourite son. Jacob became a quiet young man and was less adventurous. Rebekah loved her younger son the best.

One day, Esau came home from hunting, hungry and tired. Jacob was stirring a thick lentil stew and its spicy smell made Esau desperate for something to eat.

'Hmmm… I'd give anything for some of that! It smells delicious!' he said.

Jacob seized his chance.

'Anything? How about your inheritance?' he said.

'I will die if I don't eat something now!' said Esau. 'Have it – you're welcome to it!'

So Esau ate the stew with some bread giving no thought to what he had just given away. His birthright as Isaac's older son meant nothing to him.

Isaac began to lose his sight as he grew older. He became frail and old and realised he might not have long to live.

One day he called for his eldest son, Esau.

'Go and hunt some wild game, my son. Make my favourite meal for me,' he said. 'Then I will bless you.'

Esau took his bow and arrow and went from the tents to hunt. It was years since he had given his birthright away in exchange for a bowl of lentil stew – and he had forgotten all about it.

Rebekah had not forgotten. She had overheard everything Isaac had said and she wanted Jacob to receive Isaac's special blessing.

'Jacob! Quickly! Go and kill two goats and give them to me. I will cook for your father, and he will bless you instead of your brother.'

Jacob hesitated. His father was almost blind, but he was not stupid.

'I know we're twins, but Esau's skin is hairy,' he said. 'Father may not be able to see me very well, but I don't smell like Esau; and when Father touches me, he will know I'm not my brother.'

Rebekah already had a plan. She dressed Jacob in Esau's clothes and tied goatskin on to his arms and neck. Now he felt and smelled like his big brother. Rebekah prepared the food the way Isaac liked it and sent Jacob into his father's tent.

'Back so soon?' Isaac asked as the smell of the food reached him.

'God blessed me. It was a good day's hunting,' Jacob lied.

Isaac reached out to embrace his son. He could feel his hairy neck; he smelled the animal smell of his favourite son.

'Are you really Esau?' he asked again. 'Your voice sounds different, yet you feel and smell like Esau.'

'Of course I'm Esau,' Jacob replied.

So Isaac blessed his younger son instead of Esau, his eldest. Rebekah smiled to herself.

So Esau nursed a grudge against his brother.

When Esau returned some time later, he went to his father and asked to be blessed. Esau was very angry when he realised how he had been tricked. But it was too late now. The blessing had been given. So Esau nursed a grudge against his brother, planning to wait until his father died so that he could kill Jacob.

Rebekah did not intend to let this happen. She suggested to Isaac that Jacob go to stay with her brother, Laban. Perhaps he could find a wife from among her own people, in the same way that Isaac had done when they married? Perhaps he would stay there for a long time…

Isaac agreed and sent Jacob to his Uncle Laban, where Rebekah knew he would be safe.

Jacob set out towards Haran, the place where his uncle lived.

When it was night, Jacob lay down to sleep, with a stone for his pillow. Then Jacob dreamed. He dreamed of a long flight of stairs, stretching from the earth into heaven itself. Jacob saw angels moving up and down the staircase and at the very top, he saw God.

'I am the God of your father Isaac and your grandfather Abraham,' said God. 'I promise I will give to you and to your descendants the land you are lying on now. I will always take care of you and I will never leave you.'

He knew that he had seen God.

When Jacob awoke, he knew that he had seen God and he was afraid. He took the stone he had used as a pillow and stood it up like a pillar to mark the special place.

'If you look after me as you have promised,' said Jacob, 'I will follow you always. You will be my God as well as the God of my ancestors.'

Jacob continued his journey to Haran, until he reached the place where his uncle lived with his family. There he met some shepherds and their sheep waiting by a large well.

'Where are you from?' Jacob asked.

'Haran,' they replied.

'So you know Laban?' he asked hopefully.

'Yes,' they replied. 'Look, over there - that's Rachel, his younger daughter,' said one of the shepherds.

Jacob looked towards a shepherdess who was leading her flock of sheep towards the well. Jacob went to meet her and helped her water her sheep from the well. Then he kissed her and told her that he was her cousin. She was so pleased, she ran to tell her father.

Laban hurried to meet his nephew and greeted him like a father. He took Jacob home and made him welcome. Soon Jacob felt like part of the family.

Jacob helped his uncle take care of his sheep and goats. After a month, Laban asked him how he should be paid.

'Name your price,' Laban said.

Jacob thought carefully. He knew that he had fallen in love with Rachel while he had been staying in Haran.

He wanted her to be his wife.

'I will work for you for seven years,' Jacob answered, 'if you let me marry Rachel.'

Laban smiled. Seven years of a strong young man working with him as part of the family – it was worth a lot to Laban. Laban agreed.

Jacob worked hard. He saw Rachel every day and knew that the time would soon come when he could have Rachel as his wife.

When the time came for the wedding, Laban organized a big feast to celebrate his daughter's marriage. His daughter was dressed as a bride and wore a veil over her face as was the custom. Jacob was so happy that the day he had worked for was finally here.

But Laban had always intended to trick Jacob. Laban had another daughter, Rachel's older sister, Leah. The custom was that the older daughter should marry first. So when the wedding took place, instead of finding Rachel under the veil, Jacob found that he had married Leah.

'Why did you trick me?' asked Jacob angrily. He wanted Rachel, not Leah.

'It is our custom,' replied Laban. 'But don't be angry, Jacob. We can make this right. You can marry both

---

'I will work for you for seven years,' Jacob answered, 'if you let me marry Rachel.

---

of my daughters. You can marry Rachel now if you agree to work for me for another seven years.'

Jacob agreed. He loved Rachel very much.

God saw that Jacob did not love Leah and so he blessed her with children. She had six sons, Reuben, Simeon, Levi, Judah, Issachar and Zebulun, and a daughter named Dinah.

Rachel loved Jacob but she had no children, so, just as Sarah had done many years before, she asked Jacob to give her children by taking her maid as his wife. So Dan and Naphtali were born.

Leah gave Jacob her maid also and so Gad and Asher were born.

It was a long time before Rachel gave birth to a son of her own. She and Jacob were delighted with baby Joseph. He soon became Jacob's favourite son.

Laban liked being a grandfather. He also saw that while Jacob had been with him, God had blessed him. So when, after twenty years, Jacob told him he wanted to go home to Canaan, Laban begged him to stay.

'Very well,' Jacob said reluctantly. 'But if I stay, let me build up flocks and herds of my own. Let me have any of the spotted or speckled sheep or goats that are born.'

Laban agreed, but secretly he had no intention of letting Jacob go. So to make it difficult, Laban removed all the spotted and speckled sheep so that Jacob could not breed his own from them. Now Jacob would have to stay longer in Haran, he thought.

Jacob had plans of his own to trick his uncle. He found a way to increase the number of sheep and goats that were spotted and speckled and because God blessed all he did, Jacob soon owned all the strongest animals in Laban's flocks.

Laban and Jacob knew they could not trust each other. Jacob began secretly to prepare his wives and children for a long journey. He did not tell Laban that his daughters and grandchildren were moving somewhere else.

Jacob had arrived in Haran with nothing but by the time he left he was a man with a large family and great wealth. God had kept his promise to Jacob.

But Jacob was worried about returning to Canaan. He had never made up with his brother Esau. He knew it was time to say sorry.

Jacob had sent his family ahead on camels. He wanted time to think, so he sat alone by the River Jabbok.

Suddenly there was someone there – wrestling with him. Jacob was taken by surprise and together Jacob and the stranger struggled all night long, each one trying to overpower the other. The man wrenched Jacob's hip so that he was in terrible pain, but still Jacob would not give in.

You have struggled with God and have not been defeated.

Then gradually dawn broke and the person spoke.

'Let me go now. The sun is rising.'

'No!' said Jacob. 'I will not let go until you bless me.

'What is your name?'

'Jacob!' he said.

'From now on you will not be Jacob but Israel, for you have struggled with God and have not been defeated.'

Jacob was alone again. He limped away. He knew that this had been some sort of test. He had not been wrestling with an ordinary man but with an angel sent by God.

CHAPTER 5

IN AND OUT OF CANAAN

JACOB WAS ON HIS WAY HOME.
HE KNEW THAT HIS BROTHER ESAU
WAS COMING TO MEET HIM, BUT HE
HAD NOT EXPECTED HIM TO BRING 400
MEN WITH HIM. JACOB WAS SURE THAT
ESAU PLANNED TO TAKE REVENGE FROM
WHEN HE HAD TRICKED HIM OUT OF
THEIR FATHER'S BLESSING.

Now Jacob was frightened. He
had sent messengers on ahead with
gifts for his twin brother of sheep and
goats, donkeys and camels. Jacob had
prayed to God.

'I am going home to the land you
promised me,' said Jacob. 'You also

promised to protect me. Please help
me now!'

Jacob divided his family and herds
of animals into small groups. He
hoped if Esau attacked one, there was
still hope for the others. Jacob was
still a man who planned and plotted.

Jacob went alone to meet his
twin brother. He bowed down to
the ground. But he was surprised
by Esau's response. Esau had not
come to fight his brother – instead
he threw his arms around him and
hugged him. Both men started to
weep. Many years had passed and
Esau had forgiven Jacob long ago.

He was no longer angry. Neither man was jealous of the other. Jacob introduced Esau to his wives and children and they were friends and brothers once more.

Jacob made his way to Bethel where he settled with his large family. He made an altar to thank God for keeping him safe and giving him so much. God now called him Israel, and promised that he would have many descendants, as many as the grains of sand in the desert. They would be known as the Israelites.

Jacob moved his tents on towards Bethlehem. Rachel, his much-loved wife, was expecting her second child any day.

While they were on the journey, Rachel began to have labour pains. She eventually gave birth to another little boy. But Rachel was weak. She lived only long enough to know that her husband had named him Benjamin.

Jacob buried his wife near Bethlehem but then returned to the land of Mamre near Hebron where Abraham and Isaac had made their home. He saw his father again but Isaac was dying, having lived to a great age. Not long afterwards, Isaac died, and his twin sons buried him.

Jacob now had twelve sons, but Joseph was still his favourite. By the time he was seventeen, Joseph helped his older brothers to look after his father's flocks. But Joseph watched them and listened to them, and then told his father the bad things they said and did.

Jacob made Joseph a gift of a very special long-sleeved coat. When Joseph's brothers saw it, they knew that he was loved much more than they were and they hated him.

He was loved much more than they were and they hated him.

One night, Joseph dreamed. His dream was so strange that he told his brothers the next day. He had not yet learned when it was wise to tell people things and when it was wise to stay silent.

'Listen to this!' he said. 'Last night I dreamed that we were all binding sheaves of corn when my sheaf stood up straight, and your sheaves bowed down before mine.'

Joseph's brothers exchanged angry looks. Their hands formed fists. They were even angrier than when their father gave him a beautiful coat.

'So...' one of them said, 'I suppose you plan to rule over us now?'

Then Joseph dreamed again. He didn't see the warning signs. This time he told his father too.

'I had another strange dream,' he said. 'I dreamed that the sun, the moon and eleven stars all bowed down before me!'

Even Jacob told Joseph not to boast in this way. The meaning of the dream was clear to all of them.

'Do you really think your mother and I as well as your brothers will bow down before you?' he asked.

While his brothers hated Joseph even more, Jacob wondered what the dreams could mean. What did Joseph's future hold for him?

A day came when Joseph's brothers had taken the sheep to graze. Jacob sent Joseph to find out how they were.

Joseph walked many miles across the desert wearing his special coat. He found his brothers not far from the ancient city of Dothan. But his brothers saw him coming. His coat marked him out from other people even when he was far off.

'Here comes that dreamer,' one muttered to another. By the time Joseph had come within hearing distance, they had formed a plan to make sure their brother didn't bother them any more.

They had formed a plan to make sure their brother didn't bother them any more.

He was saved by Reuben. Reuben didn't like his younger brother, but he didn't want to be part of a plan to murder him either.

'I've a better idea,' Reuben said. 'Let's throw him down this empty well.'

So as soon as Joseph reached them, the brothers surrounded him and pulled off his coat. They marched him to the well and forced him down it.

Despite his confused cries for help, they were sitting eating their midday meal when they saw a train of Midianite traders, loaded up with spices, on their way to Egypt. It was not long before Judah had suggested a plan to sell their brother.

So Joseph was pulled out of the well, sold for twenty pieces of silver and taken to Egypt to be sold as a slave. His brothers then slaughtered one of their father's goats and dipped Joseph's fine coat in the blood. They returned to their father and said they had found it.

Jacob was devastated. He listened to their story and believed that his much-loved son had been attacked by a wild animal and was dead. He was overcome with grief.

Joseph was sold for twenty pieces of silver.

Meanwhile Joseph was taken to Egypt. The journey was long and dusty and all the time he was trying to work out how this had all happened. How could his brothers have treated him this way? Would he ever see his father again?

In Egypt he was just another man for sale. No one was interested in who Joseph was. No one cared about the promises God might have made to his father…

Joseph was sold as a slave to Potiphar, the captain of the king's guard.

Joseph's life had changed. But he made a decision. He would work hard. He would make the best of what had happened. God blessed Potiphar's home because of Joseph. Soon Potiphar trusted him with everything he owned – and Joseph became his chief servant.

Joseph's problems were not over yet. He had grown into a strong, good looking young man. Potiphar was married to a beautiful woman who appreciated beautiful things. When she saw Joseph day after day, she wanted him for herself. But Joseph had learned some wisdom. He was a good servant to his master – and he kept away from his master's wife.

He had done the right thing but everything had gone wrong.

Now Potiphar's wife was angry. She was used to getting what she wanted – and she planned to make Jospeh suffer. She told her husband lies – and Potiphar believed them. He threw Joseph into prison.

Once more Joseph found that his life had changed. He had done the right thing but everything had gone wrong. But God did not abandon him. He blessed Joseph again so that soon he was put in charge of the other prisoners. He worked hard, even though things were difficult for him.

While he was in the prison, Joseph was put in charge of the king's cupbearer and baker. Both had upset the king and also been thrown into the prison. Soon they were talking to Joseph as if they were old friends.

One night each of the men had a strange dream. Joseph told them that God could help them to understand the meanings of their dreams. This meant bad news for the baker – he was executed by Pharaoh soon afterwards. But there was good news for the cupbearer, who was released, as Joseph had predicted.

'Don't forget me!' Joseph called out as the cupbearer shook off the dust from the prison. 'I am innocent! Tell the king!'

But the cupbearer did not speak up for Joseph when he was free again. He forgot all about him.

Two long years went by and Joseph remained in the prison in Egypt.

Then things changed very quickly. The king, Egypt's great Pharaoh, had strange and disturbing dreams. No one could explain them to him, but he was troubled. He believed they must mean something important.

Then the cupbearer remembered Joseph.

'There is a man in your prison who might help,' he said, and he told Pharaoh what had happened when he and the baker had also had strange dreams in prison.

Pharaoh sent for Joseph. He was shaved and cleaned up and found himself listening to what the king of Egypt had dreamed.

'In the first dream, seven thin cows ate up seven fat, healthy cows,' said Pharaoh. 'In the second dream, seven thin, straggly ears of corn swallowed up seven healthy ears of corn.'

Everyone in the court listened, waiting to hear what this prisoner would say.

'Only God can help you understand the meaning of these dreams,' Joseph said, 'and both dreams have the same meaning. God is sending you a warning. There will be seven years of good harvests in the land – so much that your barns will be overflowing. But then there will be seven years of famine. People

God is sending you a warning.

will starve and die. But if you store the grain wisely during the first seven years, you and your people will survive. You need someone to manage the situation so everyone will benefit.'

Pharaoh knew immediately who should help him store the grain and look after the good harvests: he put Joseph in charge of the whole land of Egypt. He put a ring on Joseph's finger and a gold chain around his neck. Pharaoh made him ride in a chariot dressed in fine robes, and wherever Joseph went, people bowed down to him.

Joseph was 30 years old when his dreams began to come true.

Over the next seven years there were abundant harvests. Joseph made sure that all the extra grain was stored carefully. Then, as year after year passed, the harvests failed in Egypt and in all the lands around them. The people were hungry.

Joseph opened the storehouses and sold the grain to the people of Egypt. Everyone had what they needed to get through the seven years of famine.

Back in Canaan, Jacob heard that there was grain for sale in Egypt. He heard that others were going to buy food there and sent ten of his sons to buy some. Jacob kept only his youngest child, Rachel's son Benjamin, at home with him.

When Joseph's brothers arrived, they went to the Egyptian governor and bowed down before him. Many years had passed since they had sold their brother into slavery. They did

Wherever Joseph went, people bowed down to him.

not expect to see him there; they did not expect to see him dressed as a ruler with power to save their lives. None of the brothers recognised Joseph in the richly dressed man who stood before them.

Joseph, however, knew that the men on their knees were his father's sons. He did not speak to them in the language of the Israelites, but used an interpreter, so they would not know he understood them.

'Are you spies?' Joseph asked them.

'No, sir,' they replied. 'We are brothers from Canaan. Our youngest brother is at home with our father. We are hungry and have come to buy food.'

'I don't believe you!' Joseph said. 'You must prove this by bringing your brother here to me.'

Then Joseph had them put in prison to think for a while about what he had said.

After three days, Joseph released his brothers from prison.

'Return home,' he said, 'but as proof that you are not spies, you must leave one brother here and return with your father's youngest son.'

The brothers turned away and discussed the matter.

'This is all our own fault!' they said to each other. 'Joseph pleaded with us for his life but we wouldn't listen. We did a terrible wrong and now we are being punished!'

Joseph understood all they said. He hid his tears from them as he

We did a terrible wrong and now we are being punished!

remembered all the wasted past years when he had not been able to be part of their family.

Then Joseph had Simeon taken from them and bound up. He sold grain to his other brothers and sent them home, but secretly had all their silver replaced in their sacks.

That night, the brothers opened their grain sacks to feed their donkeys, and found that the money they had paid for the grain had been returned. They were frightened.

What could have happened? What would happen to them now?

When the brothers returned to their father Jacob, they told him everything. They explained that they must return with Benjamin or Simeon would die.

Jacob shook his head.

'Once I had twelve sons,' he said. 'Joseph was lost many years ago;

now I have lost Simeon. Benjamin is the only son left to me from his mother, Rachel. I cannot let him go. If anything happens to him, I will surely die of sorrow.'

So Benjamin did not go. The family lived through the famine by eating the grain they had brought back from Egypt until there was no more left.

'You must go back to Egypt for more grain,' Jacob said to his sons, 'or we will all die of hunger!'

Judah would not return without Benjamin.

'We were warned what would happen,' he told his father. 'You will lose all your sons if you will not take this risk. Either we go with Benjamin or we die here of starvation.'

So Jacob made sure that his sons packed not only silver to pay for more grain, but also enough to replace the silver they had brought back from Egypt. Then he packed honey and spices, pistachio nuts and almonds, as gifts for the Egyptian governor.

Then, very sadly, Jacob let his youngest son go with them to Egypt.

When the brothers arrived, they went to the governor with Benjamin. They quickly explained to Joseph's steward that they had found their silver in their grain sacks and had brought it back.

'Don't be afraid,' the man told them. 'Your God is taking care of you. I was paid for the grain you bought. God made sure that you had silver to return to your country.'

Then Simeon was returned to them safely and all the brothers were invited to a feast at Joseph's house. They gave him their gifts, but they still did not realise that the great man before them was their lost brother, Joseph.

Don't be afraid. Your God is taking care of you.

Joseph asked after their father, and then, when he saw his younger brother, Benjamin, he wept privately for joy. When the brothers sat down to the feast, Joseph made sure that Benjamin had more to eat and drink than anyone else. The brothers could not understand their good fortune.

When the time came for the men to return to their father, Joseph arranged for them to be given as much grain as they could carry. As before, he made sure that their silver was also put back in their sacks. Finally, he asked his servant to put his own silver cup in Benjamin's sack.

As the brothers left the city, Joseph ordered his men to catch up with them and accuse them of stealing the silver cup.

The brothers were shocked. They denied that any one of them could be guilty of stealing from the man who had treated them so well. They were so sure that they said that if anyone was found to have stolen the cup, that brother would die, and all the others would become slaves in Egypt…

Their bags were searched, beginning with the oldest brother. When the silver cup was found in Benjamin's sack, the brothers tore their clothes in disbelief.

They returned to Joseph. Judah put himself at Joseph's mercy.

'Please don't harm Benjamin!' Judah pleaded. 'We will all become your slaves rather than that!'

'There is no need,' Joseph said. 'You may all go back to your father. I will make only Benjamin my slave.'

Then Judah asked to speak to Joseph alone. He explained that his father would die of grief if anything happened to Benjamin. He begged to be allowed to take his place for the sake of his aged father.

Joseph could barely keep the tears from his eyes. He ordered his servants to leave him alone with the men from Canaan. Then he wept so loudly that all his household heard him.

'I am your brother, Joseph,' he told them. 'You sold me into slavery, and you wished that harm would come to me. But God, our God, meant only that good should come of it. He has protected me here in Egypt and now he will take care of you too. There will be famine for another five years yet. God made sure I was here in Egypt to help you; he made sure that I was known to Pharaoh so that your lives could be saved.

'Now you must return to your father and mine. Tell him that I am governor of all Egypt and that it is safe for him to come here. There is plenty of room for your families. You will live in the land of Goshen with your families and sheep and goats

and all that you own; and you will have plenty to eat during the famine.'

Joseph's brothers wept for joy. God had blessed them in ways they could not have imagined.

So Joseph sent his brothers home to Jacob in fine clothes and with more food – and with carts to collect all they wanted to bring with them.

'Don't argue with each other on the way!' he shouted after them.

When Jacob heard all that had happened, he could hardly believe it. His son Joseph was still alive! Only this would have made him agree to leave the land of Canaan and take all his children and grandchildren with him to live in Egypt.

Joseph went in his chariot to meet his father in the land of Goshen. There was much weeping as the two men threw their arms around each other.

Jacob and his family then settled in Goshen and made it their home. God blessed them. Soon they had property there, and many grandchildren and great grandchildren

were born to Jacob. He lived in Egypt
for seventeen years, and when he
knew it was time for him to die, he
made Joseph promise that he would
be buried in the land of his ancestors,
not in Egypt.

Joseph had married long before
and had two sons of his own:
Manasseh and Ephraim. Joseph
brought the boys to see his father as
he lay dying.

'I never thought I would see you
again, my son,' he said to Joseph.
'Now I am able to see not just you,
but also your sons. God will be with
you all. He will take you back to
the land he promised to give to my
grandfather, Abraham, to my father,
Isaac, and to me, and he will bless
you.'

Jacob blessed each one of his
sons, and then he died. Joseph
wept over his father and then he
had him embalmed in the way of
the Egyptians. He asked permission
from Pharaoh, and then he took his
father's body back to Canaan to bury
him.

Joseph lived to see his own
great great grandchildren. Before his
death, he told his brothers that God
would one day take them back to the
Promised Land.

God made sure that I was known to Pharaoh so that your lives could be saved.

When Joseph died, he was
embalmed and buried in a coffin in
Egypt.

CHAPTER 6

SUFFERING IN EGYPT

MANY YEARS PASSED. JACOB'S DESCENDANTS HAD INCREASED TO HUGE NUMBERS IN THE LAND OF EGYPT. A TIME CAME WHEN THERE WAS A NEW PHARAOH. HE SAW HOW MANY ISRAELITES THERE WERE IN THE LAND AND HE WAS AFRAID.

'There are too many Israelites,' he said. 'How do we know they won't join with our enemies and overcome us? We will lose our land. No! We must make the Israelites our slaves! We will work them hard and make them build us new cities. Then they will have no power to overcome us.'

So the Egyptians made life unbearable for the Israelites. They made them work hard for them and

---

Kill all the baby boys born to the Israelite women.

---

ill-treated them. But the Israelites were strong. God blessed them with many children and still their numbers grew.

So Pharaoh came up with a new plan to reduce their numbers. It was cruel and harsh. He ordered the midwives to kill all the baby boys born to the Israelite women. The

let them take her baby away.

When her little boy was too big to hide any longer, she put him in a basket and coated it with tar to make it waterproof. She hid it among the reeds beside the river and told Miriam to watch to see what would happen.

Now the soldiers could not hurt him. He belonged to the princess.

When Pharaoh's daughter came to bathe in the river, she saw the basket and found the little baby. She felt sorry for him.

Miriam came out from her hiding place.

'Shall I find someone to nurse him for you?' she asked.

'Yes,' said the princess. 'I want to keep this baby. I will call him Moses.'

Miriam went to fetch her mother.

'Look after this baby until he is old enough to live with me,' said the princess. Jochebed took her little son away to care for him. Now the soldiers could not hurt him. He belonged to the princess.

Moses grew up strong and healthy. His mother took care of him

midwives were shocked. They would not obey Pharaoh; but they told him that the women were strong and gave birth before they arrived to help. So God blessed the Egyptian midwives for helping his people. But Pharaoh would not give up. In his latest plan he ordered his soldiers to throw all new baby boys into the River Nile. The babies would be drowned.

Jochebed had two children already, Miriam and her little brother Aaron. When she gave birth to another son, she was frightened for his life. She kept him hidden until he was three months old. She could not

while he was very small but when he was older he lived in the palace with the Egyptians. But he never forgot who he was. He saw how badly his own people were treated.

One day, Moses stood and watched the Israelites working under the hot sun. He saw the marks on their bodies where they had been beaten. He saw the sweat dripping from their brows. Then he saw an Egyptian beating one of them until

---

He never forgot who he was. He saw how badly his own people were treated.

---

the man fell to the ground in pain. Moses had seen enough.

Looking around to make sure no one was watching, Moses seized the Egyptian slave-driver and killed him. Then he buried the man's body in the sand.

The next day, Moses saw two Israelites fighting.

'Why are you hurting each other?' he asked them.

'What does it matter to you?' one of the men replied. 'Are you going to kill me as you killed that Egyptian?'

Moses was frightened. He realised someone had seen him after all. The news of what he had done soon reached Pharaoh. But by the time Pharaoh had sent someone to arrest him, Moses had left the palace and run away through the desert to Midian.

Moses turned his back on Egypt. Now he would make his home in Midian.

Moses met his future wife when he stopped by a well. The priest there had sent his seven daughters to fetch water but they had been chased away by some shepherds. Moses came to their rescue. He was invited back to their home to eat and soon became part of the family.

He married Zipporah and some time later she gave birth to his son, a little boy they called Gershom.

Moses exchanged his life in the palace for the job of a shepherd. He looked after his father-in-law's sheep and was often out in the desert. That was when something happened that changed his life for ever.

Moses saw something strange, something that was different from the sheep he took care of day after day. In the distance there seemed to be a bush on fire – but the leaves were still green – the flames did not burn them up. Moses went over to take a closer look.

'Moses! Moses!' called a voice from the flames. Moses was startled!

'Yes, here I am,' he replied nervously.

'Take off your shoes!' The voice came from an angel who was there in the burning bush. 'You are on holy ground.'

Moses was so afraid, he hid his face.

'I am the God of Abraham, the God of Isaac and the God of Jacob. My people, the Israelites, are suffering as slaves in Egypt. They call out to me to help them. Now I want them to be free to live in the land I have promised them. I want you to go to Pharaoh and bring my people out of Egypt.'

Moses was amazed.

'But I can't go to Pharaoh,' said Moses. 'Why would he listen to me?'

'I will help you,' replied God.

Moses exchanged his life in the palace for the job of a shepherd.

Moses was afraid. He did not want to be the Israelites' leader. He could not be their leader.

'The people will not believe me,' Moses dared to argue. 'What shall I say?'

'Tell them that the God of Abraham, the God of Isaac and the God of Jacob sent you to bring them out of their slavery in Egypt.

'Take your stick and throw it on the ground.'

Moses threw it. The stick hit the ground and turned into a snake. Moses ran from the snake!

'Now pick it up by its tail,' said God.

As Moses picked it up, it changed back into a stick.

'Put your hand inside your cloak,' said God.

Moses did as God asked. When he took his hand out from under his cloak, it was white with leprosy. Quickly, he put it back and when he removed it, his hand was whole and healthy again.

'Show them these things,' said God, 'and they will know that I have sent you. If they still have any doubts, then take some water from the River Nile. As you pour it on to the ground, it will turn to blood.'

Moses had one last objection.

'I do not speak well,' he said. 'I have always found it difficult to speak to people. Please – send someone else.'

When he took his hand out from under his cloak, it was white with leprosy.

'I made you, and I know all about you,' God said. 'I can help you with all I have asked you to do. Trust me. Your brother Aaron can also go with you and he will help you. But take your stick. You will need it to prove that I have sent you.'

So Moses went back to his father-in-law and explained that he had to return to Egypt.

God sent Aaron to meet Moses. Moses told his brother that he had met with God and that they had a difficult task ahead of them. Then Moses and Aaron went to the people who were slaves, and told them that God had heard their prayers and everything was about to change.

They performed the signs that God had given them – and the people believed that God had sent Moses to help them.

Then together, Moses and Aaron went to see Pharaoh, the king of all of Egypt.

'We have come with a message from the Lord, the God of Israel: "Let my people go, so that they can worship me,"' they said.

The great king looked down at the two men.

'I don't know your God,' said Pharaoh, 'and nothing will make me let my slaves go. They belong to me and I need them to work. I will not let them go!'

When Moses and Aaron had gone, Pharaoh gave new orders to his slave-drivers.

'Let the Israelites gather their own straw to make bricks. They will need to work even harder to produce just as many bricks as before.'

The Israelites cried out to Pharaoh.

'How can we make the same number of bricks without straw?'

'That is your problem,' said Pharaoh. 'You are lazy. Get back to work!'

Some of the Israelites went and complained to Moses and Aaron.

'This is your fault!' they said. 'You have made Pharaoh hate us even more!'

Moses spoke to God.

'Why have you allowed me to cause such trouble?' he asked. 'Things are worse now than before.'

'They are my people,' promised God. 'Trust me; I will rescue them.'

Moses and Aaron went to see Pharaoh again.

'The Lord, the God of Israel says, "Let my people go, so that they can worship me,"' they said.

'They are my people,' promised God. 'Trust me; I will rescue them.'

Just as before, Pharaoh refused to let the Israelites go.

Then God spoke to Moses.

'Tell Aaron to stretch out his stick,' he said.

Aaron stretched out his stick, and the water in the River Nile turned to blood. All the fish died; the smell was terrible.

Moses and Aaron went to see Pharaoh again.

'The Lord, the God of Israel says, "Let my people go, so that they can worship me,"' they said. 'If you refuse, God will send a plague of frogs.'

'I will not let them go!' said Pharaoh.

Aaron stretched out his stick and Egypt was covered in frogs. There were frogs in the markets and frogs in the homes. Frogs hopped out of ovens and beds and appeared wherever the people were. It caused huge panic.

'All right! All right! Take the frogs away and I will let these people go,' said Pharaoh.

Moses asked God and he took the plague away. But once the frogs had gone, Pharaoh changed his mind. He refused to let the Israelites go.

Seven more times Moses and Aaron asked Pharaoh to let the Israelites go. When Pharaoh refused, God sent plagues of gnats, flies and locusts; another plague caused every Egyptian animal to die; and another brought boils to cover their skin; violent hailstorms battered the land, and finally, the whole of Egypt was plunged into darkness.

As soon as God took away the plague, Pharaoh changed his mind.

After each plague Pharaoh agreed to let the Israelites go, but as soon as God took away the plague, Pharaoh changed his mind.

'I will give Pharaoh one more warning,' said God to Moses. 'If he still refuses to listen, every Egyptian, including Pharaoh, will want you to leave.'

Then God told Moses that this time the firstborn of every living creature in Egypt would die – including Pharaoh's own son. It would be like the day when Pharaoh drowned their baby sons in the Nile. But God would protect his people and keep them safe. He gave Moses special instructions to follow.

Moses warned Pharaoh, but Pharaoh would not listen. He did not want the Israelites to leave Egypt.

That night every Israelite family coated their door frames with blood from the lamb they were to roast that night. This would be a sign for the angel of death so that he would pass over them. Thousands of Israelites ate the lamb with herbs and unleavened bread with their cloaks wrapped round them, their sandals on their feet, and a stick in their hands.

The Egyptians gave the Israelites gold and silver – all they asked for, as long as they would leave.

'This night must never be forgotten,' Moses told the people. 'We must tell our children and our grandchildren everything that happens tonight.'

That night, after midnight, every firstborn Egyptian died. The crying and wailing of the Egyptians could be heard throughout the land.

Pharaoh called Moses and Aaron.

'Take your cattle and sheep and leave this land!' he shouted. 'Go – and never come back!'

The Egyptians gave the Israelites gold and silver – all they asked for, as long as they would leave.

Then Moses told the people that God would lead them to Canaan, the land he had promised to their ancestors.

By day God appeared to the people as a pillar of cloud leading them, and by night as a pillar of fire. God did not take them by the dangerous road that crossed the land of the Philistines but by the desert road towards the Red Sea.

But back in Egypt, it was not long before Pharaoh began to regret that he had let his slaves leave their work. For the last time, Pharaoh changed his mind. He decided to pursue them and bring them back.

Pharaoh took 600 of his best chariots and every other chariot he could find in Egypt; he took horses, horsemen and troops on foot. When the Israelites realised that the Egyptians were coming after them, they were terrified.

'Were there no graves in Egypt?' they demanded of Moses. 'Have you brought us all the way out here into the desert to die?'

But Moses was not afraid. He trusted God; he knew that God would save his people.

The pillar of cloud moved behind the people so that it stood between them and the Egyptians and it brought confusion to Pharaoh's men.

A dry pathway opened up across the sea.

Then Moses stretched out his hand over the Red Sea. God sent a wind to blow back the waters through the night. A dry pathway opened up across the sea so that all the Israelites – thousands upon thousands of men, women and children – could pass over safely to the other side on dry land.

None of them survived.

When all of God's people had crossed, the Egyptians tried to follow them, but Moses stretched out his hand again, now from the safety of the far bank, and God sent back the water to cover the pathway. Pharaoh and his army and chariots were stuck in the Red Sea. None of them survived.

When Moses and the Israelites saw what had happened to the Egyptians, they wanted to tell God how great and wonderful he was: he had saved them from years of suffering. So Moses led the Israelites in a song of praise.

'Our God is great and mighty!' they said. 'He threw horses and riders into the sea. Our God is strong and mighty! He came to rescue us all. God came for us as he promised. He loves us and leads us.'

Then Miriam, Moses' sister, took her tambourine, and began to play and to dance to thank God for all that he had done. The other Israelite women saw what she did, and they followed her, dancing and playing tambourines.

'Sing to the Lord God,' sang Miriam. 'He is the greatest!'

CHAPTER 7

GOD'S HOLY PEOPLE

MOSES LED THE ISRAELITES INTO THE DESERT BEYOND THE SEA. AT FIRST THEY WERE HAPPY BUT AFTER THEY HAD WALKED IN THE HEAT OF THE SUN FOR THREE DAYS, THEY WERE TIRED AND THIRSTY. THEY COULD FIND NO WATER; AND WHEN THEY DID FIND WATER, IT TASTED BITTER AND THEY COULD NOT DRINK IT.

The people grumbled and complained to Moses. Then Moses spoke to God.

'Throw that piece of wood into the water,' said God.

Moses obeyed God, and the water became sweet to drink.

The people were happy to rest and drink the fresh water and then they travelled on through the desert. But soon they were grumbling again.

'If only we had died in our beds in Egypt!' the people said to Moses. 'At least we didn't go hungry there.'

God heard the grumblings of his people and he answered them.

'In the mornings I will make bread fall from the sky like rain. In the evenings I will provide quail for you all to eat. Everyone is to collect just enough for their daily needs, and on the day before the Sabbath day, collect twice as much so that the

Sabbath can be a day of rest.'

Everything happened just as God had said. They called the bread that God gave them 'manna'. It looked like a thin layer of frost on the ground and it tasted like wafers made from honey. God continued to provide bread for the people every day that they wandered in the desert. They did not go hungry again.

The Israelites continued to wander through the desert, moving camp as God led them on.

Soon they were grumbling again. They could find no water to drink.

'We must have water!' they complained to Moses.

So Moses called to God to help him. He was sure the people

In the mornings I will make bread fall from the sky like rain.

were angry enough to kill him if he couldn't find water for them.

God answered Moses. He told Moses to take with him some of the people and go to the rock at Horeb where he should hit it with his stick. If he did this, said God, water would pour from the rock and the people would have good water to drink.

Moses did as God instructed and water poured from the rock in front of the people, just as God had said.

For a long time, they walked peacefully through the desert. But when the Israelites reached a place called Rephidim, they met the hostile Amalekites, the tribal people who lived in that part of the desert. It was clear that they would not let them through. The Amalekites wanted to fight. Moses had no choice but to defend the Israelites.

He told Joshua to choose men to make up an army.

The next day, Moses, his brother Aaron and Hur went up the hill overlooking the desert valley where a battle would take place. Moses held out his stick over the fighting men and watched the battle. For as long as he held up his stick, Joshua's men were the stronger side; when Moses tired and lowered the stick, the Amalekites seemed to take control of the battle. So Hur and Aaron found a large stone for Moses to sit on. Then they stood on either side of him and supported his arms so Moses could hold up the stick until sunset, when the Amalekites were finally defeated.

Then Moses made an altar to thank God for protecting them against the enemy. He called it 'The Lord is my banner' because he had lifted his stick high in the air.

After three months in the desert, the Israelites reached the foot of Mount Sinai. They made camp there.

Moses climbed the mountain alone, while the people watched and waited. Then Moses met with God and God told him what he was to tell the people.

'You have seen how I saved you from the Egyptians and brought you safely across the Red Sea. Now I will make a promise to you: you will be my special people if you will obey me, and keep your side of the agreement.'

Moses told the people what God had said and they promised to obey.

God told Moses that he would come down and speak to him on the mountain when they heard the sound of a ram's horn. The people were to prepare themselves and keep their distance until then.

Three days later, thunder and lightning struck, and there was a thick cloud over the mountain. At the sound of a trumpet blast, Moses led the people to the foot of the mountain. There was fire and smoke, the ground shook, and the trumpet sounded over and over again. All the Israelites trembled.

Then God came to the mountain top, and Moses went up to meet him.

God gave Moses the laws for his people to obey. He engraved them on two large pieces of stone, in his own handwriting.

'I am the Lord your God, who brought you out of Egypt where you were slaves. Do not worship any god but me.

'Do not make idols that look like anything in the sky or on the earth or in the ocean under the earth. Don't bow down and worship idols.

'Do not misuse my name. I am the Lord your God.

'Remember that the Sabbath day belongs to me. You have six days when you can work, but the seventh day of each week is special. Take time to rest and worship me. Don't work on that day.

Then God came to the mountaintop, and Moses went up to meet him.

'Respect your father and your mother, and you will live a long time in the land I am giving you.

'Do not plan to take another life with hate in your hearts. Do not murder anyone.

'Be faithful to the person you have married.

'Do not steal.

'Do not tell lies about others.

'Do not look at the things other people have and desire them. Don't look with desire at anyone's house, wife or husband, slaves, oxen, donkeys or anything else that belongs to them. Be happy with what you have and do not be controlled by your desire to own things.'

God gave Moses commandments so they would know how best to live good lives, live peacefully with each other and be happy; but he also told Moses how he wanted the people to worship him.

God told Moses that they were to build a special tent, a tabernacle. It would have linen curtains made from blue, purple and scarlet coloured yarn. The altar should be made of acacia wood and all the bowls and shovels and meat forks should be made of bronze.

There should be a golden lampstand with six branches, the cup of each one shaped like almond flowers. The table should be decorated with gold.

The priests should wear fine linen garments with a breastplate decorated with twelve beautiful stones – ruby, topaz, beryl, turquoise, sapphire, emerald, jacinth, agate, amethyst, chrysolite, onyx and jasper – each one to represent one of the twelve tribes of Israel.

'I have chosen Bezalel and Oholiab to do the work,' God said to Moses. 'I have filled Bezalel with my Spirit so that he can use his special gifts to work with many different materials. I will help all the craftsmen to use their talents to give the best results.'

When God had finished talking to Moses, he gave him the two pieces of stone and Moses took them down the mountain.

Moses had stayed on the mountain talking with God for forty days and forty nights.

At first the people had waited, wondering what news Moses would bring from God. Day by day had passed. But the longer the people had waited, the more tired and restless they had become.

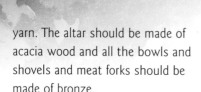

Moses had stayed on the mountain talking with God for forty days and forty nights.

'Where has Moses gone?' they asked Aaron eventually. 'Anything could have happened to him in all this time. We have waited long enough. We need gods we can see with our own eyes!'

Aaron knew immediately what to do. The Israelites had seen the Egyptians worship many golden statues while they had been Pharaoh's slaves. Aaron told the people to give him all their gold jewellery. Then he melted it down, and made it into the shape of one of the Egyptian gods. It was a golden calf.

The people were delighted. They thanked the golden calf for leading them out of Egypt. They worshipped something made with human hands. Then, because Aaron knew that making an idol was against God's law, he built an altar too and announced that the following day would be a festival to the Lord God.

Meanwhile God had seen his people making the golden calf.

'Go back to the people,' God told Moses. 'They have already forgotten that I have brought them out of Egypt. They have made an idol and they are worshipping it.'

Moses hurried down the mountain, carrying the two stone tablets on which God's ten commandments were written.

Joshua was waiting for him. Together they heard the noise the people were making.

'The people are shouting! What's happening? Are we being attacked?'

'This is not the sound of battle!' Moses replied. 'This is the sound of singing and dancing. The people are having a party.'

Moses went closer. He saw the golden calf and the people dancing around it. He saw that already God's laws had been broken. Moses threw the pieces of stone down at the bottom of the mountain. Now they were also broken.

Moses was furious with his brother, Aaron. He destroyed the golden calf.

'How could you let this happen?' he asked Aaron angrily.

'The people wanted this,' muttered Aaron. 'I gave them what they asked for.'

'God will punish those who have broken his commandments!' said Moses. Then he turned to the people.

'Who is on the Lord's side?' he asked them. 'Anyone who still loves God, come here to me.'

Many of the people came to Moses; many more did not.

'God will bless those people who stand firm and worship only him. But he will punish those who do not. I will speak to God and ask for his mercy.'

But a plague swept through the people and many died because the people had worshipped the golden calf.

'I made a promise to Abraham, Isaac and to Jacob which I cannot break,' said God. 'I promised that their descendants would live in a land that I would give them. Leave this place, take the people who will go with you and go to the Promised Land. But because they have disobeyed me, I will not go with you.'

When the people heard what God had said, they were sorry. They wanted God to stay with them.

Moses used to pitch a special tent away from the main camp. Joshua would stand outside the tent. When Moses needed to ask God something, he would go inside and a pillar of cloud would cover the tent entrance. Once inside, God would speak to Moses as if he were his special friend.

The Israelites would stand at the entrances of their own tents and watch. They would worship God until Moses returned to the camp.

Now Moses spoke to God on behalf of all the people.

'*I will not leave you,*' *God said. '*I love my people.*'*

'If you are not angry with me, Lord, and if you will listen to me, please help me now. Teach me your ways. Help me to serve you better. You have called us your own people. But if you will not go with us, how are we different from any other group of people? We need you. Please don't send us on alone to the Promised Land.'

God saw that Moses wanted to obey him and save his people.

'I will not leave you,' God said. 'I love my people. I know you and I love you.'

'Now let me know you better,' asked Moses bravely. 'Let me see your glory.'

'No one can see my face and live,' said God. 'But there is a place where you can stand on the mountain and I will pass by you. You must stand in the cleft of the rock and I will cover you with my hand to protect you. But you cannot see my face.'

God told Moses to come alone to the mountain the following morning with two new pieces of stone.

Moses stood in the cleft of the rock on Mount Sinai. God came and passed in front of him as he had promised. Then God spoke.

'I am the Lord. I am faithful and compassionate. I love the people I have made and I long to forgive their disobedience.'

Moses fell on the ground and worshipped the one true God.

'I will make a covenant with you, a special promise,' said God. 'I will lead you to the land I promised to give Abraham and his descendants.

But if the people disobey my laws, they will be punished.'

God wrote the commandments on the two new pieces of stone and gave Moses other laws to help the people obey him. Then Moses came down from the mountain.

When the people saw Moses, they were afraid to go near him, for his face shone like the sun. He had been in the company of God himself.

Moses told the people about the special tent they needed to make for God.

'We need to make an ark, a table, an altar and a lampstand, and there will be special clothes for the priests to wear. If you are willing, give God anything you have that can be used.'

The people brought their gold, silver, bronze and precious jewels. The women spun linen and made cloth out of goat's hair. They brought the best spices and the purest olive oil. They worked for six days of the week, and rested on the seventh, as God had commanded.

When the people had finished making everything for the special tent, Moses placed the pieces of stone inside the ark and this was put in the 'Holy of Holies', a special place separated by a curtain.

Aaron and his sons prepared themselves to be God's priests. They washed themselves and dressed in the special clothes God had designed for them.

Moses set a courtyard around the special tent, made with more curtains. Then a cloud covered the tent, and God's presence filled it. His presence was so great that Moses could not enter.

God's presence remained with the Israelites, just as he had promised. When the cloud lifted, it was time to move on, with God leading the way.

CHAPTER 8

REBELLION IN THE DESERT

FOR SOME TIME THE ISRAELITES TRAVELLED THROUGH THE DESERT. WHENEVER THE CLOUD RESTED, THEY MADE CAMP. WHEN THE CLOUD LIFTED, THEY MOVED ON TOWARDS THE LAND GOD HAD PROMISED THEM.

But they found their journey hard. They started to complain about the hot sun and the dry land; they complained about the food. They began to wish they were back in Egypt where they had meat whenever they wanted it and sweet melons and cucumbers. They forgot about the slavery and the beatings. They blamed Moses for everything.

Even Miriam and Aaron complained. They gossiped about Moses' wife, and criticised their brother.

'Why is Moses so special?' they asked. 'Can God not also speak through us?'

God heard what they said.

'Listen carefully to what I have to say,' said God. 'I have spoken to Moses face to face and he is faithful to me. Who are you to challenge him?'

When the cloud of God's presence lifted, Miriam saw that her skin was covered in leprosy.

'Forgive us, Lord!' cried Aaron to Moses. 'Please don't let Miriam suffer like this!'

Moses also cried out to God for

Miriam to be healed.

'She must stay outside the camp for seven days,' said God. 'Then she can return.'

The people waited. They did not continue their journey until Miriam had come back and her skin was healed.

After some time the Israelites approached Canaan. God told Moses to send one man from each of the twelve tribes to explore the Promised Land.

Moses sent out the twelve men with detailed instructions. They were to find out what sort of people lived there; they were to see how the cities were fortified and how fertile the land was.

At the end of forty days, the twelve men returned. Joshua and Caleb carried between them a pole with a heavy branch bearing a single cluster of juicy grapes. They also brought figs and pomegranates.

Moses gathered the people, and they listened to the spies' report.

'The land is good and fertile,' said Joshua. 'It would be a wonderful place to live. Just look at this fruit!'

But it was not all good news.

'We saw strong, powerful people

We saw strong, powerful people as big as giants, living in walled cities.

as big as giants, living in walled cities,' warned the other men. 'They are too strong for us to fight; we are too weak to try to take this land.'

Then the Israelites were miserable. They cried. They grumbled.

'Let's choose another leader,' they said, 'and go back to Egypt.'

Moses and Aaron got down on their knees in front of all the Israelites. Joshua and Caleb joined them.

'God has promised to give us this wonderful land. We can trust him to help us,' they said.

The Israelites would not believe them. They planned to stone them to death. Then God's presence appeared at the special tent.

'How long will you refuse to trust me?' asked God. 'Those who cannot trust me will wander in the desert for forty years. Only their children will enter Canaan. Caleb and Joshua alone will live in the Promised Land.'

Then the Israelites were sorry.

'We will do what God wanted,' they said. 'We will go and fight the people who live in the land so that we can make our home in Canaan.'

'It's too late now!' cried Moses. 'You cannot enter the land safely without God's help. He made a promise and you refused to believe him. If you go into the land, you will be defeated. God will not go with you.'

Moses would not move from the camp. He stayed with the ark containing God's laws.

But the Israelites did not listen to Moses. Instead they went into the hill country. They were attacked by both the Canaanites and the Amalekites and were defeated.

Then the Israelites were afraid. They moved back from the borders of Canaan, and made their way towards the desert. For forty years they wandered there, eating the manna that God provided for their daily needs.

Life in the desert was hard. Many of those who had once lived in Egypt died. Their descendants arrived at Kadesh and there, Miriam also died and was buried.

For forty years they wandered there, eating the manna that God provided.

When the people were faced with no fresh water again, a new generation of Israelites began to doubt that God cared for them.

'Why did you bring us here?'

they moaned to Moses and Aaron, just as their parents had once done. 'This is a terrible place. We are thirsty and there is no water here.'

This is a terrible place.

Aaron and Moses left the people and went to the special tent.

'Take your stick,' said God to Moses, 'and gather the people so that they can see what I can do. But this time, just speak to the rock, and it will pour out water.'

Moses took his stick and gathered the people to watch him. But Moses was angry. He had heard their fathers moaning and their descendants were no better. Instead of obeying God, he held his stick in the air, and then hit the rock with it twice.

Immediately, water poured out from the rock and the people had plenty for their needs.

But God was not pleased with what Moses had done.

'Moses,' said God, 'you were angry. You did not do as I asked. It is time for someone else to lead my people into the Promised Land.'

As the Israelites approached the land of Edom, they sent messengers to ask if they could go through their country.

'You cannot pass this way,' warned the Edomites. 'We will come with swords if you try!'

The Israelites asked again – but the Edomites came with a large army and turned God's people back from their borders.

So the people came instead to Mount Hor. Here God told Moses to call Aaron to go to the top of the mountain with his son Eleazar.

'It is time for Aaron to pass on his priestly duties to his son before he dies,' said God. So Moses took Aaron's special clothes and dressed his son in them. When Aaron died, he was mourned by all the people for thirty days.

As the people travelled towards

the Red Sea, they began to grumble once more. First it was the lack of water; then they grumbled about the bread that God provided for them. When poisonous snakes slithered through the camp and bit them, they realised God was angry with them.

'We have sinned,' they cried to Moses. 'We're always complaining. We don't trust God as we should. We know God has been good to us and saved us from our enemies. Please ask him to take the snakes away.'

So Moses prayed.

God has been good to us and saved us from our enemies.

'Make a bronze snake and put it on a pole,' said God. 'Anyone who has been bitten should look at the snake on the pole and they will not die.'

Moses did as God told him. Those who looked at the snake lived.

The Israelites eventually came to the land of Moab. They asked Sihon, king of the Amorites, if they could pass through peacefully. Sihon had already fought for the land and taken it from the Moabites and he would not let them pass through. Instead he brought his whole army together and marched into the desert to defend Moab. But the Israelites fought back bravely. They began to take Sihon's land and the cities round about. When they had defeated Sihon, the Israelites settled in the land.

Moses then led the people towards Bashan near the northern end of the Sea of Galilee. King Og knew they were coming. He marched towards them from Bashan. He did not want the Israelites in his land.

'Don't be afraid of him,' God said to Moses. 'He will not win this battle.'

So Moses and the people fought King Og until he and his army were also defeated.

Then the Israelites camped along

the Jordan in the plains of Moab. The
walls of the city of Jericho were on
the other side of the river.

Balak, king of Moab, saw what
had happened to King Sihon and to
King Og. He saw the large number of
the Israelites and he was frightened
for his own land and people.

'Send a message to Balaam, the
sorcerer,' he ordered. 'Tell him to
come and curse the Israelites, so that
I can defeat them. Promise to give
him as much money as he wants.'

But God spoke to Balaam and
warned him not to listen to Balak's
messengers.

'Don't curse these people,' God
said. 'They are my people and I have
blessed them.'

Balaam heard God's warning, but

God sent an angel with a drawn sword to stand in his path and stop him.

decided to ignore it. He prepared to
go to see King Balak. He saddled his

donkey, and set off next morning.

God was angry with Balaam. He
sent an angel with a drawn sword
to stand in his path and stop him.
Balaam did not see the angel, but his
donkey did. She veered off the road,
and into the field. Balaam was angry.
He couldn't understand why she was
going the wrong way. Balaam beat his
donkey severely.

Balaam rode on towards King
Balak until the angel appeared again
in a path between two vineyards. The
donkey squeezed against a wall to
avoid the angel and crushed Balaam's
foot. Balaam shouted out in pain.
Then he beat his donkey once more.

Finally the angel blocked Balaam's
path in a place where there was
nowhere to turn. The donkey could
not go on so she lay down. Balaam
was furious. He beat her again to
make her stand up. Then God gave
the donkey the gift of speech.

'Why do you beat me?' the
donkey said to Balaam. 'Would I have
stopped if there hadn't been good
reason?'

Suddenly Balaam was able to see what the donkey had seen. He saw the angel in front of him.

'Why have you beaten your donkey?' asked the angel. 'She has saved your life! Now, you stubborn man, listen to what God wants you to do. You can go to King Balak, but you must give him the message God gives you.'

Balaam went to King Balak and asked him to build seven altars and prepare sacrifices on them. Then Balaam went to a barren hill top to listen to God's message. God told him what to say and Balaam brought the message to Balak.

'You brought me here to curse Jacob's descendants, the Israelites. But how can I curse people whom God has blessed? Everywhere around me I see them, people who are not like everyone else. They are a good people and I hope I may die as they do.'

King Balak listened with growing rage.

'Be quiet! I have brought you here to curse my enemies, not bless them!' he said.

'I can only say what God tells me to say,' replied Balaam.

Again Balak prepared seven altars and again God gave Balaam the words to say.

'God does not lie. God keeps his promises. God brought this people out of Egypt and he will be there to help them and bless them,' said Balaam.

God does not lie. God keeps his promises.

A third time Balak prepared his seven altars and a third time Balaam delivered God's blessing on his people.

'God saved his people from slavery in Egypt, and he will bless them with a land full of good things. God will make them strong against all their enemies – including you! – and no one will be able to stand against them.'

King Balak was furious! He sent Balaam away with no money for his trouble. But Balaam left him with a warning.

'No amount of money would prevent me from giving you the words that God gave me. But God has warned me that in the future someone from Israel who is so strong that he will defeat your people.'

Meanwhile Moses was talking to the Israelites. While the Moabites remained fearful of the Israelites camped on the border of Canaan, Moses reminded God's people of all that God had done since their ancestors had left Egypt.

'Live in peace and keep God's commandments,' he told them. 'You are God's special people. Don't be like the other nations. Be concerned about other people. Be generous and kind. When you enter Canaan, help those who are poor. Share what you have with those in need. If you lend or borrow money, cancel the debt after seven years if it is not repaid. Hate injustice. Be generous to one another and God will bless you.

'You will be a great nation, and your enemies will be defeated,' Moses continued. 'You will have abundant harvests, plenty of water and be blessed with many children. Other countries will watch and see that God has blessed you. But,' warned

Moses, 'God will make you a special and holy nation only if you love him and obey his commandments. He has given you a choice: life or death. Choose life and live for a long time in the land God will give you.'

Hate injustice. Be generous to one another and God will bless you.

Moses was by this time an old man. He had served God well and led his people through many years in the desert. His brother and sister, Aaron and Miriam, had died long before.

Moses spoke to the people one last time.

'I am 120 years old and I cannot lead you any more. God has told me that I will not cross the Jordan into the Promised Land. God himself will go with you and he will give you all the good things he has promised. Be strong and brave. God will go with you; you will never be alone.'

Then Moses asked Joshua to come close. He laid his hands on Joshua's head in front of all the people.

'Be strong and full of courage. God has chosen you to lead his people into the Promised Land and you must take them there and divide the land between them.'

Moses blessed the people and then he climbed slowly up Mount Nebo. God showed Moses all the land that he would give to the Israelites.

'This is the land I promised to give to the descendants of Abraham, Isaac and Jacob,' God said.

Moses looked at the land and smiled at the good things that lay ahead of God's people. But he was tired. He was content not to go any

further. Moses died in Moab and was buried there.

The Israelites mourned his death. They knew that Moses had spoken to God, face to face, and helped them for many years. He had done wonderful things and shown them how God wanted them to live.

Moses had spoken to God, face to face.

God's Spirit came to Joshua now. Joshua was wise and obedient and the Israelites listened to him.

CHAPTER 9

THE PROMISED LAND

JOSHUA KNEW WHAT LAY AHEAD OF HIM. THE WALLED CITY OF JERICHO WAS JUST OVER THE RIVER. FIRST THEY HAD TO CROSS THE RIVER JORDAN. THEN THEY HAD TO GET THROUGH THE FORTIFIED CITY BEFORE THEY COULD ENTER CANAAN. SO JOSHUA SENT TWO SPIES ACROSS THE RIVER TO SEE WHAT THEY COULD FIND OUT ABOUT THE PEOPLE WHO LIVED THERE.

The spies went secretly to a house built into the city walls. Rahab, the woman who lived there, was willing to talk to them. But the king of Jericho was told that there were strangers in his city, that there were spies in Rahab's house. He sent a message for her to hand them over to his soldiers.

Rahab had other ideas. She hid the spies under the flax drying on her roof. Then she sent a message to the king saying that the spies had left earlier by the city gate.

Rahab watched as the king's men went in pursuit of the spies. When it was safe, she went to the men who were hiding and made a bargain with them.

'All my people know that your God dried up the waters of the Red

We are all afraid because God is on your side.

Sea. They know he saved you from the Egyptians. We know that he is with you now and will give you the city of Jericho. We are all afraid because God is on your side. Promise me that you will help me and save my family when you come to capture the city.'

The spies agreed. They told her to hang a scarlet cord from her window in the city wall and to have her whole family there in the room when the Israelites came into the city. Then they would make sure she was kept safe. The spies left by the window and climbed down the city walls, escaping to hide in the hills.

The spies brought Joshua the news that the people of Jericho feared for their lives. God had already gone before them so that they were sure to capture the city.

Now Joshua had to cross the River Jordan with all the people – thousands of men, women and children. God spoke to him.

'Today, everyone will know that I am with you, just as I was with Moses,' said God. Then he told Joshua how he would lead the people into the Promised Land.

Immediately, the waters that ran downstream stopped flowing.

At Joshua's command, the priests carried the ark into the river and stopped in the middle. Immediately, the waters that ran downstream stopped flowing. The priests stayed in the middle of the river, and the Israelites crossed over on dry land, thousands upon thousands of them.

'Choose one man from each of the twelve tribes,' said God to Joshua. 'Tell them to take one stone each from the middle of the river bed, and to place them near where you camp tonight. Then your children and grandchildren will know what I have done for you today.'

When all the people had crossed the river, the priests carrying the ark with God's ten commandments in them walked to the other side too. Only then did the river waters flow again.

No one wanted to fight against the Israelites when they heard what had happened. Everyone in Canaan heard what God had done for them.

Joshua camped with the people outside Jericho. They celebrated the Passover and waited until God told them what to do next.

Then a man with a sword in his hand appeared in Joshua's path. Joshua knew he had been sent by God, and fell to his knees.

'I am the commander of God's army,' said the man. 'I have come to tell you what to do. Seven priests must lead you in a march around the city walls. The priests must walk in front of the ark, each blowing a trumpet, for six days. On the seventh day, they must march around the city walls seven times, blowing their trumpets. On the long trumpet blast, signal to the people to shout. Then the city walls will collapse.'

'I am the commander of God's army,' said the man. 'I have come to tell you what to do.'

The gates of the city of Jericho stood before Joshua and his army, firmly closed against them. The people inside watched and waited.

For six days the priests marched with the armed guard as God had told them. On the seventh day, at the sound of the long trumpet blast, the people shouted, and the walls of Jericho crumbled and fell down.

The Israelites marched into the city. God had given them the victory! But they found Rahab and her family and kept them safe as they had promised.

'Don't take anything for yourselves when we march into the city!' Joshua had warned his troops as they entered Jericho. 'Everything here belongs to God.'

But Achan found a beautiful robe, some silver and gold. He wanted them for himself. He stole them and hid them secretly under his tent.

Joshua then sent 3000 soldiers into the city of Ai. Spies had been sent in and reported that it could be defeated without the whole army in place. But everything went wrong. The Israelites were defeated at Ai and thirty-six soldiers were killed.

Joshua prayed to God.

'Why have you let us be defeated, Lord? We trusted you to help us.'

'Not everyone has trusted me,' said God. 'Someone has disobeyed me. They have stolen from Jericho and kept riches for themselves. Then they have lied about it.'

Joshua found out that Achan was the guilty man.

Joshua gathered the people together. Tribe by tribe, family by family, he eventually found out that Achan was the guilty man. Joshua challenged him.

'Tell me what you have done,' he said. 'Men have died because of your greed. Hide nothing from me.'

Achan admitted that he had stolen and cheated and lied, and Joshua sent his men to find the stolen items. Achan paid the ultimate penalty for his crime – he was put to death.

God told Joshua that the time was now right to attack the city of Ai.

'Don't be discouraged,' said God. 'This time, you will win the battle.'

Joshua chose his army.

'Half of you must go by night and hide on the far side of the city,' Joshua said. 'In the morning, the rest of us will attack the city gates. The king of Ai will chase us, and we will lead his army away from the city. Then we can capture Ai while it is not defended.'

Joshua and his army advanced. The king and his troops ran out to fight the Israelites as they had done before and chased them as far as the desert.

God told Joshua to give the rest of the army the sign they had agreed – and the rest of the army came from behind and burned the city to the ground. When the Israelites saw the smoke, they turned back to fight the soldiers of Ai. They were now surrounded.

Joshua's men drove them into the desert. God had given them the victory once more.

As time went on, Joshua took the Israelites further into Canaan and saw that all the kings around grew afraid.

The people of Gibeon decided not to fight and lose. They preferred to make a pact with Israel. So they dressed in old clothes and loaded their donkeys with cracked wineskins and stale bread to deceive the Israelites.

'We have come from far away,' they lied. 'We want to make a peace treaty with you.'

Joshua and his leaders did not ask God what they should do. They made a peace treaty with the Gibeonites. When they realised that these men were their enemies, and lived in Canaan, they were angry.

'We will not break our promise,' said Joshua, 'but you must now work for us, cutting wood and carrying water for us.'

'Your God is a great God,' the Gibeonites told Joshua. 'We know that he has promised to give you this land. We wanted peace. We will work for you rather than die.'

King Adonizedek from Jerusalem heard about the pact the Gibeonites had made with Joshua.

He feared what Joshua could do with their help so he joined forces with four other kings in Canaan.

'Come with me and let's attack Gibeon!' he said.

Once the attack had begun, the Gibeonites sent for help.

'Joshua! Come and rescue us! The Amorite kings want us dead!' the message reported. 'We are your servants. Help us!'

God spoke to Joshua.

'Don't be afraid. I will help you defeat the Amorites.'

So Joshua marched towards Gibeon and took the Amorites by surprise. As the enemy armies fled, God sent huge freak hailstones from the sky, which battered the enemy soldiers to death.

Then, in the middle of the day Joshua prayed.

God sent huge freak hailstones from the sky, which battered the enemy soldiers to death.

'Don't let the sun go down till we have the victory!' he said.

And God answered him. The sun did not set until the battle was won.

As Joshua led the Israelites northwards, King Jabin of Hazor watched his progress.

'Come and fight these Israelites with me!' he said to his allies. They gathered a huge army, with horses and chariots, and set out to confront the Israelites.

When Joshua confronted them, it seemed that there were more of their enemies than grains of sand on a beach.

'Don't be afraid,' said God to Joshua. 'By this time tomorrow you will have defeated them.'

Joshua trusted God. He made a surprise attack at Merom Pond. By disabling the horses and burning the chariots, Joshua was able to defeat his enemies.

Joshua led the Israelites in victory over thirty-one kings. Canaan was theirs at last. Now the Israelites could settle in the land that God had promised them and enjoy it.

The Israelites had the land of Canaan before them. Joshua's last task was to divide the land between all the tribes of Israel.

Jacob had had twelve sons. The sons of Levi were priests and did not take a share of the land; the land that should have been Joseph's was divided between his two sons. So it was that the land was divided into twelve parts.

The sun did not set until the battle was won.

Now, at last, the people could stop wandering and receive their inheritance, their new home.

'Don't forget all that God has done for you,' said Joshua. 'Remember to love him and keep his laws and he will never forget his promises to you. You will live safely in the land as long as you don't marry the people on your borders or worship their gods. The Lord is our God. He has made an agreement with us as he did with Abraham, Isaac and Jacob.'

Many years had passed since Joshua and Caleb had been spies sent into Canaan by Moses. They alone had been allowed to see the day when the people would settle in the land God had promised; they alone had believed God would keep his promises when the other spies would not trust him. Joshua and Caleb had seen God help them conquer their enemies. Now it was time for Caleb to receive the reward Moses had promised.

'Forty-five years ago, Moses promised that I would have a share of the land to pass on to my children,' Caleb said to Joshua. 'Now I am eighty-five! But God has kept me fit and well for this day. Please give me the hill country of Hebron. I know the people there are unfriendly but I am still strong and God will take care of me.'

Joshua blessed his old friend, Caleb. He knew that he loved God and trusted him still. He gave Caleb the area of Hebron as his special reward.

Then there was peace in the land of Canaan.

Joshua lived to be 110 years old. When he knew that his death was near, he called together the leaders of the people to say goodbye.

'I am old and must soon die,' he said to them. 'You have seen for yourselves how God has kept his promises and given us this land as our home. Now you must be strong and continue to keep God's laws always. You must keep yourselves separate from the other nations around you. You must love God with all your hearts.'

You must be strong and continue to keep God's laws always.

Then Joshua brought together all the people with a message from God.

'Remember that I the Lord God brought Abraham out of a land where they worshipped other gods. I brought him to Canaan and gave him Isaac; I gave to Isaac sons, Esau and Jacob. When Jacob's family went into Egypt, I sent Moses and Aaron to lead them out of slavery. Then I brought you across the River Jordan and helped you defeat all the Amorites and the other people who lived in Canaan. Now this land is yours.'

Then Joshua challenged the people again not to be tempted to worship foreign gods.

Choose today which god you will trust and worship. As for me and all my family, we will serve the Lord.

'Choose today which god you will trust and worship. As for me and all my family, we will serve the Lord.'

Then the people promised to trust and obey God alone. Joshua took a large stone and placed it under an oak tree at Shechem.

'This stone will be here always as a reminder of your promise to serve the living God.'

Joshua died and the people buried him. Aaron's son, Eleazar, the priest, died and was buried also. And the bones of Joseph were brought from Egypt and buried at Shechem.

CHAPTER 10

A NATION UNDER THREAT

IT WAS NOT LONG BEFORE A WHOLE GENERATION OF ISRAELITES WHO LOVED AND SERVED THE LORD HAD DIED. THEIR CHILDREN QUICKLY FORGOT WHAT THEY HAD BEEN TAUGHT. THEY FORGOT JOSHUA'S WARNING. THEY CHOSE NOT TO FOLLOW GOD'S LAWS BUT WORSHIPPED THE GODS OF THE PEOPLE AROUND THEM.

Soon the Israelites began to marry people from neighbouring countries. They were no longer God's separate people. They worshipped Baal and Ashtoreth – the gods made of wood and stone that the Canaanites believed gave them rain to grow their crops and large families to carry on their family name.

The Israelites forgot the promises their ancestors had made and broke the rules God had given them to live in peace with others.

They no longer asked God for help. Without God's help, raiders plundered their lands and they were defeated in battle. Then Cushan-Rishathaim, king of Aram, overpowered them. For eight years. he ruled over them.

The Israelites were no longer free.

Then they began to call out to God for help once more.

God had not been happy that they had chosen to forget him. But God was kind and loving. He had compassion on his people; he did not forget them.

Caleb's nephew was called Othniel. God blessed him so that he was wise and able to guide the people back to the laws God had given to Moses.

Othniel went to war against Cushan-Rishathaim and with God's help, he overpowered the king of Aram so that the Israelites were free once more. Then for a while there was peace in the land of Canaan.

For forty years Othniel guided the Israelites but when he died, the people returned to their old ways. They rebelled against God's laws and were cruel to the poor. They forgot about justice and kindness.

Then Eglon, the king of Moab, made a pact with Israel's enemies, the Ammonites and Amalekites. Eglon gathered an army and

captured Jericho, the city of Palms. The Israelites were once more overpowered and were Eglon's subjects. This time it took eighteen years before they called to God for help.

God heard the cries of his people and he sent Ehud, from the tribe of Benjamin, to rescue them. When King Eglon demanded a tribute from the Israelites, the people chose Ehud to take it to the king.

It took eighteen years before they called to God for help.

Ehud, a left-handed man, made a long double-edged sword and strapped it to his right thigh, underneath his tunic. First Ehud bowed before the king, and gave him the tribute. He dismissed the men who had helped him carry the gifts and then whispered, 'I have a secret message for you, your majesty.'

Eglon was intrigued and sent his attendants away. He invited Ehud to enter the upper room of his summer palace, not realising that his visitor was armed.

Ehud approached the king, who was a very a large, fat man.

'I have a message from God for you,' he said. Ehud reached for his sword and plunged it into the king's belly, killing him. Quietly, Ehud left the room, locked the doors behind him, and made his escape.

When Ehud reached the hill country, he blew his trumpet. The Israelites rushed down the hills.

'Follow me!' cried Ehud as he led the people into battle. 'God has helped us defeat the people of Moab!'

The Moabites then became subject to the Israelites and there was peace in the land for eighty years.

When Ehud died, the Israelites stopped following God's ways yet again. It was not long before one of the kings who lived in Canaan oppressed them.

King Jabin had a large and fierce army under the command of a man called Sisera. He equipped his troops with 900 iron chariots, and for twenty years he oppressed Israel. The Israelites suffered and cried out to God to help them.

Deborah, Lappidoth's wife, loved God and still listened to him. People would come to her when they had disputes to settle. She was good and wise.

God spoke to Deborah now about King Jabin. Then Deborah sent for a warrior called Barak.

'I have a message to you from God,' Deborah told Barak. 'He has a great task for you. You must take 10,000 troops and march to Mount

Tabor. God will lure Sisera and King Jabin's army toward the River Kishon. Then they will be trapped, and you can defeat them.'

But Barak was frightened.

'I cannot do this alone,' he said. 'You must come with me.'

Deborah was disappointed by Barak's response, but she agreed.

'Be warned, Barak,' she said. 'Because you do not trust God to help you, everyone will say that this victory was won by a woman.'

When Sisera heard that Barak was leading an attack, he gathered his army and 900 chariots by the River Kishon and waited.

Barak went up to Mount Tabor with his troops where they were safe from the chariots.

'Attack!' signalled Deborah to Barak. 'This is God's plan. Today we will defeat our enemies.'

Barak charged down the hillside, attacking Sisera's army, slashing with their swords. But God also sent a storm which caused the river to flood. Sisera's 900 chariots became stuck in the mud. There was chaos.

Sisera abandoned his chariot and his men and ran. He deserted the battle scene, knowing that his army could not win. Instead he made his way towards some tents belonging to a man called Heber.

'I'll be safe here,' thought Sisera. 'I can hide. Heber and King Jabin are friends.'

Heber's wife, Jael, saw Sisera. She knew who he was.

'Don't be afraid,' she said. 'No one will find you here in my tent.' Sisera went inside and asked for a drink. Jael gave him some milk and hid him under some covers.

She drove the peg through his head and killed him.

'Keep watch!' he pleaded. 'If someone comes looking for me, don't tell them I am here!' He was so exhausted that he was soon fast asleep.

But Jael did not keep watch. She was on God's side. Instead, she took a tent peg and crept up to the sleeping soldier. She drove the peg through his head and killed him.

Barak charged through Heber's camp, looking for Sisera.

'Look no further,' said Jael. 'I will show you the man you have come for.'

Barak saw the body of his enemy, killed by a woman, just as Deborah had prophesied. Now King Jabin was unable to fight back.

'Praise the Lord!' sang Deborah and Barak. 'He has defeated our enemies.'

The Israelites enjoyed peace in their land for another forty years, but then, as before, they forgot all the things that God had done for them. They behaved as if they were not God' special people – and, without God's help, the Midianites came to attack them.

The Midianites would wait till the Israelites had grown their crops, then they would swoop down on camels and spoil the land or steal what they had grown. As a result the Israelites were weak from hunger and frightened for their lives. They hid in the mountains and were afraid to stay in the open. They lived like this for seven years.

Eventually the Israelites cried to the Lord for help. God sent them a prophet and a man to help them.

'We have disobeyed God!' the prophet warned the people. 'That is why we are being attacked by our enemies.'

Gideon was the son of Joash. Like everyone else, he was working out of sight, trying to thresh wheat in secret. An angel came to sit under an oak tree and watched him.

An angel came to sit under an oak tree and watched him.

'God is with you, mighty warrior!' the angel said to Gideon.

'Then why are we in so much trouble?' Gideon answered. 'God brought our ancestors out of Egypt only to let us die under the Midianites!'

'You can change that,' said the angel. 'God wants you to save Israel from the Midianites.'

'But why would God send me? I am no one at all! I belong to the smallest clan in my tribe; I am the least in my family!'

'You can do this because I will be with you,' said the angel. 'We will save Israel together.'

Gideon was amazed. At first he had been angry. Now he was listening – and he was afraid.

But why would God send me? I am no one at all!

'Please show me a sign,' said Gideon. 'Prove to me that this is not just a dream.'

Gideon rushed home and returned with food as an offering.

'Put the food on a rock,' said the angel.

Gideon did so and the angel touched it with his stick. The food caught alight; and the angel vanished. Now Gideon was able to believe that he had been in the company of an angel sent by God.

That night, God told Gideon to destroy the altar to Baal and the Asherah pole that belonged to his father, and build in its place an altar to the living God.

Gideon did this secretly while everyone was sleeping, but in the morning, when the local men saw what had happened, they came to find him.

'Hand him over!' they demanded of Gideon's father. 'Your son must die!'

'Whose side are you on?' asked Joash. 'If Baal is really a god, surely he can defend himself!'

The mob decided to listen to Gideon's father – and left them alone.

The Midianites joined forces with the Amalekites. They crossed over the River Jordan and made camp.

Then Gideon was filled with God's Spirit. He blew his trumpet and gathered together the Israelite men from every tribe. Gideon asked God to help him.

'I need to be sure that you want me to save Israel,' prayed Gideon. 'I will put a sheepskin on the ground this evening. In the morning, if the sheepskin is wet and the ground dry, I will know that you want me to lead Israel.'

In the morning Gideon squeezed the sheepskin. It was wet, but the ground all around was dry.

'Don't be angry with me, Lord, but I must be sure. Let me put the sheepskin out again, only this time let the ground be wet and the sheepskin dry.'

In the morning the ground was covered with dew, and the sheepskin was dry. God had given Gideon his answer.

Gideon gathered together the men who would form his army and made camp.

'You have too many soldiers,' said God to Gideon. 'When the battle is won, the people will say that they did it in their own strength. Tell anyone who is afraid that they may go home.'

That day, 22,000 men went home. Only 10,000 remained.

That day, 22,000 men went home. Only 10,000 remained.

'There are still too many,' said God. 'Ask the men to go to the river and drink.'

Some of the men knelt down to drink, while others stood up and lapped the water out of their hands like dogs.

'I will use the men who stood up and lapped the water,' said God. 'Send the others home.'

Gideon obeyed God. He now had an army of just 300 men to fight the Midianites.

'It is time!' said God to Gideon during the night. 'Now you will defeat your enemies! But first, go down to the enemy camp and listen to what they are saying. Then you will not be afraid to attack.'

Gideon went silently with his servant to the enemy camp. There were tens of thousands of men. There were more camels than grains of sand on the seashore. But Gideon had just 300 men.

'I've had a terrible dream!' Gideon heard one man say to another. 'A huge, round barley loaf rolled into our camp and hit the tent so violently it collapsed!'

'I know what that means,' said the other. 'God is on Gideon's side. They will win the battle.'

Gideon thanked God for what he had heard. He returned and woke his men.

'Come! God has already won the battle for us!' he told them.

Gideon divided the men into three groups and gave each man a trumpet and a burning torch covered by an empty jar. In the darkness, the Israelites surrounded the enemy camp. At Gideon's signal, he and his men blew their trumpets and smashed the jars.

'For the Lord and for Gideon!' they cried.

The Midianites and the Amalekites were terrified by the loud noise coming suddenly upon them. They stumbled and fell upon each other in the darkness. They killed each other with their swords. Those who remained fled to the hills.

They stumbled and fell upon each other in the darkness. They killed each other with their swords.

It was just as God had said. God had rescued the Israelites once again.

Then the people went to Gideon and asked him to rule over them.

'No,' he answered. 'The Lord God will rule over you. You need no other king,' he said. 'Neither I nor my sons will be your ruler.' But one of

Gideon's sons had other ideas.

Gideon had many wives and children. One of his sons, Abimelech, went to his mother's home town of Shechem after Gideon's death and spoke to his relatives.

'Choose me as your leader. Don't let any of my half-brothers rule over you.'

Abimelech's relatives agreed and he hired a band of men to follow him. Then he went to his father's home town, and killed all his half-brothers. Only the youngest, Jotham, escaped. Then Abimelech returned to Shechem where the people crowned him king.

When Jotham heard about it he went to Shechem and climbed to the top of Mount Gerizim.

'Remember what my father did for you!' he cried. 'Now think about what you have done to his family!'

Abimelech remained as ruler of Israel for three years, but God had seen the terrible crimes he had committed.

A while later, a man called Gaal came to Shechem. Before long he had a number of friends and supporters.

'What's so special about Abimelech?' he asked. 'If you followed me, I would easily defeat Abimelech and his whole army.'

Zebul, the governor of Shechem, was angry when he heard Gaal's boasting.

'Gaal is stirring up trouble,' he warned Abimelech. 'Make a surprise dawn attack and destroy him and his followers.'

As Abimelech approached Shechem, Zebul went to Gaal.

'So, you think you can destroy Abimelech's entire army, do you?' he sneered. 'Well, now's your chance!'

Gaal and the citizens of Shechem fought Abimelech, but they were driven out of the city. The next day, when Abimelech attacked Shechem again, the people hid in the stronghold of the temple. But Abimelech and his men chopped down branches and lay them against the stronghold. They set fire to them so that the people inside were all killed.

Abimelech then marched on to Thebez. The people fled from their homes and locked themselves in a strong tower. Abimelech made his way towards the entrance to burn it as he had before, but this time one of the women saw what Abimelech was trying to do. She lifted a heavy

She lifted a heavy millstone, and flung it down on top of him.

millstone, and flung it down on top of him. It landed on Abimelech's head and cracked his skull.

'Kill me with your sword,' Abimelech begged his servant. 'Don't let them say a woman killed me!'

The servant obeyed. When the Israelites saw what had happened, they knew they were free to leave the city. Abimelech had met a violent death, matched only by the terrible things he had done in his lifetime.

Some time later, the Israelites found themselves victims of the Ammonites. The elders of Gilead went to the great warrior Jephthah and asked him to be their leader.

'If God helps me defeat the Ammonites, will I still be your leader?' asked Jephthah.

'We promise,' they replied.

First Jephthah sent a peaceful message to the Ammonite king.

'Why are you treating us this way?' he asked. 'What have we done to you?'

'You took my land when God brought you out of Egypt,' said the king. But Jephthah knew this was not true.

'We did not take your land – only the land of those who would not let us pass safely through on our journey out of Egypt. Then we took the land that God gave to us. We have lived here now for hundreds of years: if you really had any claim on the land, why take it now?' he asked.

Abimelech had met a violent death, matched only by the terrible things he had done in his lifetime.

When the king of Ammon refused to reply, Jephthah knew that God was leading him into battle.

'I will make a bargain with you,' Jephthah foolishly said to God. 'If you help me defeat my enemies, I will sacrifice the first thing I see when I return home in triumph!'

Jephthah led the Israelite army into victory. Then he went home. The first thing he saw was his only daughter, dancing. When Jephthah saw her, he remembered what he had promised God. He tore his clothes and wept. He knew that he had made a stupid promise to God and he could not break it.

After Jephthah died, the people returned yet again to their old ways. This time they were attacked by the Philistines. They were oppressed by the Philistines for forty years.

During this time God sent an angel to a childless woman, the wife of a man called Manoah.

'I know you have no children,' said the angel, 'but God has promised to give you a son. He will be a very special child, blessed by God, who will grow up to save Israel from the Philistines. You must drink no wine before his birth and when he is born you must let his hair grow long, as a sign that he has been dedicated to God.'

The woman was amazed and she told her husband. Manoah prayed to God to send the angel again so that they could be sure to do all that God asked of them. The angel came again and repeated all he had said, and Manoah realised that God had blessed them with a special task.

Some months later, the woman gave birth to a son, She called him Samson. God's blessed the child and prepared him for the work he had to do.

When Samson grew up he wanted to marry a Philistine woman.

His parents were unhappy – why couldn't he find a wife from his own people? But the marriage was part of what God had planned for him.

His parents set off to make the wedding arrangements. Samson followed afterwards. As Samson walked through a vineyard, a young lion bounded towards him, ready to attack. God filled Samson with his Spirit and gave him amazing strength. He grappled with the lion, killing it with his bare hands. But Samson told no one what had happened.

Some time later, Samson returned to the vineyard. Bees had made a nest within the lion's carcass and there was honey inside. So during the wedding feast, Samson told his Philistine companions a riddle.

'Out of the eater, something to eat; out of the strong, something sweet. Tell me the answer to my riddle within seven days, and I will give you a prize. If not, you must reward me.'

The Philistines had no idea how to solve the riddle, but they did not want to give Samson a prize either. Instead, they threatened Samson's new wife to find the answer out for

God filled Samson with his Spirit and gave him amazing strength.

them. She wept and she cried and she begged him to tell her the secret of the riddle until finally, Samson gave in. Then his wife told her people.

So the Philistines were able to give Samson the answer to his riddle.

'What is sweeter than honey? What is stronger than a lion?' they cried.

Samson knew he had been deceived. The only way for them to know the answer was for them to have cheated. Samson was very angry. He wanted revenge.

Samson went from the wedding feast and brought back the prize he had promised to give the Philistines. But he left his wife there and returned to his father's house alone afterwards. His father-in-law assumed Samson did not want his daughter after all, so he gave Samson's wife to another man.

When Samson had cooled down, he returned to see his wife. When he found that she was no longer his, he was furious. He planned to take revenge on the Philistines.

He went out and caught 300 jackals and tied their tails together in pairs. Then he fastened a flaming torch to every pair of tails and let them loose in the cornfields. The corn was burned to the ground.

The Philistines soon came looking for Samson. They sent men from Judah to capture him.

Samson allowed himself to be tied up by the men, but as soon as the Philistines came towards him,

God gave him enormous strength. Samson broke through the new ropes as if through butter. Then he used the jaw bone of a dead donkey to fight and kill 1000 of his enemies. Samson was a terrifying fighting machine.

Samson fell to his knees dying of thirst. He prayed to God to give him water after his victory, and God caused a spring to open up so that he could drink.

He fastened a flaming torch to every pair of tails and let them loose in the cornfields.

Samson continued to protect the Israelites against the Philistines for twenty years. The Philistines hated Samson but they could not stop him because God had given him such enormous strength.

Then Samson fell in love with a woman called Delilah. The Philistine leaders seized their chance. They offered Delilah bribes.

'Find out the secret of Samson's strength,' they said to her, 'and we will reward you.'

Delilah did not love Samson. She was determined to find out the secret and win her prize.

'Tell me the secret of your strength,' she whispered to him one night.

'Tie me with seven new bowstrings, and I will be as weak as any man,' Samson replied.

The Philistines brought Delilah the bowstrings, and while they hid in the room, she used them to tie Samson while he slept.

'The Philistines are here!' she screamed. Samson leapt up, and the strings snapped under his strength.

'You lied to me,' said Delilah, some time later. 'Show me you trust me. Tell me your secret.'

'You need new ropes to bind me with,' he replied. 'Then I will be weak.'

Delilah tried the same trick again, but Samson snapped the ropes as if they were thread.

'Weave on to the loom the seven braids of my hair,' said Samson, the next time she asked. This time he broke the loom.

Delilah continued to nag Samson every day.

'If you love me, you will tell me the secret of your strength,' she said.

Eventually Samson could stand it no longer. 'My hair has never been cut,' he told her. 'If my head is shaved, I will lose my strength.'

Delilah made sure that Samson was asleep. Then one of the Philistines shaved the seven braids on his head.

Samson's strength vanished immediately. God's power left him. His enemies, the Philistines, overpowered him. They blinded Samson and put him in prison and made him work for them. He could not fight back. His strength had finally gone.

The Philistines were delighted that at last they had captured their enemy. They organised a celebration to thank their god Dagon for their success.

'Let him entertain us!' cried the people.

So Samson was brought out from the prison to amuse them. All the Philistine rulers were there; the temple was filled with the laughter of people of all ages, including 3000 on the roof. They had not noticed that Samson's hair was growing long again.

But Samson could no longer see. He asked the servant who guided him to put him between the pillars of the temple. Then Samson stretched out his arms.

'Remember me, Lord God,' prayed Samson, 'and give me strength once more. Punish the Philistines, and let me die as I have lived, destroying the enemies of your people.'

Samson pushed at the pillars with all his might. God answered his prayer and gave him back his strength. The giant pillars toppled, pulling the walls inwards and bringing the roof crashing to the ground.

God answered his prayer and gave him back his strength.

Samson had destroyed the Philistine temple, and with it, thousands of Philistines. He had died in the attempt, but killed more of his enemies by his death than he had in his lifetime.

CHAPTER 11

LOVE AND LOYALTY

THERE WAS A FAMINE IN ISRAEL DURING THE TIME THAT THE LEADERS AND JUDGES HELPED GOD'S PEOPLE AGAINST THEIR WARRING ENEMIES.

A man named Elimelech took his wife Naomi and left his home in the area around Bethlehem. His sons, Mahlon and Kilion, went too. They went to the neighbouring land of Moab to find food and started a new life.

Elimelech died while they were in Moab. Mahlon and Kilion married wives from among the local people and the family settled there for about ten years. But then Naomi's sons died too and the three women – Naomi and her two daughters-in-law – were left alone.

Naomi did not know what to do. She had heard that the famine was now over in Israel. There was no reason for her to stay in Moab any longer, so she decided to return to her home near Bethlehem.

'Stay here and return to your own mothers,' Naomi told her sons' widows. 'I will go back alone.'

But the two young women, Ruth and Orpah, did not want to leave Naomi.

'But I have nothing to offer you,' Naomi protested. 'I am too old to give you husbands again, even if I could marry. You will do better to stay here in Moab.'

So Orpah turned back and went home. But Ruth clung to her mother-in-law.

'Don't tell me to go!' she begged. 'I will never leave you. I will go with you to your country, and it will become my country. Your people will become my people and your God will become my God. I will go where you go, I will die where you die, and I will be buried there.'

Your people will become my people and your God will become my God.

Naomi saw that Ruth was serious. She was happy to have Ruth's companionship. So the two women went on to Bethlehem. They arrived there at the beginning of the barley harvest.

With no one to provide for them, Naomi and Ruth were among the poor and helpless there. And they were hungry.

'I will go and pick up the leftover grain in the fields after the workers,' Ruth told Naomi.

God blessed Ruth, and she found herself working in the fields belonging to Boaz, a relative of Elimelech. She worked hard, and Boaz asked his workers who she was.

'She is Naomi's daughter-in-law,' the man replied. 'She came from Moab to keep her mother-in-law company, even though her husband had died.'

Boaz went over to talk to Ruth.

'Stay and gather grain in my fields,' he said, 'and take some water whenever you are thirsty.'

'Why are you being so good to me?' Ruth asked.

'I have heard of your kindness to Naomi,' he replied. 'You have come to ask help from Naomi's God. May God now bless you and reward you for your loyalty to her.'

Boaz provided Ruth with food that day and there was enough over for her to take some home to Naomi, as well as the barley Ruth had gleaned. Boaz had made sure that plenty was left for her to collect.

May God bless you now and reward you for your loyalty.

Naomi was amazed at the amount she had gathered.

'Where did you go?' she asked. 'Someone has surely been kind to you.'

Ruth told Naomi about the kindness of the landowner. 'His name is Boaz,' she added.

'But he is a relative of ours!' exclaimed Naomi. 'This is wonderful. You must go to his fields again tomorrow.'

Ruth worked in Boaz's fields until the end of the harvest and she and Naomi did not go hungry. But at the end of that time, Naomi spoke to Ruth about her future.

'It's my duty to try to find a better home for you,' she said. 'We know that Boaz has been kind to you, and we are also related to him. It is our custom that if a man dies leaving a young wife, a relative should marry her to care for his family.'

'What must I do?' asked Ruth. 'Tell me and I will do it.'

Ruth did all Naomi told her. Ruth went to the threshing floor where Boaz had been celebrating the end of the harvest. That night, when he lay down to sleep, Ruth lay down at his feet and waited. When he woke in the night, he was surprised.

Everything was taken from me, but God gave me Ruth, who was better than all that was taken away.

'Who's there?' he asked.

Ruth told him why she had come.

'I will look after you,' said Boaz kindly, 'but there is another relative who should be asked first. If he is happy to let you go, I will take care of you and Naomi.'

When Ruth returned home, she told Naomi all that had happened. Then together they waited.

Boaz went to the town gate and found Naomi's relative. In front of the elders of the people, Boaz asked him if he wanted to buy Elimelech's land, marry Ruth and raise children for her dead husband, Mahlon. The man decided that he could not do it, and offered the opportunity to Boaz.

Boaz was happy. He married Ruth and God blessed them all. Some time later, Naomi found herself not only happy in Boaz's household but proudly looking after her first grandchild.

'Everything was taken from me, but God gave me Ruth, who was better than all that was taken away. Now I have Obed, too, my grandson, and God has blessed me.'

Obed grew up to have a son called Jesse, who himself had eight sons. The youngest son was called David.

Chapter 12
The prophet Samuel

EVERY YEAR ELKANAH AND HIS TWO WIVES, HANNAH AND PENINNAH, WENT TO SHILOH TO WORSHIP GOD AND MAKE A SPECIAL SACRIFICE — AN OFFERING THAT SHOWED GOD THAT THEY LOVED HIM.

Peninnah had many children but, though Hannah longed to have a baby of her own, she had none.

Hannah cried so much she couldn't eat.

Peninnah often teased Hannah until Hannah cried so much she couldn't eat.

One year, Hannah went to the place of worship and poured out all her sorrow.

'Lord God,' she prayed in her heart, 'please answer my prayer! Please let me give birth to a baby, a little son. If I could hold him in my arms and love him for a while, I will promise to give him back to you when he is older, so that he can learn to serve you all his life. Please hear me. Please help me!'

When Eli, the priest, saw Hannah's lips moving but heard no sound, he thought she had been drinking and rebuked her. But when

Hannah told him of her unhappiness and what she had asked God, he was kind.

'May God answer your prayer and bless you with a child,' he said.

Hannah returned home. God did answer her prayer and bless her. Before long she found that she was expecting a baby. She was overjoyed. Hannah gave birth to a son, and called him Samuel.

God did answer her prayer and bless her.

Hannah cared for her baby son for several years and she loved him dearly. But then, just as she had promised, Hannah took Samuel to the place of worship in Shiloh and went to Eli the priest.

'Do you remember the unhappy woman who came here and asked God to bless her with a baby son?' she asked him. 'I am that woman; but I am no longer unhappy. God has blessed me, and now I must keep my promise. My son must live here in the temple and learn how to serve God.'

Every year after that, Hannah came to visit Samuel and brought him a new robe that she had made for him.

Eli asked God to bless Hannah so she would have other children. In time she had three more sons and two daughters.

Eli had two grown up sons of his own called Hophni and Phinehas. They had become priests like their father but both were selfish men. They broke God's rules and did not serve God as well as their father.

Eli was sad when he saw how his sons behaved and he warned them that God would be angry with them. But Hophni and Phinehas did not listen.

Samuel became Eli's helper. God watched as Samuel grew up and he blessed him.

As Eli grew older, his eyes became weak and he depended more and more on Samuel's help.

One night, while the golden lampstand was still alight, and everyone was asleep, God called to Samuel.

'Samuel! Samuel!' God called.

Samuel woke at the sound of the voice but he did not know who it was. He got up and rubbed his eyes. He went to Eli.

'Here I am,' said Samuel. 'You called me?'

'No, I didn't call,' said Eli. 'Go back to sleep, Samuel.'

Before long Samuel heard the voice calling him again.

'Samuel! Samuel!' God called.

He went again to Eli.

'I didn't call you,' said Eli. 'Go back to your bed.'

Then Samuel heard the voice for a third time.

He went once more to Eli. But this time Eli understood who was calling him.

'It is God who is calling you,'

said Eli. 'Go back to your bed. But this time, if the voice calls your name, reply, "Speak, Lord, for your servant is listening."'

God called Samuel again and he answered just as Eli had taught him. Then God told Samuel of his plans for his people and for Eli's sons.

From that day God spoke to Samuel and Samuel learned to listen and to act on all that God asked him to do.

Eli and all the people saw that God was with him and that he spoke with God's authority. God had chosen Samuel to be a prophet. God would speak through him and help his people again.

'If the voice calls your name, reply, "Speak, Lord, for your servant is listening."'

Some time later, the Israelites went into battle with the Philistines. The Israelites came home to camp, defeated. They decided that if they took with them the ark, the box that contained God's laws, God would be with them and help them to win. So next time they went into battle, Eli's sons, Hophni and Phinehas, went with the ark.

The Philistines saw how brave the ark made the Israelite soldiers. They began to tremble and be afraid. These were the same people whose God had brought them out of Egypt!

Both sides engaged in battle, but although the ark was there, God was not with the Israelites that day. Hophni and Phinehas died along with 30,000 men; and the Philistines captured the ark and carried it away with them.

A young man ran from the battle line to tell the Israelites what had happened. When he told the people, they were all very afraid.

Eli was sitting at the gate, waiting. He was almost blind now and very frail.

'What has happened?' Eli asked. 'Tell me everything.'

'Our people have fled from the enemy; we have lost a great many men today in battle. I am sorry to tell you that your two sons are dead and the Philistines have captured the ark.'

When Eli heard about the capture of the ark, the shock was too much for him. He fell down dead. His daughter-in-law, Phinehas' wife, was expecting a baby at that time. When she heard the news that her husband had been killed, she went into labour and gave birth to a son whom she named Ichabod, because she believed that God had left his people.

Your two sons are dead and the Philistines have captured the ark.

The Philistines took the ark to Ashdod where they put it next to their god, Dagon, in the temple there. They thought that God would bless them now they owned it. But the next day, the people went into the temple and found that the statue

'Take the ark away!' cried the people. 'Send it back to the Israelites or we will all die!'

So the ark was put on a cart with some gifts of gold and hitched up to two cows. They put it on the road and set it on its way.

'If the cows go straight to the country of the Israelites, we will know their God has sent these plagues,' they said. 'But if not, then all of our suffering has just been a coincidence.'

But the cart went in the direction of the Israelites' country.

The Israelites rejoiced to see the ark returned to them! They sacrificed the cows that had pulled the cart, and worshipped God.

Now that Eli had died, Samuel waited to see when the people would call out to God again for help. When he thought they were sorry that they had worshipped other gods, and were ready to try again to follow God's ways, Samuel called them all together.

of their god had fallen on its face in front of the ark. They lifted the statue and put it back again but next morning, it had not only fallen again, but its head and hands had broken off.

Then there was a plague on the people of Ashdod and they were overrun with rats. They suffered terribly. They began to see that God was not blessing them – the ark should not stay in their town. They moved it to Gath, but then there

They were overrun with rats.

was a plague on the people of Gath. They moved it to Ekron, and the same thing happened there.

'Are you ready to return to God? Can you love him with all your hearts? Then you must show it. Destroy all the idols you own. Promise to serve God alone,' Samuel said. 'Then God will drive out the Philistines and there will be peace in the land.'

The people listened and acted. They destroyed all the images of Baal and the Ashtoreths they had collected. They began to worship God once more.

Then Samuel told them he would pray for them.

'We have sinned, Lord, and we are sorry. Please forgive us,' he prayed. 'Be our God as you were the God of our ancestors, Abraham, Isaac and Jacob.'

When the Philistines next threatened to attack the Israelites at Mizpah, the people were afraid. But Samuel offered sacrifices to God and kept on praying.

God heard the prayers of his people. He sent thunder, which threw the Philistines into confusion and gave the Israelites the opportunity to attack and defeat their enemy.

Samuel set a stone in the ground. He called it Ebenezer to mark the fact that God had helped his people there.

From that time on, Samuel the prophet became Israel's leader.

From that time on, Samuel the prophet became Israel's leader. Samuel judged the people wisely and helped them to follow God's ways.

Chapter 13

The first king of Israel

S AMUEL GREW TO BE OLD. HE HAD SONS, BUT, LIKE ELI'S SONS, THEY DID NOT LISTEN TO GOD OR OBEY HIM.

'We want a king like all the other nations!' cried Israel's elders as they stood before Samuel. 'You are old and there is no good man to follow you who serves God.'

Samuel was sad. Then he was angry with the people. He prayed to God.

'Listen to them,' said God. 'It is not that they are rejecting you,

---

It is not that they are rejecting you, Samuel; they are rejecting me.

Samuel; they are rejecting me. A king cannot bring them what they want; but they are just as stubborn as their ancestors before them. They must learn this for themselves. They can have a king but he will bring them great unhappiness.'

Samuel warned the people as God told him to, but they refused to listen.

So God chose a man who would be the first king of Israel. He was the son of a man named Kish. His name was Saul – and he was a tall, handsome young man.

One day Kish's donkeys wandered off into the hills.

'Take one of the servants and go to find the donkeys,' Kish told his son.

So they went first to the hill country round about, looking for the donkeys. When they did not find them, Saul and the servant went a long way from home and kept looking.

'We had better go back,' Saul said to his servant after several days. 'Soon my father will stop worrying about his donkeys and start worrying about his son!'

But the servant had heard that Samuel was in the area.

'There is a man of God nearby,' he said. 'Perhaps we could ask him about the donkeys?'

Saul agreed to go and consult Samuel before returning home.

God had already told Samuel that he had chosen Saul to be Israel's future king. When Samuel saw Saul walking towards him, he knew that this was the man God had chosen.

'We are looking for Samuel, God's prophet,' Saul said. 'Can you direct us to him?'

'You have found him,' Samuel answered. 'Come and eat with me and tomorrow I have something important to tell you. But don't worry any more about your lost donkeys. They have been found.'

The following day, Saul and his servant prepared to leave with the donkeys. Samuel told Saul to order his servant to go on a while without him.

When they were alone, Samuel took some oil and anointed Saul as the first king of Israel.

'Don't be afraid,' said Samuel. 'God will give you power to be the person who will be Israel's king. God himself will help you.'

Saul returned to his family with his father's donkeys but he kept Samuel's message a secret. He told no one about God's plans for him.

Then Samuel called all the people together.

'You have rejected the Lord God who brought your ancestors out of Egypt,' he said. 'You have chosen to have a king to rule over you instead, a man as you are, with a man's failings. Now come, so that we can see whom God has chosen to be this king.'

Samuel went through the tribes of Israel until the tribe of Benjamin – the smallest tribe – was chosen; he went through the families until the family of Kish was chosen and then he came to Saul, Kish's son. But when he asked Saul to step forward, no one could find him. Saul was hiding among the baggage. He didn't want to be brought out in front of all the people.

God told Samuel where he was hiding and so they led him out. Everyone saw that he was a tall, strong, fine-looking man.

'Long live the king!' shouted God's people.

God will give you power to be Israel's king.

Meanwhile, the Ammonites attacked the Israelite city of Jabesh. The people of Jabesh were afraid – they wanted to make peace with them.

'We will make peace on one condition,' agreed the Ammonites. 'We will blind all your inhabitants in one eye.'

When the Israelites heard this, they were even more afraid. This was Saul's opportunity to show the people that God had given him power to lead them in a victory. Saul called the people together and planned a surprise attack on the Ammonites. Saul's army was victorious – their enemies were defeated!

Then the people hailed Saul as their warrior king. He had helped them to victory and made them brave in battle. The Israelites had what they had asked for: a king like all the other nations.

God gave Samuel rules for Saul to follow so that he would be a good king. At first Saul listened and did what God told him to do. But as time went on, Saul became more confident. He made his own decisions. He started to act without God's blessing. Saul was like any other man, with a man's failings.

'You have disobeyed God,' Samuel told Saul. 'Now he will look for another king, a man who listens to him and obeys him.'

One day King Saul and his army were preparing themselves for a battle with the Philistines who continued to raid Israel. Saul was married with grown-up children by now. Saul's son, Jonathan, left the group unnoticed, taking his armour bearer with him.

'Let's find out what the Philistines are doing,' Jonathan said. 'God can use just the two of us if he will bless us and give us victory.'

They began to climb up into the rocky mountains.

'We'll let the enemy see us,' Jonathan told his armour bearer. 'If they say, "We're coming to get you!" we'll stay here. But if they say, "Come here and get us!" we'll know God will help us defeat them.'

As soon as the Philistines saw Jonathan, they dared him to come and fight. Then Jonathan knew what

God wanted him to do. He climbed over the rocks, while his servant followed behind. The Philistine army fell back as Jonathan approached, and soon Jonathan and his armour bearer were pursuing them, killing each of them in turn. Then God sent an earth tremor. The Philistines panicked and killed each other with their own swords.

God had given the Israelites victory through Jonathan, Saul's son.

King Saul, however, became more and more stubborn. He did not listen to Samuel and did not listen to God. He continued to do what he thought was right even when it was the opposite of what God told him to do.

God wants your obedience, not your sacrifices on altars.

He gave in when the people wanted to take plunder from his enemies and this made Samuel grieve.

'God wants your obedience, not your sacrifices on altars,' Samuel told him. 'You have rejected God's guidance, Saul. Now he is rejecting you as his people's king.'

Samuel wept for Saul's disobedience. He left him to himself and stopped advising him, waiting to see what God would do next.

'Fill your horn with oil, Samuel,' said God one day. 'I have chosen the man who will be king after Saul. I want you to travel to Bethlehem and invite a man called Jesse to a feast.'

So Samuel went to Bethlehem and held a feast for all the people.

When Samuel saw Jesse's eldest son, he felt sure that he must be the man God had chosen to replace Saul. But God said no.

'I have not chosen him, Samuel. You see what a person looks like on the outside, but I can see what's inside their heart.'

Then Samuel met Jesse's second son. But he was not the one God had chosen either.

When Samuel had met seven of Jesse's sons, and none of them was the one God had chosen to be king, Samuel asked whether Jesse had any more sons.

'Well, there's my youngest son, David,' he said. 'He is looking after the sheep.'

So they sent for David and brought him to the feast. 'This is my chosen king,' said God, when Samuel met David. So Samuel anointed him with oil in front of all his family, and God's Spirit filled him. But the time had not yet come for David to replace Saul.

> ## You see what a person looks like on the outside, but I can see what's inside their heart.

King Saul now suffered from depression. He was moody and his mind was full of bad, unhappy thoughts.

'Let us find someone who plays soothing music to help you,' his servants offered.

Saul agreed and asked them to find someone.

'One of Jesse's sons plays well,' suggested a servant. 'He is a fine young man, who loves God.'

So King Saul sent a message to Jesse to bring his son, David, to him.

Jesse loaded a donkey with gifts of bread and wine and a young goat and took David to see the king.

David played his harp for King Saul. It soothed him to hear David play and so David visited often, whenever the king suffered from his unhappy moods. Saul asked Jesse to let David stay and become one of his armour bearers.

David made up his own songs and sang these when he played his harp.

'You, Lord, are my shepherd. I will never be in need.

You let me rest in fields of green grass.

You lead me to streams of peaceful water, and you refresh my life.

You are all that is good and true and you lead me along the right paths.

I may walk through valleys as dark as death, but I won't be afraid.

You are with me, and your shepherd's stick makes me feel safe.

You entertain me at a feast while my enemies watch.

You treat me as your special guest and you fill my cup until it overflows.

Your kindness and love will always be with me each day of my life, and I will live in your house for ever.'

The Philistines continued to trouble the Israelites. King Saul had good reason to be depressed. Day by day, the Israelite battle line was gathered on one hill; the Philistines were on the other. In between them was a valley, and in the valley was the Philistine champion, a giant of a man named Goliath.

Goliath's huge head was protected by a bronze helmet; his huge body was protected by bronze armour; his muscular legs were protected by bronze greaves and he carried a bronze javelin on his back. In his hand was a spear with a heavy iron point. Day by day, Goliath walked up and down in front of the Israelites, mocking them and daring them to send a man to fight him.

Saul had his head in the hands. The Israelite soldiers were terrified.

No one wanted to take up the challenge. No wanted to fight the giant.

One day David came to the Israelite camp bring food supplies for his older brothers who were soldiers. He saw Goliath walking up and down and shouting, and he saw that no one was ready to stand up to him.

'How dare he challenge us!' said David to the men around him. 'He is just a man; but we have the living God on our side.'

The soldiers looked at David who was not yet a man. It was easy for him to talk. David wasn't in the army.

But King Saul heard the rumours among his soldiers that David was not afraid. Saul sent for David.

'Our army should not be afraid

of this warrior,' David told the king. 'I will go out and fight him.'

'This giant is a professional fighter,' Saul said. 'You are still a boy.'

'I look after my father's sheep,' answered David, 'and I have to fight off lions and bears to protect them. If God can save me from the paw of the lion and bear, he can surely save me from this Philistine.'

Saul was amazed at his bravery. He decided to let David try. He gave him his own armour to wear but it was too heavy and clumsy. Saul let him try his helmet but it was far too big. Instead David took his own sling and chose five small stones from the stream. Then he walked out to the amazement of the soldiers on both sides.

When Goliath saw him, he sneered at him. He thought David was a joke!

'You have sword and spear and javelin,' David shouted at Goliath, 'but I have the living God on my side! Today the whole world will know that there is a God in Israel who has the power to save us.'

David slipped a stone into his sling and whirled it around his head. The stone shot through the air and landed on the only unprotected part of Goliath's forehead. The huge man sank to the ground to the cheers

---

Today the whole world will know that there is a God in Israel who has the power to save us.

---

of the Israelite army. Their enemy's champion was dead and his army had run away.

After David had defeated Goliath, he became a hero of the Israelites. He became firm friends with Jonathan,

King Saul's son, and he married one of the king's daughters.

Saul gave David many things to do, and he saw that God blessed him in everything he did. Saul then promoted him to a position of great authority in his army. David was both popular with the people and successful.

Saul watched all that happened. He was pleased that David was on his side. But soon Saul felt jealous that David was everything he thought he should be as king.

One day when David was playing his harp, Saul was gripped with such anger and jealousy towards David that he picked up his spear and hurled it at him. Saul missed. David was not hurt but Saul had intended to kill him.

After that Saul sent David away. He could not bear to have him close by. But Saul saw that God blessed David and made sure that he led the Israelites in battles with the Philistines.

One day Jonathan went to see his friend David.

'David, you must hide,' warned Jonathan. 'My father wants to kill you. You are not safe here. I will speak to him and try to persuade him

Saul was gripped with such anger and jealousy towards David that he picked up his spear and hurled it at him.

that you mean him no harm. But he is not happy.'

King Saul listened to Jonathan and promised not to kill David. But at the next opportunity, the king threw his spear at David again. Once more David escaped.

'I don't understand why your father wants to kill me,' said David at one of their secret meetings. 'How can I trust him and be safe?'

'He tells me everything,' said Jonathan, 'and you are my closest friend. I will not let him hurt you. Now, he will expect you at the New

Moon Feast. If it is safe for you to come, I will send you a sign. But if your life is in danger, then you will also know.'

When everyone except David came to the feast, King Saul asked his son where David was. Jonathan made excuses for his friend but Saul burst into a furious rage.

'What kind of son are you to side with my enemy! I know you are protecting him! Now go! Bring David here so I can kill him!'

Jonathan went out into the field and fired some arrows. He sent a boy to fetch them, giving the agreed sign.

Now go! Bring David here so I can kill him!

Then David knew his life was still in danger. Jonathan was warning him to run away.

David could only think of one place in which to hide from King Saul. He went to the priests who lived at a place called Nob.

'I'm here on a secret mission from the king,' David said. 'I left in a hurry and have no weapon. I need something to eat and a sword or spear, if you have one.'

Ahimelech the priest only had the special holy bread but he gave this to David to eat. The only weapon there was Goliath's sword. David took the sword away.

David moved on, but Saul's head shepherd, Doeg, was there that day. He went to tell Saul that David had been there and the direction he had taken. He also told Saul that the priest had helped David.

'I will have all the priests killed for their part in David's escape,' Saul said in his anger.

Saul's own men would not hurt the priests, but Doeg went and killed not only Ahimelech and the other priests but slaughtered everyone who lived in the town of Nob. Only one man escaped. He was Abiathar, Ahimelech's son.

Abiathar fled. He found David and the men he had gathered around him. David was angry when he heard what Saul had done, and very sad for all the lost lives.

'This is all my fault,' he told Abiathar. 'You must stay here and I will keep you safe.'

David and his men kept on the move to escape from King Saul. But when he heard that the Philistines were attacking the town of Keilah, David asked God what he should do.

'Go and protect the town,' said God. 'They need your help against their enemies.'

So David and his men fought and defeated the Philistines and saved the people of Keilah. But Saul heard of the victory and came looking for David with 3000 men.

David was camping in the hills of En Gedi when Saul came searching for him. Saul entered the entrance to the cave where David's men were hiding but he did not realise that they were there in the darkness deep inside the cave.

'Look,' one of his men signalled to David. 'God has given you this opportunity to kill your enemy!'

David crept up to Saul very quiety and in the darkness he cut off a part of Saul's cloak. The king suspected nothing. But David would not kill him. Saul was still the man God had made king. David waited until Saul had left the cave, then he went out and called to him.

'King Saul!' David called as he went on his knees. 'Look here at the cloth cut from your cloak. Now do you believe that I don't want to kill you? I mean you no harm!'

Saul wept at the sound of David's voice.

'You have been good to me today and I don't deserve this. God has blessed you and he will make you king after me. But promise that when you are king, you will not kill all my family.'

David promised and Saul went home. But David continued to hide from Saul. He could not trust him.

By now, the prophet Samuel had become an old man. When he died, he was buried at Ramah. Samuel did not live to see David become king.

Now do you believe that I don't want to kill you?

David and his men lived rough in the hills. They knew they were not safe from King Saul.

For some time they had protected the shepherds of a foolish man called Nabal. As the time for sheep-shearing and feasting came near, David sent some of his men to ask if any food could be spared for them. Nabal was very rich.

Nabal was not a generous man. He saw no reason to be kind to David and his men so he sent the men away rudely with nothing.

David was angry. He told his men to arm themselves to fight.

Nabal's wife, Abigail, did not know how rude and unkind her husband had been until a servant came to tell her. Abigail was beautiful but she was also wise and she knew what danger Nabal had placed them all in.

Abigail took control of the situation. She prepared a feast for David's men – bread and wine, roasted sheep and plenty of grain, cakes of raisins and pressed figs – and without telling her husband, she rode out on a donkey into the mountains to meet David.

'Please forgive my husband's bad manners,' she said. 'Don't be angry with us, but accept these gifts of food. We know that God has blessed you and protects you from your enemies. Now please – we don't want any trouble.'

David accepted her gift and praised God for preventing him from killing the men there.

'Thank you for coming to see me,' he said to Abigail, 'and thank you for this food. Go home. No one will harm you.'

Nabal was drunk when Abigail returned home so she didn't tell him what she had done until the next morning.

Not long after this, Nabal became ill and died. David did not forget what Abigail had done to help him. When he heard that her husband was dead, David asked her to become his wife.

But Saul was still searching for David. He took his 3,000 men and hunted him down.

David's spies watched from their secret hiding places while Saul and his army made camp. The king was surrounded by his troops and Abner, the commander of Saul's army, was by his side.

He took his 3,000 men and hunted him down.

'Who will come with me to see Saul?' David asked his friends.

'I will,' offered Abishai.

When it was dark, the two men crept down to Saul's camp, where everyone was sleeping deeply. Close to King Saul's head lay his spear, its point stuck in the ground; by his side was a water jug.

'Let me kill Saul while we have the chance,' whispered Abishai to David. 'God has given us an opportunity – he means for us to take his life.'

'No!' ordered David. 'Don't touch him! He is still God's chosen king.'

Instead David told Abishai to pick up the spear and water jug, and they left the camp as quietly as they had come.

When they were at a safe distance, David shouted to Saul's commander.

'Speak to me, Abner!' shouted David. 'You haven't been protecting your king very well! Where is your

---

Don't touch him! He is still God's chosen king.

---

master's spear and water jug?'

Saul recognised David's voice and looked around him anxiously. He realised what had happened. Once more David was close enough to kill him – but he had spared his life.

'God bless you for not killing me,' the king shouted back.

David knew that King Saul might be grateful now but he would soon be searching for him again. He took 600 of his men and escaped to the land of the Philistines. The Philistine King Achish knew that Saul and David were enemies and he let David settle in his land. Achish preferred to have David as his friend rather than an enemy.

Meanwhile Saul prepared to lead the Israelite army. He needed Samuel's advice – but Samuel was dead. Saul then broke an important rule – he disguised himself so no one would know he was the king and went to Endor to find a woman who claimed to be able to speak to the dead.

'I must talk to Samuel,' he told her.

'Surely you know that King Saul has forbidden anyone to talk to the dead! It is against God's law,' she said.

Saul reassured her that she would be safe and she called to Samuel. But as soon as she saw the dead prophet, she was afraid. She knew that the disguised man in front of her was King Saul himself.

'Tell me what Samuel says,' Saul commanded. 'You need fear nothing from me.'

But Samuel had no good news for Saul.

'Why do you call me?' asked Samuel. 'You have done all those things that God told you not to do. You know that God has left you. No good can come to you now. Tomorrow, you will be defeated by the Philistines. You and your sons will all die.'

King Achish gathered his army to fight the Israelites. He wanted David to fight with him against his own people, but the Philistine commanders were unhappy about this. They told King Achish that they did not want David fighting on their side.

You know that God has left you. No good can come to you now.

So when the battle took place, David was not there. The Philistines defeated the Israelites the next day, but David was not there to watch his friend Jonathan killed in battle, or to see King Saul fall on his own sword rather than be killed by the Philistines.

Israel's first king was dead.

CHAPTER 14

DAVID'S WARRING SONS

A FTER SAUL'S DEATH, DAVID WANTED TO RETURN TO HIS OWN LAND.

'Shall I go back to Judah?' David asked God.

'Yes,' said God. 'Go to the town of Hebron.'

So David took his two wives, the men who had fought with him and their families and they all settled in Hebron. Men from the southern tribe of Judah came to Hebron and welcomed David. They made him their king.

Meanwhile Abner, the commander of Saul's army, had made Saul's son, Ish-Bosheth, king over the northern part of the land. Here they did not accept David as their king. So the land was divided: Israel included the tribes in the north and Judah was made up of those in the south.

David's army, under the command of Joab, sat on one side of the pool of Gibeon. Ish-Bosheth's army, under Abner's command, was on the other side.

'Let's choose twelve champions and let them fight!' said Abner. 'Whichever side does best will win the battle.'

There was a keen contest

between the two sides but all of the soldiers died; there was no clear winner. Then war broke out with both armies fighting each other. David's men were stronger, and Ish-Bosheth's army was defeated.

Abner fled from the battle, followed by Asahel, Joab's brother.

Abner turned and tried to reason with Asahel.

'Stop pursuing me!' shouted Abner. 'I don't want your death on my conscience.'

But Asahel would not give up. Abner killed Joab's brother with a spear.

Abner then tried to agree a truce with Joab. At sunset, he and his men called to Joab from the hilltop.

'We should be on the same side,' Abner said. 'This fighting is senseless. Let's stop now!'

Joab agreed to end the battle, but he knew Abner had killed his brother; he would not forget.

Over time David married more wives. He had six children, each with a different mother.

The trouble between the lands of Judah and Israel continued but David's side was always stronger. King Ish-Bosheth made Abner very angry. Eventually Abner decided to go over to David's side.

When Joab discovered that King David had made peace with Abner, he was furious. He still bore a grudge against him. He waited for the right time and when he was alone with Abner, he murdered him to avenge his brother's death.

David was very sad when he heard how Abner had died. He knew that he had been a brave soldier, and he mourned him openly. He didn't want people to think he had been involved in Abner's death.

Ish-Bosheth also heard that Abner was dead. Now he was afraid. The whole of Israel was afraid.

Then one day, while Ish-Bosheth was taking his rest in the heat of the afternoon, two strangers arrived. They crept into the house and found the king lying on his bed. They stabbed him and killed him then cut off his head. Thinking that they would please King David, they took his head as a trophy and brought it to Hebron.

'We have brought you the head of your enemy,' they told David.

You have murdered an innocent man while he slept in his own bed!

David could not believe what they had done. 'You have murdered an innocent man while he slept in his own bed!' he cried. 'How could you think I would approve of such a thing? This is a crime – and you must die for it.'

The two men were taken out and executed. David made sure that Ish-Bosheth's head was buried with Abner.

Once people realised that Ish-Bosheth was dead, they came together at Hebron.

'Years ago we were one nation, and we fought together against our enemies,' they said to David. 'God promised that you would look after us as a shepherd looks after his sheep. We want you to be our king now.'

So when David was thirty years old, he was made king of all Israel. The two kingdoms were united again.

David gathered together an army and marched towards the fortified city of Jerusalem, which was set on a hill. The city was occupied by the Jebusites, a Canaanite tribe.

'You are no match for us here!' they boasted. 'Not even David will be able to defeat us.'

But David found the tunnel which had been dug under the city to bring in water from the Gihon spring. He surprised the Jebusites by entering the city through the water tunnel and was able to capture Jerusalem.

David made the fortress his capital and Jerusalem became known as the City of David.

Now that he was king and living in Jerusalem, David wanted to bring the ark there as a sign of God's presence. So the ark was placed on a new cart, and carefully guided along the road.

Suddenly one of the oxen stumbled. Uzzah put out his hand and touched the ark to stop it from falling. But at that moment, he fell down, dead.

David was angry. He knew that the ark was holy and that the instructions were clear about not touching the ark, but David believed that God had struck him dead. It seemed unfair.

'I can't bring the ark back to Jerusalem now,' said David. 'The day is spoiled.'

So David left the ark in Obed-Edom's house.

Three months later, David was told how much God had blessed Obed-Edom because he was looking after the ark. David knew he had to bring the ark back to Jerusalem so that God would bless the whole nation.

Everyone gathered as the ark was carried into Jerusalem. They sang to God and David celebrated by joining the people and dancing before God.

Michal, one of David's wives, saw him dancing in the streets.

'What a fool he is making of himself!' she thought.

When the celebrations were over, Michal went out to meet David.

'I saw you today, dancing with the people!' she sneered. 'You didn't behave the way a king should.'

'It doesn't matter what you think of me,' said David to his wife. 'I was praising God and dancing for God. And he chose me to be king rather than your father, Saul, because God knew what was in my heart.'

David built a palace made of cedar wood in Jerusalem. All his enemies knew that God had blessed him and Israel enjoyed a time of peace.

He chose me to be king because God knew what was in my heart.

One day David spoke to Nathan, the prophet, about the ark.

'It does not seem right that I live

here in a palace while the ark lives in a tent,' said David. 'I think I should build a temple fit for God.'

That night Nathan heard God speaking to him.

'I don't want David to build a temple for me,' said God. 'I have been happy to move from place to place with my people. My plan for David is to make Israel into a great nation. I will make him a great king and I will never stop loving him. After David will come one of his sons. I will also love him, and he can build me a temple. David's family will be kings for a long time to come.'

Nathan told David everything that God had said. David was amazed at the plans God had for him, and he was humbled.

'I don't know why you have chosen me or looked after me,' said David, 'or why you have told me your plans. But I do know that you are a great God and you always keep your promises.'

Then David wrote a song as a prayer to God.

'You have looked deep into my heart, Lord, and you know all about me,' David wrote. 'You know when

I'm resting and when I'm working and although you are in heaven, you know what I am thinking. You notice everything I do and everywhere I go. Before I even speak a word you know what I will say and with your powerful arm you take care of me

> ## You know what I am thinking. You notice everything I do and everywhere I go.

and protect me. I can't understand any of this! It's amazing to think that you who are so great are concerned about what I do. Where could I go to hide from you? How could I escape from your sight? Would you still see me if I were to climb into the highest heavens? Yes – you would be there! Would you find me if I were to go down to the world of the dead? Yes – you would be there too. Suppose I could fly over the ocean on rays of morning light? Even then your powerful arm would guide and protect me. Perhaps I could hide in the shadows until I am cloaked in the darkness of night? But daylight and

darkness are all the same to you –
you would always be able to see me.

You are the one who created
me; who put me together inside
my mother's body and gave me
this curious and amazing body and
the power to think and feel and
love. Lord, I praise you because you
made me and everything you do is
marvellous!

'Nothing about me is hidden
from you! I was secretly woven

Your thoughts are far beyond my understanding, much more than I could ever imagine.

---

together deep in the earth below,
but with your own eyes you saw
my body being formed. Even before I
was born, you had written in a book
everything I would do. Your thoughts
are far beyond my understanding,
much more than I could ever

imagine. I try to count them but they
outnumber the grains of sand on the
beach. And when I wake from sleep, I
find you nearby.

'Look deep into my heart, God,
and find out everything I am thinking.
Don't let me follow evil ways, but
lead me in the way that is true and
good and right.'

David often thought of his friend
Jonathan, who had died in battle.

'Does Saul have any family still
living?' David asked one day. 'I would
like to be kind to one of his relatives
for Jonathan's sake.'

'There is one called
Mephibosheth,' Ziba told the king.
'He is Jonathan's son. He was
dropped when he was five years old
and both his feet are damaged.'

'I'd like to help him,' said David.
'Bring him here.'

Mephibosheth was anxious about being brought before King David.

'There is no need to be afraid, Mephibosheth,' David told him. 'Your father was my greatest friend. I promised to look after his family. Come and live in the palace with me and I will give you the land that belonged to your anestors.'

Mephibosheth was amazed that a great king like David should keep his promise and take care of him. From that time on Mephibosheth lived in Jerusalem and was treated as part of David's family.

David was a good man but like every man and woman who had lived before him, he was not perfect. David had his faults. One evening in springtime, when the Israelite army was away fighting, King David went out on to the palace rooftop. As he looked across the city, he saw a woman bathing in the courtyard of a nearby house. She did not know she was being watched. She was a very beautiful woman.

David called a servant and asked who she was.

'That's Bathsheba,' the servant replied, 'Uriah's wife.'

David knew Uriah. He was a soldier in his army. But at that moment, David did not care whose wife she was. He wanted Bathsheba for himself.

'Bring Bathsheba here,' he ordered.

Bathsheba came to the palace, and David knew that he loved her. He spent the rest of the day with her. Some time later, Bathsheba sent a message to David.

David did not care whose wife she was. He wanted Bathsheba for himself.

'I'm pregnant,' she said. 'The baby I am carrying is yours.'

David put his head in his hands. This was not good news. He quickly thought of a plan to cover up the wrong he had done. David sent a message to Joab at the battlefront, asking him to send Uriah home. Perhaps he could arrange things so that no one would ever know what had happened.

Uriah returned to Jerusalem and went to see the king. David asked him about the progress of the war with the Ammonites. Afterwards David told him to go home and relax and spend time with his wife. But Uriah was an honourable soldier. He would not go home.

'How can I enjoy myself while all my fellow soldiers are fighting?' he said. 'It would be wrong.'

Sadly, David let Uriah return to the battlefield. He asked him to take with him a letter for Joab.

'Make sure Uriah fights on the front line,' the letter said. 'Leave him undefended so that he will die.'

It was a terrible thing to do.

Joab had besieged the city. He let Uriah fight close to the city walls so that he was killed by an arrow, along with a number of the soldiers.

A messenger was sent from the battlefront to King David, telling him

---

Make sure Uriah fights on the front line, leave him undefended so that he will die.

---

that some of his men had died; Uriah was one of them.

David felt relieved. Now he could hide what he had done wrong.

Bathsheba mourned her husband's death. But then David brought her to the palace and she became his wife.

Time passed and Bathsheba gave birth to her child, a baby boy. But God knew all that had happened, from David's deceit through to his arranging of Uriah's death. As David had once written, there is nothing that God doesn't know. Now God was angry with David.

God sent the prophet Nathan to David with a message.

'There were once two men,' said Nathan. 'One of them was a wealthy farmer with many sheep and cattle. The other man was poor with just one little ewe lamb. That lamb was very special to him. One day a guest came to stay with the rich man. Instead of killing one of his own sheep for their meal, he stole the little ewe from the poor man and cooked it.'

David was furious.

'That's a terrible thing to do,' he said. 'The rich man must surely be punished!'

'But you are the rich man,' said Nathan quietly. 'This is God's message for you, David. God has given you so much. He made you king over his people and saved you from Saul's anger. He gave you wives and children of your own. Yet you took another man's wife and made sure that the man himself died. God is angry. Don't you think you deserve to be punished for this?'

Then David put his head in his hands. He knew that everything Nathan had said was true.

'I am so sorry,' said David. 'I have sinned against God.'

'God will forgive you,' said Nathan. 'But there will still be consequences of the wrong that you have done.'

> **God will forgive you, but there will still be consequences of the wrong that you have done.**

David prayed to God after Nathan had left.

'Have mercy on me, oh God, because your love is great and constant. Wash away my sin and let me feel your forgiveness. I know that what I have done is wrong; I cannot forget how terrible it is and I am so sorry. I know, too, that you are holy and it is you that I have wronged; I have betrayed your trust and let you down. Wash away my sin, Lord; take away my guilt. Forgive me; don't hold this wrong against me for ever. I know you don't want empty sacrifices or outward signs of my guilt; you

Give me back the joy I have in loving and serving you.

want only to know that I am really sorry and that I will not sin in this way again. Make my heart pure and help me to do only what is right. Give me back the joy I have in loving and serving you so that others may know and love you too.'

Not long after this, Bathsheba's son became very ill and although for a whole week David could do nothing except pray to God for his life, the little boy died. David comforted Bathsheba as best he could. In due time, she had another little boy. They named him Solomon.

David had many sons, but because they had different mothers, they were often jealous of each other.

David's daughter, Tamar, was very beautiful. Amnon, David's eldest son, fell in love with her. Tamar was his half-sister. She knew that they could not be husband and wife but Amnon could not resist her beauty. When Tamar's brother, Absalom, found out that he had forced her to have sex with him, he was angry. He hated Amnon so much that he waited for the right opportunity and arranged for him to be killed.

When David heard that Amnon was dead, he was grief-stricken. He

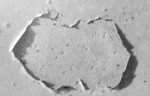

had lost two sons: one was dead and the other had fled the country. Absolom knew he had to stay away from his father. But David loved all his sons. He missed Amnon because he was dead; but although he was angry with Absalom, he also missed him.

Joab could see how sad David was. After some years had passed, he persuaded David to let Absalom come home.

Absalom was strong and handsome and popular with the people. He was also ambitious. Absalom dreamed of being king one day. He moved to Hebron and gathered a band of men around him.

Before long a messenger came to David in Jerusalem.

'Absalom has been proclaimed king in Hebron!' he announced.

'Then we must go from here quickly!' said David to his men. 'Absalom will let nothing stand in his

I may be his father — but he will kill us all.

way. I may be his father — but he will kill us all.'

So David and his friends fled from Jerusalem. When he found that his friend Ahithophel had also joined Absalom, David wept. He had been betrayed by his son and by his trusted adviser.

'Oh, God,' prayed David, 'please make Ahithophel give Absalom bad advice.' Then David turned to Hushai. 'Return to Jerusalem and pretend to join Absalom. You will be able to advise against any plans Ahithophel may have.'

When Absalom arrived in Jerusalem, Hushai came to meet him.

'Long live the king!' said Hushai.

Absalom was suspicious.

'Why are you here?' he asked. 'Is this how you serve your friend, my father David?'

'I will serve the man God and all the people have chosen as king,' Hushai replied. 'I will serve you now as well as I have served your father in the past.

Absalom then turned to Ahithophel and asked him what he should do next.

'Let me choose 12,000 men to attack David tonight,' said Ahithophel. 'He and his men will be tired and anxious. It will be easy to kill David and then I will lead his troops back to Jerusalem. Then there will be peace.'

It was a good plan, but Absalom was undecided.

'What do you think?' he asked Hushai.

Hushai thought quickly. 'Ahithophel has not given you good advice,' he said. 'David will know you will try to come after him. He will hide away from his men. Wait for a while, and then go after him but make sure you lead the army yourself.'

Absalom liked Hushai's plan. Secretly, Hushai sent a message to David and warned him. But when Ahithophel heard that Absalom had not followed his advice, he went home and killed himself.

David prepared for battle. He divided his men into three groups and planned to go with them to fight.

'You must stay here,' they told him. 'If anything happens to you, everything is lost. You can send us help if we need it.'

David decided to do as they

He went home and killed himself.

wanted, but he had one request. He made sure everyone heard it.

'Do what you have to do, but please do not harm Absalom!'

The two armies engaged in battle in the forest and the fighting was fierce. David's soldiers defeated Absalom's men but thousands of men died.

Then Absalom came riding through the forest, weaving his way through the trees, his thick hair flowing behind him. Suddenly, his hair caught in the branches of an oak tree.

He was pulled from his mule and left dangling in mid air. His mule ran on without him.

'I saw Absalom hanging in a tree,' said one of the soldiers to Joab.

'What do you mean you saw him? Why then didn't you kill him?' asked Joab. 'I would have rewarded you.'

'King David gave instructions that we shouldn't hurt his son,' the man said. 'I wouldn't dare disobey such an order.'

But Joab wasted no time. He and his ten armour bearers found Absalom and killed him.

Two men ran with the news of their victory to David. But Joab warned them not to say that Absalom was dead.

'The victory is ours!' cried Ahimaaz who got there first.

'Is Absalom alive?' asked David. But Ahimaaz claimed not to know.

'Is Absalom alive?' David asked the other messenger.

'I wish all your enemies would end up like him,' the messenger replied.

Then David knew that he was dead. He wept for his son.

'Oh, my son, Absalom,' cried David. 'I wish I could have died instead of you!'

King David was growing older. By the time he was an old man he became unwell and soon the affairs of the nation were of less importance to him. He kept to his room and was nursed day and night by a beautiful woman called Abishag.

David's fourth son, Adonijah, decided to take over from his father and rule the people.

'Oh, my son, Absalom,' cried David. 'I wish I could have died instead of you!'

Joab supported him but Zadok, Benaiah and Nathan, the prophet, remained loyal to David.

Nathan went to see Bathsheba.

'Have you heard that Adonijah has made himself king?' Nathan asked her. 'You had better warn King David. Didn't he promise you that Solomon would be king after his death?'

Bathsheba went to see King David and told him what she knew. Nathan confirmed it.

'I will keep my promise,' David assured Bathsheba. 'Solomon will be king. Let Benaiah take Solomon to Gihon, riding on my mule so that he can be anointed.'

Solomon was prepared and taken to Gihon where Zadok took the horn of oil and anointed him king.

'Long live King Solomon!' shouted the people. Then there was a great joyful procession with the people making pipe music and singing and shouting.

Adonijah had been feasting with his friends and supporters. They heard the sound of music and celebration and came to find out what was happening.

'David has made Solomon king!' a messenger announced. 'Zadok the priest has anointed him.'

Adonijah's supporters realised they might now be in danger for siding with a rival king. They hurriedly made their way to their own homes, leaving Adonijah alone. Adonijah was certain Solomon would kill him and fled to the temple for sanctuary.

'I will not harm my brother as long as he does not betray me,' promised King Solomon.

When David knew that he was dying, he sent for Solomon.

'I am soon to die, and go the way that all of us must. The throne of Israel will belong to you and to your descendants. Remember to obey God and to follow all the laws that

---

If you do as God says, he will bless you in everything you do.

Moses left us. If you do as God says, he will bless you in everything you do. But watch Joab,' warned David. 'Remember that he is a murderer. Make sure that he is punished.'

Solomon listened carefully to his father. Not long afterwards, David died and was buried in Jerusalem. He had ruled for forty years, and under his leadership, Israel had become a strong nation.

Solomon sat on David's throne and ruled as king. But Adonijah still hoped to take some power for himself. He went to Bathsheba with a request.

'Solomon will listen to you,' he said. 'Please ask if I may marry Abishag now that our father is dead.'

Bathsheba told Solomon what Adonijah had asked for, but Solomon knew he wanted much more.

'Adonijah cannot be trusted,' Solomon told his mother. 'We will not be safe till he is dead.'

Solomon sent Benaiah to execute Adonijah, and when he was dead, Joab ran away and hid, knowing that he was in danger for supporting him.

But Solomon had also given orders for Joab's execution for the murders he had committed. Benaiah found Joab and killed him too.

We will not be safe till he is dead.

Then Solomon promoted Benaiah so that he was commander of the army in Joab's place. He also made Zadok the priest. Solomon was now properly in control of Israel.

CHAPTER 15

WISDOM AND FOOLISHNESS

SOLOMON LOVED GOD AND FOLLOWED HIS FATHER'S ADVICE BY KEEPING ALL GOD'S COMMANDMENTS.

One night, after a day of worshipping God at Gibeon, Solomon had a strange dream in which God appeared to him.

'Ask for anything you want,' God said, 'and I will give it to you.'

Solomon replied, 'You blessed my father David, and you gave him a son who would rule after him. You have already been so good to me, allowing me to be king in his place. But I know nothing; I am young and inexperienced. What I want most of all is the ability to make wise judgements so that I can rule the people fairly.'

God was pleased with Solomon's answer.

'You have asked for wisdom,' said God, 'when you could have chosen wealth, or revenge over your enemies, or a long life. I will give you what you have asked for, so that everyone will be amazed at your wisdom and will always remember you for it, but I will also give you wealth and power. And if you obey me, I will give you long life too.'

When Solomon woke up, he clearly remembered his dream and all that God had promised him.

One day, two women came to see Solomon.

'Your majesty,' cried one of the women, 'this woman and I live in the same house. I gave birth to a baby son while she was in the house with me. Then three days later, she also had a baby son.

'We both went to sleep with our babies cuddled up next to us. But this woman rolled on her baby while she was sleeping and he died. She came to me while I slept and swapped her dead baby for my living son. When I awoke, I knew that the dead baby was not mine.'

'That's not true!' shouted the other woman. 'My son is alive; yours is dead!'

She came to me while I slept and swapped her dead baby for my living son.

'Bring me a sword!' ordered Solomon. 'Divide the baby into two parts so that each woman can have a share!' But Solomon knew that the real mother would not let her child suffer and die in this way.

Divide the baby into two parts so that each woman can have a share!

'Don't harm him!' the first woman pleaded with the king. 'Let her have the baby.'

'No, what the king says is fair!' replied the other woman. 'Then neither of us can have the baby!'

Immediately Solomon knew which woman was the baby's mother.

'Give the first woman her baby,' Solomon ordered. 'She is his mother.'

Everyone in Israel was amazed.

They knew that God had given him wisdom to judge between them fairly.

Solomon made many good judgements; but he also brought together much wise teaching about how to live and wise proverbs that warned people about what was important in life and what bad things should be avoided.

'Listen to what your parents tell you,' Solomon advised. 'Their teaching will build a good character in the same way as good clothes make you look smart.

'A wise child pays attention when parents correct him, but a foolish one never admits that he is wrong.

The start of an argument is like a hole in a dam. Stop it quickly before it gets out of control.

'If you love your children, you will correct them when they are naughty.

'The start of an argument is like a hole in a dam. Stop it quickly before it gets out of control.

'There is nothing but sadness and sorrow for a parent whose child does foolish things.

'Discipline your children while they are young enough to learn. If you don't, you are helping them to destroy themselves.

'Children are lucky if they have a father who is honest and does what is right.

'Anyone who thinks it isn't wrong to steal from his parents is no better than a common thief.'

Solomon didn't just talk about parents and children. He said wise things about all kinds of relationships. He believed in forgiveness and generosity.

'A gentle answer can turn anger away, but a fierce reply can make things worse.

'Gossip is spread by wicked people; they stir up trouble and break up friendships.

'It is better to eat bread and water with your friends than to eat a feast with your enemies.

'If you want people to like you, forgive them when they do something wrong. Remembering wrongs can break up a friendship.

It is better to eat bread and water with your friends than to eat a feast with your enemies.

'If you want to stay out of trouble, be careful about what you say.

'Don't make friends with people who have hot tempers. You might learn their habits and find it hard to change.

'A friend means well, even if he hurts you. But if an enemy starts pretending to be your friend, trouble is bound to follow.

'You will never succeed in life if you try to hide your sins. Confess them and God will show mercy and forgive you.'

Solomon thought it was important to search for knowledge but also to be careful about when to speak and when to remain silent; he believed in the important of justice and of kindness and warned people not to think too much about money.

'Trust in the Lord with all your heart. Don't rely on what you think you know. Ask for God's help in all you do and he will guide you.

'Be careful how you think; your life is shaped by your thoughts. Speak only the truth; have nothing to do with lies.

Be careful how you think; your life is shaped by your thoughts

---

'Sensible people will see trouble coming and avoid it, but a foolish person will walk into trouble and regret it later.'

'Do good to those who are in need whenever you can. Don't tell someone you will help them tomorrow if you can help them today.

'Be generous, and you will do well. Help others and you will be helped.

'If you want to be happy, be kind to the poor. Never despise or belittle other people.

'If you oppress poor people, you insult God who made them; but kindness to the poor is an act of worship.

'Do what is right and fair; that pleases God more than any gift you can offer him.

'Don't wear yourself out trying to get rich. Your money can disappear in a flash as if it had grown wings and flown away.

'It is better to have no money and be honest than to be rich and dishonest.'

The people knew that they had a good, wise king and for a time, there was peace in Israel. This was the right time for Solomon to build a temple for God.

King Hiram of Tyre had been a friend of King David's. When he sent ambassadors to his son, Solomon sent back a message.

'God told my father that a temple would be built after his reign at a time when there was peace in the land. Now that time has come and I want to build a temple for God. I

It is better to have no money and be honest than to be rich and dishonest.

want you to fell the best cedar trees in Lebanon so I can start building. I will pay you whatever you ask.'

The king of Tyre was happy to make an agreement and he supplied him with all the wood he needed, making rafts out of the logs of cedar and pine and floating them down the coast to Solomon.

God told Solomon how the temple should be designed and constructed. The stones were prepared in the quarry and brought to the chosen site. Solomon lined the internal walls with highly carved wood, and covered them with gold. He filled the temple with all the things that God wanted, taken from the tent of meeting.

Finally, in front of all Israel's elders, the ark, which contained the stone tablets bearing God's laws, was brought to the temple and put into the Holy of Holies. The cloud of God's presence filled the temple so that the priests were dazzled by the light.

Then Solomon asked God's blessing on the people.

'Lord God of Israel, you are like no one else,' prayed Solomon. 'No one in heaven above, no one beneath the earth shows such love and compassion; no one else keeps promises as you do.'

'I have built this house for you, Lord, but I know that you cannot live in a house made by men. Even heaven cannot contain you, for you are a great God! Let this temple be a place where your people can come when we need your help. Whether we bow before the altar here, or whether we bow in its direction when we are far away, hear our prayers.

'We will come if we fear our enemies; we will come if there is drought or famine; we will come when we have sinned – for there is no man, woman or child, who does not sin and break your laws – and we will ask your forgiveness. Then Lord, hear us from heaven and have mercy on us. Keep the promises that you made to Moses and our ancestors, that we will be your people, and that you will be our God.'

The Solomon turned to the people and prayed again.

'We ask that God will be with us and bless us and help us to keep his laws; so that all the peoples on earth will know that the Lord is God, and that there is no other.'

God appeared to Solomon some time after this and spoke to him.

'I have heard your prayers, and I will bless you and this house that

you have made for me. But,' God warned Solomon, 'remember to follow my laws. Keep to the right path. If you don't, your children will not be kings, and this house will become a ruin. People will pass by and know that it is because you did not obey my laws and because you did not love the God who brought you out of Egypt.'

Reports about Solomon's wealth and wisdom were carried to people far from Israel through the traders who passed through his land.

Far away, the queen of Sheba heard stories of Solomon's greatness. She prepared for the long journey across the desert sands of Arabia and along the Red Sea coast. She rode by camel on a beautiful four poster bed covered in cushions, with a roof to protect her from the sun. She rode up into the land of Moab and crossed the River Jordan to arrive in Jerusalem. She journeyed for months to see Solomon for herself.

Her arrival was greeted with great interest. The queen had brought with

---

The queen had brought with her nearly 800 camels, mules and donkeys, all laden with gifts.

---

her nearly 800 camels, mules and donkeys, all laden with gifts for King Solomon – gold and precious stones, exotic spices and items of furniture.

The queen saw the magnificent ornamented palace that Solomon had built with lavish crimson and purple curtains; she walked in his fruitful vineyards, beautiful gardens and by refreshing pools; she saw his many fine horses and chariots; she tasted the best food and wine. She noticed the expensive clothing his servants wore and listened to singers with exotic musical instruments.

She watched Solomon worship God in the temple and found that he could answer questions about so many things – his wisdom was inexhaustible.

'I heard all about you in my country,' the queen said to Solomon, 'but I couldn't believe it was true. Now I know that you are even greater than your reputation. Let me praise your God for making you such a great and wise king!'

Solomon planted olive, spice and nut trees and studied the ways of spiders, locusts and harvesting ants. He knew all there was to know about plants and animals, birds, reptiles and fish.

As Solomon's reputation grew, he became richer and richer. Many visitors came to consult him and ask for his help; each one brought expensive gifts. He traded with many different nations, and his fleet of ships brought him back gold and silver, ivory, apes and peacocks.

Silver was worthless because there was so much gold.

Soon Solomon had so much gold that everything in his palace was made of it; silver was worthless because there was so much gold. Solomon's throne was made out of ivory, with golden armrests and golden embroidery and a calf's head carved on the back of it. On either side of the throne was a huge golden lion. Six steps led up to the throne and on each side of each step was another golden lion. No one had ever seen anything so spectacular before.

But Solomon had a weakness. Like many before and after him, he could not resist a beautiful woman.

But Solomon had a weakness.

He married foreign wives, who bowed down to idols and did not know the one true God. He had forgotten God's warnings.

As the years passed, Solomon not only loved his many wives, he also began to worship their gods.

'I warned you not to worship these idols as the other nations do,' said God. 'You have broken your promise to me. I will not take the kingdom from you yet, because I made a promise to your father, David. But I will take the kingdom from your son.'

A young man called Jeroboam worked very hard for Solomon. One day as Jeroboam was walking on the road outside Jerusalem, the prophet Ahijah came to him. Ahijah took off the new cloak he was wearing and ripped it into twelve pieces.

'Take them!' he said, giving ten pieces to Jeroboam. 'This is a picture of what God will do for you. Once Solomon is dead, God will make you king over ten of the tribes of Israel. Remember to follow God's commandments and serve him well.'

Solomon heard what had happened and tried to kill Jeroboam. But Jeroboam escaped to Egypt and hid there.

CHAPTER 16

A DIVIDED NATION

WHEN SOLOMON DIED, JEROBOAM LEFT EGYPT AND JOINED WITH THE PEOPLE FROM THE NORTHERN TRIBES OF ISRAEL AT SHECHEM.

Solomon's son, Rehoboam, also went to Shechem, hoping that the people would proclaim him king. Instead they challenged him.

'Your father, King Solomon, made us work hard. If you want us to make you king now, you must promise to make our work easier.'

Rehoboam didn't know what to do. He told the people to return in three days, and meanwhile he consulted his father's old officials.

'It's the only thing to do,' they advised him. 'Make their workload lighter.'

Rehoboam listened but he didn't like their advice. He went instead and asked his friends what he should do.

'Don't give in!' said his friends. 'Tell them that you will make them work harder, and they'll regret it if they don't!'

So when the men returned after three days, Rehoboam gave them the answer his friends had suggested. It was not the right answer!

'You are not one of us; you are

not our king! We will not serve you or work for you.'

Rehoboam had made his first mistake. He returned to Jerusalem where only the tribe of Judah followed him. The ten northern tribes of Israel made Jeroboam their king.

The kingdom of Israel was divided again. Now there was no longer one nation but two.

Jeroboam was anxious. He had built two cities at Shechem and Penuel but the temple was in Jerusalem – under Rehoboam's control. If he let the people return to worship God, they might decide to follow King Rehoboam instead. He couldn't let that happen.

So Jeroboam made two golden calves.

'These are your gods!' he said to the people. 'Now you don't need to go to Jerusalem to worship.'

Jeroboam placed one of the statues in each of his two cities, and went to worship them himself. He made priests out of people who were not Levites, and he introduced new feast days.

He was challenged one day by a prophet from Judah.

'Be careful!' the man shouted. 'God has seen what you've done. He has chosen Josiah, one of King David's descendants, to overthrow all the bad things you have done. And so that you know that what I say comes from God, your altar will crumble and the ashes of the sacrifice will fall on the ground.'

Jeroboam was angry.

'Seize him!' he said, pointing at the prophet. But at that moment Jeroboam's hand was paralysed. He could not move it.

Jeroboam watched helplessly as the altar cracked and crumbled before his eyes, scattering the ashes over the ground.

'Ask God to help me!' he begged. 'Give me back the use of my hand.'

The prophet prayed for Jeroboam and his hand was restored. But Jeroboam soon forgot the prophet's warning. He continued to disobey God.

Then Jeroboam's son, Abijah, became ill. It became clear that he might die.

'Go to Ahijah, the prophet in Shiloh,' Jeroboam told his wife. 'Ask him what will happen to our son. But disguise yourself; don't let him know that you are the king's wife.'

Jeroboam's wife took some bread, cakes and honey as gifts for the prophet, and went to Shiloh.

Ahijah's sight was failing because he was an old man, but God told him that Jeroboam's wife was coming, and that she would be disguised. God gave Ahijah a message for her.

'I know who you are, wife of Jeroboam,' said Ahijah. 'I have bad news for you, given to me by God himself. He knows everything your husband the king has done. Your family will be punished because of his sins – terrible things will happen! But God has seen that your child is good. God will take him now so that he will be spared a worse fate. When you get home, your son will die, and his death will sadden everyone.'

It happened just as Ahijah had said. Jeroboam's wife returned home to find that her son had died.

As time passed the kingdom of Judah becoame stronger. Rehoboam fortified his cities against attack and gave each of his sons a city to rule over.

But Rehoboam also built many shrines and altars to other gods and his people followed him. He did all

God will take him now so that he will be spared a worse fate.

those things that his ancestors had done which had made God angry. He did not follow God's commandments or love him as his grandfather, David, had done.

God allowed Shishak, the king of Egypt, to attack Jerusalem. Shishak plundered the temple and the palace, removing the golden treasures that Solomon had made.

Then Israel and Judah – God's people – fought each other. Peace between the nations was over.

Kings came and went in Israel – Nadab, Jeroboam's son was overthrown by Baasha; Elah, Baasha's son was overthrown by Zimri; Omri overthrew Zimri. Each king was worse than the one before. Not one of them served God as King David had. All God's commandments were broken again and again.

When Omri's son Ahab became king, violence, corruption and injustice was greater than it had ever been. Ahab married a woman called Jezebel, daughter of the King of Sidon, who worshipped the fertility god, Baal.

Ahab openly worshipped Baal too and made a temple for his statue.

The people who had once worshipped God as creator of all the world now bowed down to idols they had made with their own hands.

But in the mountains of Gilead, there lived a man called Elijah, a prophet who heard God speak and – unlike so many of the people of Israel at that time – he tried to follow God's ways.

God chose Elijah to go to see King Ahab.

'God – the one true God – has sent me here,' said Elijah. 'There will be no rain, not even any early morning dew, for some years. There will be a drought until God chooses to send rain again.'

The king was angry at the news; Elijah did not stay to see what he would do next.

Day after day, the hot sun beat down and the dawn brought no dew.

'Leave this place now and go eastwards,' God told Elijah. 'You will find all you need at the Cherith Brook.'

Elijah found the brook on the eastern side of the River Jordan. He made himself a shelter there and drank the water from the brook. God sent ravens with food for him to eat and Elijah had everything that he needed.

It did not rain. Day after day, the hot sun beat down and the dawn brought no dew. The ground became dry and parched. After a while, the water in the brook dried up.

God had already provided for Elijah's needs.

'Go to Zarephath,' God told Elijah. 'There is a woman there who will provide you with food.'

Elijah travelled to Sidon and when he reached the city gates of the place called Zarephath, he saw a woman gathering sticks for firewood.

'Some water, please,' Elijah asked her. 'And a little bread to eat?'

'I have no bread baked,' she replied, 'for the drought has made us all hungry. I have only a little flour and oil left, and I am here gathering these few sticks to make a fire. I will cook the last meal for myself and my only son. Then we must die, for there is no more.'

'Don't be afraid,' said Elijah. 'Go and bake this bread as you were planning to do. Only share a little of it with me and God will bless you. Your flour and oil will not run out until God sends rain again.'

The woman went home and baked the bread. She shared it with Elijah and her son – and there was still enough flour and oil for another meal.

Again the woman used the flour and oil so they could share their last meal. Again there was just enough left. Many days passed. God made sure that the woman was rewarded for helping Elijah. They all had enough to eat.

During this time, Elijah stayed in a room in the woman's house.

One day, the woman's son grew ill. She sat by his bedside, watching, holding him in her arms until he drew his last breath and died. The woman was overcome by grief and anger.

'Why did you come here?!' she sobbed. 'What have I done to you that my son should die like this?!'

> ## I will cook the last meal for myself and my only son. Then we must die, for there is no more.

Elijah took the dead boy in his arms and carried him upstairs to his own room. He laid the boy on his bed and prayed.

'Lord God,' he cried, 'why have you allowed this to happen to the woman whose home I have shared? Please give the boy back his life!'

God heard Elijah's prayer. Suddenly, the boy started to breathe again. Elijah lifted him gently and carried him back to his mother.

'Look! Your son is alive!' Elijah said.

The woman was amazed. She hugged her son and smiled at Elijah, the tears still in her eyes.

Suddenly, the boy started to breathe again.

'Now I know you are God's friend,' she said, 'and that what you say is truly from the living God.'

In all this time it had not rained. Nearly three years had passed.

King Ahab sent the prophet Obadiah to search for any green place left in the land where food might be found for the animals. If none could be found, the animals would have to be slaughtered. But while Obadiah

was searching, he met Elijah. Elijah asked him to bring the king to him for he had another message from God.

'My Lord,' said Obadiah, 'you must know that King Ahab has had people searching the whole country for you! I cannot go and tell him that I have found you now! You are sure to disappear as you did before – and the king will kill me!'

But Elijah promised he would stay until Ahab came to meet him.

Obadiah brought King Ahab to meet Elijah. He was very angry.

'You are a troublemaker!' he shouted at him.

'No - you are the one who has brought trouble to the land,' said Elijah, 'because you stopped worshipping God and started to worship false idols. Now we will settle this matter. Call all the people to Mount Carmel, and bring all the false prophets who are your wife's friends.'

King Ahab sent for all the people and for all the prophets of Baal and Asherah. The word went out that there would be a contest between them and the one true God who had protected Elijah through the years of drought. The people came and with them the 450 prophets of Baal. They gathered on Mount Carmel.

Elijah stood in front of King Ahab and all the people.

'Today is the day you must choose,' said Elijah. 'Who will you serve? If the living God is the real God, then choose him – and follow him! If Baal is God, then serve and follow him. It is time to make up your minds and do what is right.

Who will you serve? If the living God is the real God, then choose him!

'I am the only prophet here who worships the one true God,' he said, 'while there are 450 prophets here who worship Baal. We will each prepare a sacrifice. You must call upon Baal to send down fire to burn it up; I will ask my God to do the same. Then we will see who is real. We will see who has the power to send down fire.'

The prophets agreed. They prepared a bull for the sacrifice and all day they prayed to Baal to send down fire.

Nothing happened.

'Is your god asleep?' Elijah asked. 'Is he on holiday so that he can't answer you?'

The prophets prayed and shouted even louder, but still there was no answer. The prophets of Baal had failed. There was no fire on the altar they had prepared.

Now it was Elijah's turn.

Elijah did not just make an altar as the other prophets had done. He used twelve stones to represent the twelve tribes of Israel and remind the people that they were God's people. He dug a deep trench around the altar and then prepared his sacrifice. Finally, Elijah asked for large jars to be filled with water and poured all over the wood and the sacrifice so that it ran down into the trench. Elijah's sacrifice was soaking wet; no accident could cause it to burn.

'Is your god asleep?' Elijah asked.

Then Elijah stepped out in front of the people and prayed. Elijah prayed that God would hear him so that the people would believe once more that he was their God too, and would worship him.

When Elijah stopped praying, God answered.

God sent down fire. God sent down fire which burned the bull, the stones and the water from the trench. And the people fell on their knees and cried out, 'The Lord is God! The Lord – he is God!'

Elijah called for the false prophets to be put to death. Then he watched as black clouds began to form and the wind rose – and God sent rain once more upon the land.

When Ahab told Queen Jezebel that Ahab had killed all her prophets, she was furious! She threatened to kill Elijah. Elijah did not wait around for her to find him – he ran away into the desert, terrified.

Elijah found a quiet place under a broom tree and sat in the shade. He was tired and he was frightened. He felt he couldn't take any more.

'Let me die,' he said to God. 'I have had enough.' In his exhaustion, Elijah fell asleep.

After a while, an angel came and touched him.

'Get up; have something to eat,' said the angel.

Elijah looked up and saw some water and freshly baked bread. He ate the bread and drank the water. He felt a little better. Then he fell asleep again.

The angel touched Elijah for a second time.

'Eat some more and refresh yourself for the journey ahead,' the angel said.

Elijah ate again. Then he set out for Mount Horeb, the mountain of God.

God sent down fire which burned the bull, the stones and the water from the trench.

When Elijah reached Mount Horeb, he found a cave and sheltered there for the night.

'What are you doing here, Elijah?' asked God.

Elijah had been thinking about all that happened since he had been serving God as his prophet. He had tried to encourage God's people to obey him, but everyone seemed to disobey and go their own ways.

'I have done my best to serve you,' said Elijah, 'but no one listens; no one hears and tries to follow you. And now they are trying to kill me!'

God heard what was in Elijah's heart and understood that he was discouraged and frightened.

'Stand on the mountain,' said God, 'and watch me pass by.'

A powerful wind suddenly stirred and ripped through the mountains, shattering and splintering the rocks in its path. But God was not in the wind.

Then there was an earthquake, cracking open the rocky ground and moving everything in its path. But God was not in the earthquake.

Then there was a fire. But God was not in the fire.

Finally, there was a gentle whisper. God was there in the gentle comforting whisper.

Elijah left the cave, and stood on the mountain with his cloak wrapped round him.

But Elijah was still unhappy; he did not understand God's message.

God was there in the gentle comforting whisper.

'Go back the way you have come,' said God. 'Anoint Jehu to be king of Israel, and Elisha to succeed you as prophet. Those who have disobeyed me will be punished.'

But there are some left who have remained faithful and not worshipped foreign idols. I will save them.'

Elijah went to find Elisha. He found him ploughing a field with a pair of oxen.

Elijah went to him, took off his cloak and flung it around Elisha's shoulders. The young man knew what this meant: it was his turn to serve God. But first he would learn from Elijah and help him. Elisha left his oxen and ran after Elijah.

'Let me first go back to say goodbye to my parents and then I will come with you,' he said.

Elisha burned his ploughs, killed the oxen and cooked them. He gave the cooked meat to the people to eat. Now his past life was over. He was ready to follow Elijah and serve God as a prophet.

Near King Ahab's palace lived a man called Naboth who owned a vineyard. Ahab wanted a garden near the palace and thought Naboth's vineyard would suit him very well.

'Your vineyard would make an ideal garden for me,' the king said to Naboth one day. 'Name your price and sell it to me – or I will give you a better vineyard somewhere else.'

His past life was over. He was ready to follow Elijah and serve God.

But Naboth's vineyard had belonged to his father and his grandfather. He didn't want to sell it to anyone.

Ahab had set his heart on the vineyard. He had not expected the answer no. He went home, shut himself away in his room and sulked.

Queen Jezebel couldn't believe what she saw.

'What are you doing here, feeling sorry for yourself? You're the king! You can have anything you want!'

So Jezebel plotted against Naboth to get the king what he wanted. She organised for Naboth to be invited to a feast where two men would be paid to lie about him and accuse him of treason in front of all the people.

The plan worked. Naboth was taken and stoned to death. Now there was no one to stop King Ahab taking the vineyard for himself.

But God had seen all that happened. He sent Elijah to him with a message.

Ahab was walking around the vineyard making plans when he saw Elijah. He knew it could only mean trouble.

'Did you really think God would be happy if you killed a man to take what he owns?' said Elijah. 'You will die for what you have done to Naboth. Your queen will die for her part in this and your family will be punished.'

Ahab listened to Elijah. First he was sorry; then he was afraid. God decided to give him another chance. For the next few years, there was peace in Israel.

In Judah, King Jehoshaphat had become not only powerful but feared by all the nations around him. Unlike King Ahab in Israel, Jehoshaphat destroyed foreign idols and tried to love and follow God's ways as David had before him.

One day he went to visit King Ahab. Ahab prepared a great feast for him. He wanted Jehoshaphat's help.

'Join with me and fight against Ramoth Gilead!' Ahab asked.

'I will help you,' Jehoshaphat replied. 'But what does God say? Is there a prophet here we can consult?'

King Ahab brought various prophets to Jehoshaphat, all of whom said that God would give them victory. But Ahab said that there was one man, Micaiah, who always brought bad news. Jehoshaphat wanted to hear what he had to say.

Naboth was taken and stoned to death.

'Go to war and you will be successful!' Micaiah said. But Ahab did not trust his message.

'You never bring me good news,' he said. 'Tell me what God has told you!'

'God wants you to be lured into battle and to your death. He has told all your prophets to tell you to fight so that this will happen.'

Ahab was angry and had Micaiah locked up. But he would fight, with or without God's help. He told Jehoshaphat to wear his royal robes into battle; but Ahab rode his chariot in disguise. He did not want the enemy to know he was the king.

The enemy only wanted King Ahab's death. With God's help, they found him. An arrow pierced the chinks in his armour and wounded him. He watched the battle, propped up in the chariot till sunset, when finally, King Ahab died.

Elijah had been God's prophet for a long time – all the time that Ahab had been king. Now it was time for Elijah's ministry to end. Elisha knew that he was spending his last day on earth with the prophet he had learned so much from.

Elisha walked with Elijah from Gilgal.

'Stay here,' Elijah said to his friend. 'God has sent me to Bethel.'

But Elisha refused. 'I will come with you,' he said.

When they reached Bethel, the prophets there spoke to Elisha.

'Do you realise that God will take Elijah today?' they asked.

'Yes, I know,' he replied.

The same thing happened when they walked on to Jericho and then again to the Jordan.

Then Elijah took off his cloak, rolled it up, and struck the water with it. A pathway appeared through the river so that the two prophets could cross safely to the other side.

An arrow pierced the chinks in his armour.

'Soon I must leave you. Is there anything I can do for you before I go?' asked Elijah.

'Give me twice as much of your faith and power,' said Elisha.

'This is something only God can give. If you see me leave this earth, you will have what you have asked for,' said Elijah.

Then a chariot and horses made of fire appeared in the sky and separated Elijah from Elisha. Elijah was taken into heaven in a whirlwind.

In the silence that remained, Elisha picked up Elijah's cloak and rolled it up. He struck the River Jordan as Elijah had done. A pathway appeared through the water.

Some prophets had been watching from a distance.

'God has given to Elisha the faith and power of Elijah,' they said to each other.

Joram, Ahab's son, became king after his father's death. The king of Moab would not respect him as such, however. He refused to send him the lambs and wool which they had previously sent Ahab in return for peace.

Joram joined with King Jehoshaphat and the king of Edom and they rode out together across the desert to fight against Moab. Before long they had run out of water for themselves and their animals.

'Is there no prophet here so that we can find out what God wants us to do?' asked King Jehoshaphat.

'Elisha is here,' an officer answered. 'He used to help the prophet Elijah.'

The three kings went down to Elisha, but he would not speak to King Joram.

Is there no prophet here so that we can find out what God wants us to do?

'Bring a harpist here, so that I may hear what God has to say. But I am doing this only because of King Jehoshaphat,' he said.

Then God spoke to Elisha. He told the kings that God would both send water and give them victory over the people of Moab.

The next morning, as God had promised, water was flowing from the land of Edom. It filled the desert. They had plenty to drink and to water their animals; but more than this, the people of Moab came and saw the sun shining on the water, red as blood. It seemed to them that the kings had killed each other in battle. They thought it would be easy to come and plunder what remained of their camp. When they did so, the armies chased them away, invaded their land and had victory over Moab, just as Elisha had told them.

One day a woman came to ask for Elisha's help. Her husband had been a prophet, but when he died, he owed money.

'I cannot pay back the money,' she told Elisha. 'The man wants to take my two sons away to be his slaves and cancel the debt.'

'What do you have in your home?' Elisha asked her. 'Tell me how I can help you?'

'I have nothing,' replied the woman desperately. 'I have just a little olive oil left.'

'Go to your neighbours,' Elisha told her. 'Ask them to give you as many empty jars as they have. Collect as many as you can. Then go home to your sons, shut the door, and pour oil into all of the jars.'

The woman did as Elisha told her. She collected the jars and filled each one with oil.

'Give me another jar,' she said to her son.

The man wants to take my two sons away to be his slaves.

'There are none left,' he told her. Then the oil stopped flowing. But she had many jars full of oil by this time.

The woman returned to Elisha and told him what had happened.

'Now go and sell the oil. You will be able to pay your debt and you and your sons can stay together.'

Soon people saw that Elisha was blessed by God just as Elijah had been.

In Shunem, a rich woman offered Elisha a meal and somewhere to stay when he passed through. She and her husband had prepared a room for him on their roof. The room had a bed, a table, a chair and a lamp.

One day, when Elisha was staying at their house, he told his servant, Gehazi, to ask the woman to come to see him.

'You have been very kind to me,' Elisha said. 'Is there anything I can do to show my thanks?'

The woman shook her head. She felt she had all she needed. But Elisha's servant saw that the woman's husband was old, and she had no child. He told Elisha that perhaps the woman might wish that she had a child to care for, a son to take care of her in her old age.

'This time next year you will hold your baby son in your arms,' Elisha told her.

The woman was anxious; she did not want her hopes raised. But everything happened just as Elisha had said. A year later the woman gave birth to a baby boy.

The rich woman from Shunem loved her son dearly. Her life was completely different now God had blessed her with a child.

One day the boy was out with his father at harvest-time when suddenly he complained of pains in his head. His father sent him home in the arms of a servant. His mother took him on to her lap and nursed him, but at midday, her son died.

The woman carried him up to Elisha's room and laid him on the bed. Then she asked her husband for a donkey and one of the servants so she could visit Elisha at Mount Carmel.

When Elisha saw her coming, he was worried. He asked Gehazi to go to meet her and ask what was wrong.

Why did you give me a son just to take him away?

She would not tell Gehazi, but when she reached Elisha, she threw herself at his feet and took hold of his ankles.

'Why did you give me a son just to take him away?' she wailed.

'I could live with the pain of having no child, but I cannot live with the agony of loving him and having him die!'

Elisha was very concerned at her pain. He tried to send his servant to her home with his stick. He told him to lay it across his face to restore the boy. But the woman would not move until Elisha himself went with her.

As Elisha approached the woman's house, Gehazi came to meet him.

'There is no change,' he told Elisha.

So Elisha went into the room with Gehazi and prayed to God to restore the boy. Then he breathed into his mouth and warmed him with his own body. He went out of the room, returned and did the same thing again.

Then suddenly the boy sneezed seven times. He opened his eyes. Elisha called the woman into the room.

'Here is your son,' said Elisha to the woman. He was smiling.

One day Elisha was called on to help King Joram. It happened that in the land of Aram, an Israelite girl had been taken captive on one of the raids on nearby villages. She worked as a servant in the home of an army commander called Naaman.

Naaman was a brave soldier and highly thought of. But his skin was covered in the deadly white patches of leprosy.

'I wish my master could see the prophet in Samaria!' the Israelite girl told her mistress. 'I am sure he would cure his leprosy.'

Naaman went to the king of Aram and told him what the girl had said. The king then wrote a letter to King Joram of Israel and sent Naaman with silver, gold and other gifts.

He didn't consider that God could help him.

'I am sending Naaman to you with this letter so that you can cure him of his leprosy,' the letter said.

King Joram was upset at the letter because he thought it was a trick so that the king of Aram could wage war on him. He didn't think of Elisha; he didn't consider that God could help him. But when Elisha heard of King Joram's distress, he asked the king to send the commander to him.

'Then he will know that there is a prophet who serves God in Israel,' Elisha said.

Naaman went with his servants, his horses and his chariots and stopped outside the place where Elisha lived. A servant came out from Elisha's house with a message from the prophet.

'Go to the River Jordan and wash there seven times.'

Naaman was angry. Elisha had not even come out to greet him.

'Surely there are better rivers in Damascus where I could wash!' he said. 'I thought he would come and wave his hand over my skin and pray to his God!'

But one of his servants reasoned with Naaman.

'Sir,' he said, 'if the prophet had asked you to do something difficult, you would have done it. Don't be too proud to do this simple thing.'

Naaman listened and decided to go down to the River Jordan and wash. When he came out of the river the seventh time, his skin was clean and new and unmarked, like that of a child. He was cured.

'Now I know that there is no God in all the world, except in Israel,' he said.

Now Elijah had prophesied that King Ahab's family would all die and no king would come from their family.

Don't be too proud to do this simple thing.

No one in Ahab's family remembered or obeyed God any more but the time had come for the prophecy to come true.

Elisha sent one of the young prophets on a mission.

'Take this bottle of oil, and find Jehu, the son of Jehoshaphat,' he said. 'Ask to speak to him secretly, and then anoint him king of Israel. Don't wait to explain further – come back as fast as you can.'

The prophet found Jehu and drew

him away from his companions. Once they were on their own, the prophet poured the oil on Jehu's head.

'God has chosen you to be the king of Israel. You must kill all who remain in Ahab's family as punishment for their disobedience.' Then the prophet fled.

'What did he want?' asked one of the soldiers when Jehu returned.

'Nothing that makes much sense,' he replied. But when his friends pressed him further, he told them. 'God has anointed me king.'

The men took off their cloaks and spread them on the steps under Jehu's feet. They blew on the trumpet and shouted:

'Jehu is king!'

The kings of Israel and Judah, Joram and Ahaziah, were both in Jezreel. Jehu gathered his troops and set out to find them.

The lookout on the watchtower saw Jehu's chariot approaching.

King Joram sent a soldier out on horseback to meet him to find out what he wanted. But when the man caught up with him, Jehu told him to follow behind him. A second soldier was sent out, but Jehu made him follow behind as well.

'The man leading the troops is driving his chariot like a lunatic!' the lookout reported. 'It must be Jehu – only he drives like that!'

So King Joram of Israel and King Ahaziah of Judah went out to meet Jehu, each in their own chariot.

They met him at the place that used to be Naboth's field, the field that had caused Queen Jezebel to plot Naboth's death so that Ahab could steal the field from him.

'Have you come in peace?' King Joram asked Jehu.

'How can there be peace while your mother rules us with witchcraft and idol worship!' demanded Jehu.

'This is treason!' King Joram shouted out to Ahaziah. Then he turned in his panic to run away. Jehu aimed his arrow at his fleeing back. His aim was true, and he killed him with a single shot. Then Jehu made sure the body was left in Naboth's

His aim was true, and he killed him with a single shot

field to fulfil the prophecy that God made when Naboth was murdered.

Meanwhile King Ahaziah had also turned and fled. Jehu's men pursued him and wounded him, so that he died later in the city of Megiddo.

Jehu had not yet finished his work. Queen Jezebel was still in Jezreel. She painted her eyes and brushed her hair then watched for Jehu from a window in the palace.

'What are you doing here, you murderer?' she demanded.

Jehu looked around to see who was on his side. He appealed to some palace officials.

'Throw her down!' he called.

The men took hold of Jezebel and threw her out of the window so that she fell to her death.

Ahab's family were dead at last; their rule was ended. King Jehu was free to rule Israel as God intended. The first thing he did was plan to remove all those who worshipped false gods. He knew that there were still many worshippers of Baal in the land. So Jehu went to Samaria and called them all together for a feast.

'You know how well King Ahab served the god Baal,' he told the people. 'Well, now you will see how well I can serve him. Let all Baal's priests and all those who worship him come together here for a celebration. Anyone who does not come will be found and put to death!'

All the Baal worshippers came to the temple so that it was filled from end to end. Jehu made sure that no one who worshipped the one true God was there.

Ahab's family was wiped out in the land of Israel for ever.

Then Jehu ordered his soldiers to put to death all those who were inside. He destroyed the sacred pillar inside the temple and then the temple itself. In this way he made sure that the evil of Ahab's family was wiped out in the land of Israel for ever.

Back in Judah, Athaliah, the queen mother, had ruled for six years. She had killed the entire royal family one by one after her son's death, so that no one could take power from her or challenge her right to rule.

But her baby grandson, Joash, had escaped. He was taken to the temple where Athaliah would never find him. A priest called Jehoiada looked after him there and as Joash grew up, he taught him all about God.

In the seventh year, Jehoiada secretly sent for the palace and temple guard and asked for their support. Then he put the crown on Joash's head and a copy of God's law in his hands. He made sure the guards surrounded him with their swords drawn.

'Stay close to your king,' he ordered the guards, as they led Joash out to face the people. Then he proclaimed Joash king of Judah.

The crowd that had gathered cheered and shouted.

'Long live the king!'

Athaliah came to see what all the noise was about. When she saw that Joash was alive and had been made king, she was furious.

'Treason!' she cried. But the people had a new king. No one listened to her now.

Jehoiada made sure Athaliah was removed from the celebrations and then executed at the Horse Gate, out of the way of the crowds and of her grandson. Joash was only seven years old when he became king.

Jehoiada made sure the people knew that everything would now be different in Judah. The people who had forgotten God's laws came back to worship him. They renewed their

---

Joash was only seven years old when he became king.

---

covenant with him so that they would once more be his people and he would be their God. The altars and the idols of Baal were smashed. The temple of Baal was destroyed as it had been in Israel.

Joash had listened to everything Jehoiada had taught him about God.

He told the priests to collect money from the people so that the temple could be repaired.

Jehoiada found a large chest. He made a hole in the top of it, and put it by the side of the altar for the people to put money in. Then when it was full, the silver would be melted down and weighed and used to pay the carpenters, masons and stone cutters, and to buy the wood and stone needed to make the repairs.

So the temple was repaired, and Joash tried to lead his people back to God so that the Israelites would once more be known as those who worshipped the one true God.

Jehu's grandson, Jehoash, had become king in Israel during this time. The prophet Elisha was now very ill.

King Jehoash went to Elisha and wept. He knew how Elisha had served God faithfully but also that he and his people had failed to do so. Elisha spoke to the king from his deathbed.

'Take some arrows and shoot out of the window towards Syria,' he said. The king did so.

'You are the Lord's arrow,' Elisha told him. 'You will fight and defeat the Syrians.'

Then Elisha told the king to strike the ground with the other arrows. The king did so three times.

'If only you had struck the ground five or six times!' said Elisha. 'You will defeat the Syrians, but only three times, not completely.'

Then Elisha died and was buried.

It was a bad time for the Israelites. As time passed, king after king in Israel turned from God and failed to obey him. Evil men used their power for evil purposes and the people worshipped the gods of the nations around them again.

Chapter 17

POWERS AND SUPERPOWERS

THE ASSYRIANS WERE A GROWING THREAT TO GOD'S PEOPLE. THEIR COUNTRY BORDERED THE LANDS OF ISRAEL TO THE NORTH AND THEY WERE GREEDY TO TAKE WHAT THEY WANTED.

So when God called on Jonah, one of his prophets, to go to Nineveh, and warn them to repent of their wickedness, he was not happy. What had Israel's God to do with the Assyrians?

Jonah was so unhappy that he went to the port of Joppa to look for a ship going to Tarshish, about as far in the opposite direction as he could go…

Jonah paid his fare, boarded the ship and then went below deck where he fell into a deep sleep.

The ship had not long been out to sea when the wind grew stronger and a violent storm arose. Waves battered the sides of the ship and it lurched so dangerously that the sailors on board were sure they would drown.

The wind grew stronger and a violent storm arose.

The men prayed to their gods and threw their cargo over the side to lighten the ship. They clung to one another in fear.

Then the captain noticed that Jonah was missing. He went below deck to find him.

'Wake up!' he cried, shaking Jonah. 'How can you sleep through this storm?! Get up and pray! Perhaps your God can save us.'

By this time the sailors were sure that the storm was someone's fault. They drew lots to see who was responsible. Then they stood back and stared at Jonah. It was clear that he was the guilty one.

'What terrible thing have you done that your God is punishing us?' they asked Jonah. 'Who are you?'

'I worship the God who made the land and the sea,' Jonah replied. 'But I have run away from him. This is all my fault. There is only one thing you can do: you must throw me overboard.'

The sailors listened in horror. They did not want to kill Jonah; but they did not want to die either.

At first they tried to row back to shore, but the sea was too strong for them.

Then the sailors prayed to the living God.

'Do not blame us for taking this man's life! We can do nothing else!'

They picked up Jonah and threw him over the side.

The wind dropped straight away; the waves grew calm. The sailors were amazed and fell to their knees. They had seen the power of the living God.

Jonah, meanwhile, had sunk beneath the waves and felt himself falling down, down, down and strangled by seaweed. Then, as he felt his life draining away from him, he called to God for help. And God answered.

As he felt his life draining away from him, he called to God for help.

God sent a huge fish to swallow him whole. God saved him.

Jonah stayed inside the body of the fish for three days and three nights. He thought about what had happened and how he had tried to run away from God. He remembered that he had once promised to serve God and do whatever he asked. Then he praised God and promised to serve him again because only his God had the power to save.

God spoke to the huge fish and caused him to spit Jonah out on to dry land.

God had given Jonah a second chance. This time when God said, 'Go to Nineveh,' Jonah went.

Jonah went through the streets of the great city and he preached the message that God had given him. He warned the people that they must ask for God's forgiveness and change their ways or their land would be destroyed in forty days.

The people did not need to be told more than once. They heard what Jonah said and they believed his message. Even the king listened and acted.

'No one is to eat or drink,' said the king. Everyone must wear sackcloth and ask God to forgive them. Everyone must stop doing evil and violent deeds. Perhaps even now it is possible that God may change his mind and forgive us.'

God watched the people of Nineveh and he heard their prayers. And because God was compassionate, he forgave them. He did not destroy the people of Assyria.

But Jonah was furious that God had listened to the prayers of the Assyrians.

'I knew this would happen,' he said angrily. 'I knew you were kind and forgiving and that you would love these people if they changed their ways. That's why I ran away! They are evil people and they deserve to die! Now I might as well be dead!'

Jonah went outside the city and sulked. God let a vine grow over his head to give him shade from the hot sun. But the next day, a worm ate the vine so that it died and Jonah grew weak from the heat.

Jonah was furious that God had listened to the prayers of the Assyrians.

'Let me die!' he cried to God.

Then God spoke to Jonah.

'Why are you so angry? I let the vine grow and I let the vine die. You are unhappy about the death of the vine even though you did nothing to help it grow and did not look after it while it was alive. It is only a vine, but still you are angry. Now – try to understand. How do you think I feel about the thousands of people who live in the city of Nineveh? They hardly know right from wrong, but I made these people. I know them and care about them. I do not want them to die, Jonah. Don't be angry because I choose to save them.'

You have become rich by oppressing the poor people around you.

During the time when Uzziah was king of Judah, there lived a shepherd called Amos who also looked after the fig trees.

'Amos,' God said, 'I want you to give my people a message. Go to them and speak for me.'

So Amos went and spoke God's words to the people of Judah.

'God has told me to warn you,' Amos said. 'God has seen how you live. You are no different from the other nations around you. Although you are God's special people and know God's laws, you don't keep them. You have sinned again and again. As a result you will lose the city of Jerusalem. It will be burned to the ground.'

Then Amos spoke to the people of Israel.

'God has told me to warn you,' he said. 'You are God's people and he cares for you. Yet you ignore God's laws and you worship idols. You have plenty of money and enjoy many good things – but you have become rich by oppressing the poor people around you. You have not taken care of the poor, you have cheated the very people who most need your help. It's time to change! Put what you say you believe into practice. Learn to love what is good and hate what is evil.

'This is what God says: "You offer me gifts when you come to worship me; you sing noisy songs and play your harps. But I cannot accept any of this. I would rather you lived your lives being fair and kind to those around you. This and only this is what I want. Let justice flow like a stream through a dry land and righteousness like a river that never runs dry."'

Then God gave Amos a vision of a wall beside a plumb-line.

'I will put a plumb-line in the middle of my people. Then it will become clear that they are not like a wall built straight and true but instead they are crooked and out of line. The time is coming soon when they will lose everything that matters to them. They will be taken from their homes into exile in a foreign land.'

Hosea was another of God's messengers.

They will lose everything that matters to them.

'Your whole life will be a picture for my people in Israel,' said God. 'I want you to get married. But the woman who will be your wife will not make you happy – she will make you very sad. She will leave you and love other men. She won't care how much you love her and she will forget all about you whatever you do for her. But you will not leave her, Hosea. You will keep on loving her.'

So Hosea married Gomer and they had children. Then what God said came true. Gomer left Hosea for another man and eventually she became a slave.

'Now go and get your wife back, Hosea,' said God. 'Buy her out of slavery. Live with her and show her how much you still love her.'

Hosea paid the price to get his wife back and he loved her.

Then God explained how this was like his love for the Israelites.

'I love the people of Israel just as much as you love Gomer,' explained God. 'My people have hurt me and made me sad. They have ignored me and replaced me with things of no value. They don't care for me; they don't care what I think of them. But I have not left them and I will not stop loving them. Terrible things will happen to them and then they may realise that they do still need me. I will still be here.'

God also spoke to the people of Israel through the prophet Micah, warning them of the coming invasion of the Assyrians.

'You have sinned and rebelled against God!' said Micah. 'You are supposed to be concerned about justice, yet you hate what is good and go about doing evil things. The time is coming when you will call out to God for help, but it will be too late! All your idols will be destroyed; everything will be smashed to pieces. Your enemies will defeat you and you will be taken captive. You will be taken away from your home and be exiles in a foreign land.

'But there will be a time in the future when God will send someone to save you. God says to Bethlehem: "You are one of the smallest towns in Judah, but from you will come a ruler for Israel whose ancestors go back to the earliest times. You will be overcome and defeated by your enemies until the time when a woman gives birth to her son. Then those who have remained faithful

Do you know what God wants of you?

to God will come together. God will stand among his people, lead them and care for them as a shepherd takes care of his sheep; and at last there will be peace.

'Do you know what God wants of you? Do you know how to live so he will be pleased with you? He has already told you the answer so many times and it is so simple. You must act justly and fairly, you must always be kind and you must be humble before God, your maker.'

At the end of the reign of King Uzziah, God also spoke to the people through the prophet Isaiah.

You must be humble before God, your maker.

Isaiah was in the temple when he had a vision of God. He knew that God was calling him to serve him. Isaiah wrote down everything he saw.

'God sat upon his throne, high and exalted, and the folds of his robe filled the temple. Round him were heavenly creatures, each of which had six wings. With two wings they covered their faces; with two wings they covered their feet; and with two wings they flew.

'They called out to each other saying, "Holy, holy, holy! The Lord God almighty is holy!"

'The foundations of the temple shook at the sound of their voices and the temple filled with smoke. I felt so unworthy to be in God's holy presence. I knew that I and all my people claimed to know and worship this holy God yet we had no idea how great he was compared to how unworthy we were.

'Then one of the heavenly creatures flew down to me carrying a burning coal from the altar. He touched my lips with it and said, "Your guilt is gone; your sin is forgiven."

'Then I heard God's voice: "Whom shall I send?" he said. "Who will take my words to the people?"

'I answered: "I will go! Send me!"'

So God sent Isaiah to the people of Judah.

'God has seen all the terrible things you have done. No one can hide from him. Now time is running out. Stop doing these things. Tell God how sorry you are before it is too late.'

Tell God how sorry you are before it is too late.

No one wanted to hear the bad news Isaiah brought them. But he also had good news. He told them about a time in the future when God would do something very wonderful.

'If God's people will not listen to him, they will suffer for a time. But God will not be angry for ever. God will remember his people and give them a child who will be his own son. A child will be born who will rule over all people with justice and righteousness. He will bring light into the dark places on the earth. He will bring peace that lasts forever. This child will be called "Wonderful Counsellor", "Mighty God", "Eternal Father" and "Prince of Peace". He will be born into the family of King David, and God's own Spirit will be with him.'

When Hoshea became king of Israel, King Shalmaneser of Assyria

attacked Israel and defeated Hoshea's army. Hoshea was allowed to remain as king as long as Israel paid heavy taxes to Assyria.

Hoshea was unhappy about the situation. At first he tried to plot against Shalmaneser. He asked the king of Egypt to help him overthrow the Assyrians. But his plot was discovered and the Assyrian army poured into Israel. Shalmaneser arrested King Hoshea and had him put in prison. Then he marched on towards Samaria. The people there bravely defended themselves for three years under siege conditions before they were finally defeated.

He will bring light into the dark places on the earth. He will bring peace that lasts forever.

Then King Shalmaneser captured the people of Israel, and had them taken away to Assyria. He filled the land that God had given to the Israelites with people from other tribes, who bowed down to gods of wood and stone and did not care about Israel's God.

The warnings given by the prophets had begun to come true. God's people had rebelled against God and no longer followed his laws. Now their land had gone and they were slaves in a foreign land once more.

In Judah, things were different. There was a king at last who loved God and followed his commandments. King Hezekiah destroyed all the idols and places of pagan worship in the land; he trusted God to help him and his people. So Hezekiah defeated the Philistines, and unlike the people of Israel, he refused to pay the Assyrians the taxes they demanded.

The Assyrian army thought they could treat the people of Judah the same way as those in Israel. They swept across the land and conquered some of Judah's major towns. Then King Hezekiah acted. To raise the money he needed, Hezekiah stripped the temple of its treasures. But it was not enough. The Assyrian commander, Sennacherib, demanded more.

'Surrender to Assyria!' shouted Sennacherib's official so that everyone could hear. 'Don't listen to King Hezekiah! He thinks your God will help you! But your God is no different from the gods of all the nations around you. He has no power. He cannot save you.'

Hezekiah did not believe this. He put on sackcloth and prayed. Then he sent messengers to the prophet Isaiah for advice. Isaiah sent back a message for King Hezekiah.

'God says that you must not let the Assyrians frighten you. Trust God. The commander will hear a rumour that will make him go home to his own country – and there he will be killed.'

It happened just as God had told Isaiah.

The Assyrian commander received news of another attack and left Jerusalem. Before he went, he gave King Hezekiah a letter warning him not to trust in God.

Then Hezekiah prayed.

'Almighty Lord, you alone are God. You created the earth and the sky and everything that is in it. Now, Lord, look what is happening to us. Rescue us from the Assyrians, so that all the nations of the world will know that you alone are God.'

'God has answered your prayer,' said Isaiah. 'The Assyrians will not enter the city, nor even shoot an arrow. God will defend us.'

An angel went to the Assyrian camp. That night, 185,000 soldiers died; and Sennacherib returned home to Nineveh where he was killed by two of his sons.

King Hezekiah's faith in God was rewarded.

Some time later the king became very ill. The prophet Isaiah went to visit him with a message from God.

'It is time for you to die,' Isaiah told him. 'Make sure you have put everything in order.'

Lord God, please remember me. Know that I have tried to serve you as best as I could.

King Hezekiah turned to face the wall with tears rolling down his cheeks.

'Lord God, please remember me.

Know that I have tried to serve you as best as I could.'

As Isaiah left the palace, he heard God speaking to him again.

'Go back and give Hezekiah this message. I have seen his tears and heard his prayer. I will heal the king and let him live for another fifteen years.'

Then the shadow on the sundial moved ten steps backwards.

Isaiah rushed back to tell the king. He told his attendants to put a paste made out of figs on the inflammation on his body.

'How can I be sure?' the king asked Isaiah. 'Will God give me a sign of this?'

'Do you want the shadow on the sundial to move ten steps backwards or forwards?' asked Isaiah.

'Backwards!' exclaimed Hezekiah. 'It always moves forwards.'

So Isaiah prayed. Then the shadow on the sundial moved ten steps backwards. Hezekiah went to the temple to praise and worship God three days later. He had been healed.

God had given Hezekiah more time. In that time God blessed him with wealth and riches. Hezekiah built more cities and channelled the water from the Spring of Gihon so that it flowed through a tunnel into Jerusalem to provide fresh water.

When he died, Hezekiah was buried in the tomb of the kings.

Isaiah lived on. God gave messages of hope and comfort to him to pass on to his people.

God himself is coming to rule his people.

'"Look after my people," says God. "Be good to them. Tell them that they have suffered long enough."

'God himself is coming to rule his people,' said Isaiah. 'He will take care of you as a shepherd takes care of his sheep. He will gather you up like lambs and carry you gently in his arms.

'How can we describe our God?

Can we take the ocean and measure it in our hands? Can we take all the soil from the earth and put it in a cup? Can we pick up a mountain and weigh it in the scales? No; yet at the beginning of time, God stretched out the sky like a curtain; he led out the stars like an army and counted them.

'Do you think that this God doesn't know about your troubles? Do you believe he doesn't care if you suffer? Haven't you heard about him? He was there before time began: he created the whole world. God doesn't grow tired or weary as we do. Instead he helps and supports all those who feel weak. Anyone who puts their trust in God will find new strength. They will rise on wings like eagles; they will run and not get tired; they will walk and not grow weary.'

Isaiah also spoke to the people about the way God loved them.

'Listen, people of Israel. Listen to what the God who created you says: "Do not be afraid because I will save you. I have called you by name; you belong to me. When you pass through deep waters, I will be with you. I will not let the flood waters overwhelm you. When you walk through fire, I will not let you be burned. The flames will not destroy you. I am the Lord your God: you are precious to me and I love you.

'"Come to me everyone who is thirsty. I have cool water for you! Come to me if you have no money – I have a feast to share with you. Why do you want to spend your money on things that cannot satisfy you? Why buy things that leave you hungry again tomorrow? Come to me and I will give you life!"'

Isaiah also told the people about the child God had promised to send.

'This child will be rejected by his people. He will suffer and know pain. But his pain will be our pain; he will suffer in our place. He will die because we have sinned – not for any sin of his own. He will take the punishment that we deserve for our sins; he will die so that we can be forgiven.

He will die so that we can be forgiven.

'We are all like sheep that are lost, each wandering away from the right path and going our own way. But he will be like a lamb that goes to

be slaughtered; like a sheep waiting to be sheared. He will be arrested and sentenced to death; led away to die though he is innocent of any crime. Yet he will go to his death willingly in our place because it is God's will that he suffers. He will know that his death has achieved something good. His one death will save many people.'

Isaiah was speaking about the Saviour God had promised to send for his people.

Hezekiah's son, Manasseh, became king after his father's death but instead of worshipping God, he started to worship the sun, the moon and the stars. He sacrificed his own son to foreign gods and practised witchcraft. He brought idols into God's temple and – worst of all his evils – he slaughtered many innocent people.

Manasseh ignored the warnings of the prophets God sent to him. So when the Assyrians attacked Judah, they took him prisoner. They humiliated him and put a hook in his nose like an animal; they bound him in bronze chains, and took him to Babylon.

Only then did Manasseh remember God and ask for his help.

'I have been wicked!' he prayed. 'I am so sorry for all the things I have done. Can you forgive me, Lord?'

God heard Manasseh's prayer. He let the king return to Jerusalem. The first thing Manasseh did was destroy the altars and the idols he had made. Then Manasseh told the people that they must love God and follow his ways.

Some of the people listened, but others – including his own son, Amon, who became king after him – continued to reject God and disobey his commandments. Then Amon was assassinated by his own officials so that his son, Josiah, became king when he was only eight years old.

Josiah wanted to serve God as his ancestor King David had done. He set about repairing the temple so that he could lead the people in worshipping God.

It was while the work was under way that the high priest, Hilkiah,

discovered an old scroll which had not been read for years. In it was the covenant God had made with his people and the prophecy of how God would destroy Jerusalem because of the people's disobedience.

When Josiah heard the laws written on the scroll, he wept. He told Hilkiah to ask God what they should do.

God would destroy Jerusalem because of the people's disobedience.

'We have broken all of God's laws – he must be so angry with us,' the king said.

Hilkiah hurried to find the prophetess, Huldah. She came with some answers.

'God says that he will destroy Jerusalem,' she said. 'The people have abandoned him and worshipped idols. But God has also seen how sorry the king is. God says that he will not destroy Jerusalem in King Josiah's lifetime.'

Then Josiah asked all the people to come to the temple. The old scroll was read out so that everyone could hear it.

'I promise to serve God with all my heart,' declared Josiah.

Then everyone prayed, 'We promise too.'

Josiah began to find and destroy all the idols and altars to foreign gods that were still in the land of Judah.

When it was done, he led the people in celebrating the Passover feast. It was a long time since they had remembered how God had led them out of slavery in Egypt and thanked God for it.

Josiah was a good king. He served God with all his heart, all his mind and all his strength, and he obeyed God's commandments.

Chapter 18

The fall of Jerusalem

When Josiah had been king for twelve years, God spoke to the priest's teenage son, Jeremiah.

'Before you were conceived in your mother's womb, Jeremiah, I knew you. Before you were born, I chose you for a very special task. I want you to be my messenger.'

Jeremiah could hardly believe God's words.

'But I'm only a child,' he answered. 'I don't know how to serve you and be your prophet!'

'I will tell you what to say,' said God. 'Don't be afraid – I will always be there to help you and – even though things may be difficult – I will keep you safe.'

Then Jeremiah felt a hand touch his lips.

'I have put my words in your mouth,' said God. 'Speak for me.'

A picture started to form before Jeremiah's eyes. He had a vision. Jeremiah saw a pot full of a scalding, boiling liquid. It was tilting towards the south and the burning liquid was ready to gush out.

'The people of Judah have been disobedient,' said God. 'They have worshipped idols and ignored my laws. Soon they will be destroyed by an enemy from the north. Now go, Jeremiah, and tell them what you have seen. They will be angry and they won't want to hear it, but trust me and I will help you.'

Jeremiah went to the people of Jerusalem with God's words.

'I remember when I first brought you out of Egypt,' said God. 'You were my special people and I was

What went wrong? Why did your ancestors forget what we had agreed?

your God. You loved me and wanted to follow me with all your hearts. I protected you from your enemies and you trusted me.

'What went wrong? Why did your ancestors forget what we had agreed? What made them turn from me to worship worthless idols? When they were in trouble, I was there to help them. They only had to ask and I would rescue them. But they preferred gods made out of wood and stone. They preferred a god made with human hands rather than the God who had made them and

the world they live in. Now there is trouble ahead. Where are your gods? Let them save you if they can!

'But it's not too late. It's not too late to tell me you are sorry. Come back to me and keep our agreement. Do it now and weep for your sins; show me you are sorry. Stop doing such bad things and love me again.

'You still have a chance to put things right – but the time is coming soon when there will be no chance left. Your enemy in the north is preparing for battle. His war chariots are coming like a whirlwind! He has fast horses that will swoop down and defeat you! They have taken up their bows and swords; they are vicious and cruel. Change your ways now! You have brought this disaster on yourselves, but it is not too late to turn back to me.'

Jeremiah wept for the people.

Jeremiah wept for the people. He went to them time and time again and warned them of the punishment that was awaiting them. He told them that God would listen if they came back and said sorry. But the people had no time for Jeremiah and his bad news. Instead they laughed at him. They would not take him seriously.

One day, God told Jeremiah to go down to the potter's house.

Jeremiah stood and watched the potter at his wheel. He moulded a lump of clay, carefully cupping his wet hands around it, pulling the clay up and out into the shape of a pot. But suddenly the wheel stopped spinning. The potter was unhappy with the shape of the pot. He picked up the clay, threw it back on the wheel and began to reshape it into something better.

'I am like that potter,' said God. 'My people are like the clay. If they are rebellious and disobedient and fail to become the nation I dreamed of, then I will start again. I will reshape them into something useful and perfect. When the people of Judah suffer, their troubles will shape them into the people I want them to be.'

Then God told Jeremiah to buy a clay pot and go out to the Valley of Hinnom with some of the elders and priests. There he was to warn them about the terrible things that were to happen.

'We have filled this place with the blood of innocent people,' Jeremiah told them. 'Now God will punish us. Soon this will be called the Valley of Slaughter. The enemy will come and besiege the city and the suffering will be so terrible that people will eat one another.'

Then Jeremiah smashed the clay pot in front of the men.

'This is what God says he will do to us, because we are so rebellious,' he said. 'It will be broken in so many pieces that it cannot be put back together.'

Still the people did not believe Jeremiah. Instead they punished him for bringing such bad news. Pashhur the priest had him beaten and chained up beside one of the gates in the temple.

The priest had him beaten and chained up beside one of the gates in the temple.

The Babylonians had started to attack Jerusalem when God told Jeremiah to buy a field from his cousin, Hanamel. Jeremiah bought the field, had the papers signed, sealed and witnessed but he didn't understand why he should buy land when God had told him that everything would be destroyed.

'Lord God,' said Jeremiah. 'I know that nothing is impossible for you, but why did you want me to buy that field?'

I know that nothing is impossible for you.

'It is a sign of what will happen,' said God. 'Jerusalem will be destroyed because my people have refused to listen to me. But one day, some of them will return. They will come back to live here, and fields will once more be bought and sold. This is my promise for the future. I will look after my people. I will give them good things, and I will be their God.'

Jehoiachim was king of Judah when the prophecies about the destruction of Jerusalem began to come true. King Nebuchadnezzar of Babylon made frequent fierce attacks on them. But still no one took Jeremiah seriously.

'Buy a scroll,' said God to Jeremiah, 'and write down everything I have ever told you. Perhaps when the people hear it, and understand all that is going to happen, they will see how wicked they have been and be sorry. Then I will forgive them.'

Jeremiah dictated everything to Baruch, who wrote Jeremiah's words down on the scroll.

'You will have to take this scroll to the temple,' said Jeremiah. 'I have been banned from going there. Go on a special day, when there will be lots of people there, and read to them everything that you have written.'

Baruch went to the temple and read from the scroll. The people listened to all the things God had told Jeremiah about what would happen. When Jehudi heard about it, he told Baruch to come and read it to him and the other court officials.

Finally someone realised how terrible the situation was. They realised Jeremiah's warning must be taken seriously. They were terrified!

'Let us tell the king,' they said. 'But you and Jeremiah must stay hidden.'

It was winter, and King Jehoiakim was sitting by an open fire as Jehudi unrolled the scroll and read to him. But he had only read a few columns before Jehoiakim told him to stop. Then the king took a knife, cut the words from the scroll and threw them carelessly into the fire. The more Jehudi read, the more Jehoiakim cut from the scroll and threw into the flames, until the whole scroll was burned.

Then the king sent his men to search for Jeremiah and Baruch. He not only refused to listen to God's warning, he wanted the prophets to be punished.

'Start again,' said God to Jeremiah. 'Write on another scroll. Jehoiakim will live to regret the day when he refused to listen to me.'

Nothing could stop the Babylonians from attacking Judah. The first time they captured officials, builders and craftsmen. They captured King Jehoiachim and took him away to Babylon in chains. King Nebuchadnezzar stripped the palace and took away many of the beautiful treasures from the temple.

Then in the Spring, the Babylonians returned. All the remaining treasures were taken from the temple. This time Jehoiachin, the new king, was captured and taken to Babylon, along with 10,000 others. Among these was a man called Ezekiel.

The new king was captured and taken to Babylon, along with 10,000 others.

Once they were captives in a foreign land, the people remembered the words of warning the prophets had given them. They wished they had listened. They began to be sorry they had disobeyed God. But the people who were left in Jerusalem thought they had escaped God's punishment. Despite what had happened, they were pleased with themselves.

King Nebuchadnezzar of Babylon made Zedekiah king of Judah.

Jeremiah was one of those left behind in Jerusalem. One day he was near the temple.

'Look at those two baskets of figs,' said God. 'What can you see?'

'One basket is full of good, ripe figs,' replied Jeremiah. 'The other figs are rotten. They are fit for nothing.'

'Think about those figs,' said God. 'The people who are in captivity in Babylon are like the good figs. I will watch them and look after them, until the time is right for them to return. But the rotten figs are like King Zedekiah and all those who are left in Jerusalem.'

Outside the walls of Jerusalem, King Nebuchadnezzar had built siege walls. Day after day, month after month, the soldiers camped outside. Inside the city, food became scarce. King Zedekiah asked Jeremiah to pray to God for help.

'The Babylonians will retreat when they see that the Egyptians are coming to help you,' said God. 'But it will not last long. They will return and capture the city and then burn it down. Only those who surrender will be safe.'

Knowing that the enemy had retreated for a while, Jeremiah went out through the city gates to look at the field that God had told him to buy.

'Why are you leaving the city?' demanded one of the soldiers. 'You traitor! You are going to join the Babylonians!'

He dragged Jeremiah back, had him beaten and imprisoned him in an underground cell. He was still there when King Zedekiah sent for him to see if there were any messages from God.

'God has said that you will be handed over to the Babylonians,' Jeremiah told him. 'But why am I in prison? Please don't send me back there or I am sure it will kill me.'

Zedekiah had Jeremiah locked up in the palace courtyard instead, but while he was there, Jeremiah continued to tell anyone who would listen what God had told him.

Stay here and you will die of starvation.

'Surrender to the Babylonians and you will escape with your life! Stay here and you will die of starvation or disease! God has given Jerusalem to the Babylonians – he is punishing us because we have turned from him to worship foreign idols.'

'Stop that man!' the officials told the king. 'He is spreading fear among the soldiers! How can they put up a fight when he tells them there is no hope left?'

Zedekiah waved them away.

'Do what you like with him!' he said.

Jeremiah was thrown into the well. There was no water there, but he sank down into the mud at the bottom. As he sat in the darkness, cold and miserable, he thought he was going to die.

Ebed-Melech, one of the king's officials, heard what had happened.

'Your majesty,' he said to the king. 'Jeremiah will die if he is left in the well.'

King Zedekiah was weary.

'Bring him out before he dies,' he said.

So Ebed-Melech found some rope and some worn out clothing and some men to help him. He made sure Jeremiah put the clothing under his arms so the rope would not hurt him, and gently hauled Jeremiah up out of the well and into the light.

'Tell me what you know!' said King Zedekiah. 'What will happen to me?'

'I have told you many, many times,' said Jeremiah, 'but you do not listen. Unless you surrender to the Babylonians, you and your family will die.'

'But I'm afraid!' wailed Zedekiah. 'What will they do to me if I surrender?'

'If you obey God, you will live,' Jeremiah reassured him.

But Zedekiah did not listen. The Babylonians laid siege to Jerusalem once more. The people were starving. King Zedekiah and his soldiers tried to escape by leaving the city at night and going through the royal garden.

The Babylonians chased after the king and made him their prisoner. They killed his sons in front of him, executed his officials, then as a final cruel act, blinded him. They bound him with chains and took him to Babylon where he remained in prison till he died.

The Babylonians raided the temple of anything left that was valuable and could be carried away. They set fire to all the buildings and broke down the city walls. They put the people in chains and took them away to Babylon. Only a few poor people were left behind to work in the fields.

A captain in the Babylonian guard saw Jeremiah, who was in chains.

'All this happened just as you said it would, because the people ignored your God,' said the captain. 'I will let you go free. You can come with me to Babylon, or you can stay here if you prefer.'

Jeremiah knew that God had kept his promise and kept him safe.

Jeremiah knew that God had kept his promise and kept him safe. Jeremiah made his decision. He chose to stay with the people who were left in his homeland.

CHAPTER 19

EXILES IN A FOREIGN LAND

THE CAPTIVES WHO HAD BEEN TAKEN TO BABYLON WERE NOT TREATED BADLY. GOD LOOKED AFTER THEM, JUST AS HE HAD PROMISED.

King Nebuchadnezzar asked his chief officer to select some of the best young men to be educated and trained to work for him in the palace.

Among those chosen were four men from the royal palace in Judah: Daniel, Hananiah, Mishael and Azariah. They were given new names, Belteshazzar, Shadrach, Meshach and Abednego, and given food and wine from the king's own table. They were to be trained for three years.

Daniel was unhappy. Although he was a captive in a strange land, he did not want to eat any of the

I will lose my life as well as my job if you fall ill!

foods which were forbidden by God. He asked the king's chief officer to give him only water to drink and vegetables to eat.

'The king himself has decided what you must eat to make you fit and healthy,' he answered. 'I will lose

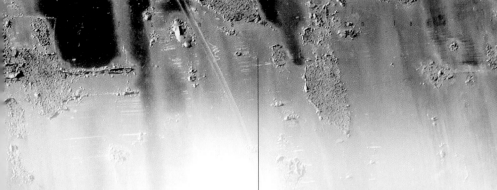

my life as well as my job if you fall ill!'

So Daniel spoke instead to the guard.

'We won't fall ill. Try it and see. Give us just water and vegetables. If we look weak after ten days, then we will eat whatever you give us.'

The guard agreed, and when, ten days later, Daniel and his friends looked healthier than the other young men, they were allowed to eat the food they had chosen. Then God blessed them and gave them special abilities so that they were the best among the captives who had been

---

God also gave to Daniel the ability to understand dreams and visions.

---

chosen. God also gave to Daniel the ability to understand dreams and visions.

When the four young men had finished their training, they were presented to King Nebuchadnezzar. He was amazed at their wisdom and understanding.

After a while the king started to have problems sleeping. His mind was troubled with strange dreams that worried him. He called his magicians and astrologers and told them the problem. But he didn't ask for help to understand the dream. His request was far more frightening.

'Tell me what I dreamed and what it means, so that I will once more be able to sleep!' said the king.

'Tell us your dream and we will explain it to you,' his wise men replied.

But the king became angry.

'No! I will reward the man who tells me what I dreamed and its meaning. But if you cannot do it, I will have you all executed – all of you!'

'It's impossible!' they cried. 'There is no man on earth who can do what you ask!'

So Nebuchadnezzar sent them away and ordered their execution.

When the king's official came to find Daniel and his friends to carry out the execution, Daniel asked what had happened to make the king issue such an order. As soon as he understood why, he went to King Nebuchadnezzar and asked for more time to interpret the dream.

Then Daniel returned to his friends. If God was God at all, he could help them.

'Pray!' Daniel urged his friends. 'We must ask God to reveal the king's dream to us, or we must die with all the wise men in Babylon.'

The four men prayed and asked God to help them, and during the night, God gave Daniel a vision so

that the mystery was clear to him.

'We praise you, Lord God!' Daniel prayed. 'Your wisdom is beyond our understanding. You are

There is a God in Heaven who can reveal mysteries.

all powerful. You reveal things hidden in darkness, mysteries that no one can understand. You have answered my prayer and given me wisdom; you have made known to me the king's dream.'

The next day, Daniel went to the king.

'Can you tell me what I dreamed?' Nebuchadnezzar asked gloomily.

'Your majesty,' said Daniel, 'there is no wise man alive who can tell you what you dreamed. But there is a God in Heaven who can reveal mysteries, and he has shown you what the future holds.

'You dreamed of a huge statue. Its head was made of gold, its chest and arms were made of silver, its belly and thighs were made of bronze, its legs were made of iron and its feet of iron and clay.

'Then out of a mountain, a rock was cut. It fell down and shattered the statue so that the gold and silver, the bronze, iron and clay, all lay in pieces. Then a wind came and blew it all away, while the rock became a mountain as big as the earth.

'This is what it means,' continued Daniel. 'God has given you everything you have. God has given you power over all you see around you. You are the golden head of the statue. After you will come other powerful kingdoms, but in time they will all fall away.

'The rock that became a mountain, stronger than everything else, is the kingdom that God will make. God's kingdom will be greater than any of them, and it will last for ever; it will never end.'

King Nebuchadnezzar fell at Daniel's feet.

'Your God is the true God!' he cried. 'He is the king of all kings!'

Then King Nebuchadnezzar gave Daniel many fine gifts and made him ruler over the province of Babylon and all the wise men in the kingdom. Daniel in turn gave his friends, Shadrach, Meshach and Abednego, important jobs in the province, while he continued to stay in the palace.

King Nebuchadnezzar made a huge statue of gold. It was placed on an open plain in Babylon and was so tall and wide that it could be seen for miles around.

Nebuchadnezzar called everyone of any importance to stand before the statue.

It was so tall and wide that it could be seen for miles around.

A herald stood up and made an announcement.

'The king has commanded all peoples, whatever language you speak, to bow down and worship the golden statue that King Nebuchadnezzar has made. As soon as you hear the sound of music,

you must bow down and worship.
Anyone who fails to do this will be
thrown into a blazing furnace of fire!'

The music sounded. Everyone
fell down to worship the statue as
they had been commanded; everyone
except Shadrach, Meshach and
Abednego.

Some of the king's astrologers
were troublemakers.

'Your majesty,' they said one day
to the king, 'you have commanded
that everyone fall down and worship
the golden statue that stands on the
plain. But there are men, men you
have made powerful, who do not
obey your decree or worship your
gods. There are three Jews, Shadrach,
Meshach and Abednego, who refuse
to bow down and worship the
statue.'

The king was very angry. He sent
for the three men who were Daniel's
friends.

'I have heard that you refuse to
obey me,' the king said. 'But I will
give you one more chance. Bow down
and worship the statue – or you will
be thrown into the blazing furnace of
fire. Then no god will be able to save
you!'

Worship the statue – or you will be thrown into the blazing furnace.

'King Nebuchadnezzar,' the
friends replied, 'there is no doubt that
you are a great man, but our God is
greater still. If you throw us into the
blazing furnace of fire, our God is able
to save us. But whether he decides
to rescue us or not, we will worship
only him. We will not bow down and
worship your golden statue.'

In a rage, the king ordered that
the furnace be heated to the highest
temperature possible, and that the

three men be tied up and thrown, fully clothed, into the fire.

Nebuchadnezzar watched. Then he stared in amazement.

'Were there not three men tied up and thrown into the fire? Yet I can see four men, and they are walking around in freedom! Their hands are not bound. Get them out, quickly!'

Our God is able to save us.

The three men stepped out of the fire. They were completely unharmed and no longer tied up. They were not burned by the fire; their clothing was not scorched; they did not even smell of smoke.

'Praise the living God!' exclaimed Nebuchadnezzar. 'He sent an angel to rescue you because you were

prepared to die rather than worship the statue I had made.'

Then Nebuchadnezzar issued another decree.

'No one of any language must say anything against the God of Shadrach, Meshach and Abednego. For he alone has the power to save.'

King Nebuchadnezzar dreamed again and called all his advisors to help him. As before, no one could help him except Daniel.

'I dreamed that I was looking at a tree that grew so tall that its top touched the sky. It could be seen

from all the ends of the earth. Its leaves were beautiful and it produced enough fruit for everyone to eat. It was so strong that all the creatures on earth sheltered under it, and all the birds lived in its branches.

'But while I watched, an angel came from Heaven. It called for the tree to be chopped down, its branches to be cut off, its leaves to be stripped and its fruit to be scattered. The animals fled from under it and the birds flew away. But its stump was bound with chains and it was drenched with dew.'

Daniel understood the meaning of the dream all too well, but he was afraid to tell the king. King Nebuchadnezzar encouraged him to hold nothing back.

'The dream is a nightmare, my King!' said Daniel. 'I wish it applied to someone other than you. But you are that tree that has grown as tall as the sky. You are the king that all the nations around know is great and powerful.

'God has seen all this but now he wants you to know that you are nothing compared to him. He wants you to change and do what is right. He wants you to be kind to those

you have oppressed. Until you do this, your mind will be destroyed, and you will live among the animals and eat grass like the cattle.'

It all happened as Daniel told the king. Nebuchadnezzar endured a time of terrible madness when he no longer looked like a king and he lived like a wild animal. But at the end of it, Nebuchadnezzar realised that God was indeed the God of all the earth. He praised God and understood that he loved kindness and justice and hated oppression and cruelty.

Time passed. When King Nebuchadnezzar died, Daniel and his friends were forgotten. Many years later, a new king, Belshazzar, gave a magnificent feast.

All the great men in Babylon were invited, and Belshazzar ordered that the wine be served in the gold and silver goblets that

Suddenly the fingers of a human hand appeared.

Nebuchadnezzar had taken from the temple in Jerusalem. The guests ate and drank; they raised their goblets and shouted:

'Let's praise the gods of gold

and silver, of bronze, iron, wood and stone!'

Suddenly the fingers of a human hand appeared and the fingers moved against the wall. One by one people stopped eating and drinking. Their mouths dropped open in astonishment. They looked at the king. His face turned the colour of ashes, his hands shook, and finally, he collapsed on the floor.

The fingers wrote: 'MENE, MENE, TEKEL, PARSIN.'

'Find someone to tell me what this means!' said Belshazzar, weakly. 'I will make him the next most powerful person in the land,' promised the king.

None of the magicians or wise men could tell him the meaning of the writing on the wall. Then the Queen Mother remembered that Daniel had helped Nebuchadnezzar with the meaning of his dreams. They sent for Daniel.

'Tell me what it means, and I will reward you,' said the king.

'I don't want a reward,' said Daniel. 'God sent this hand to write on the wall because he has seen your greed and he knows how wicked you are. He has weighed you on the scales and you have been judged unworthy. Now your rule is at an end. Your kingdom will be taken by the Medes and the Persians.'

Belshazzar knew he had heard the truth, but it was too late. That night the Persian army attacked Babylon. Belshazzar was killed.

He had heard the truth, but it was too late.

When Darius the Mede became ruler over them, he saw that Daniel was gifted and experienced and made him one of his top three administrators.

Daniel worked hard and King Darius was so impressed with him that he wanted to put Daniel in charge of the whole kingdom. But there were other officials who were jealous of Daniel. They wanted to remove him from office; they wanted to find something – anything – that would make him lose his job.

'It's useless!' they said to one another. 'The only way we will ever get rid of Daniel is if it has something to do with his God.'

They plotted and schemed and

slowly an idea began to take shape. They went to see Darius.

'Your majesty, may you live for ever!' they said. 'You are such a great king that we all think that you should issue a decree. No one must pray to anyone but you for the next thirty days. If they do, they should be thrown into a den of lions!'

Darius was flattered. It was a good idea, he thought. He even put it in writing so that it became law. And the law of the Medes and Persians cannot be changed.

When Daniel heard about the decree, he went as usual to his upstairs room where the windows faced Jerusalem. There he knelt down and prayed three times a day to God, asking him for help.

The men who had plotted against Daniel watched and smiled. Their plan had worked.

'Your majesty,' they said, 'are we right in thinking that anyone who disobeys your decree will be thrown into a den of lions?'

King Darius nodded.

'This decree cannot be altered,' he said.

'But Daniel, the man who has such power in your kingdom, ignores the decree. He does not pray to you. Instead he prays three times a day to his God.'

King Darius was very sad. He realised that the men had set out to trap him, and now he was powerless to rescue Daniel. Darius had no choice. He ordered Daniel to be thrown into the lions' den.

'May your God save you,' he said to Daniel.

That night Darius could not sleep. As soon as it was morning, he returned to the lions' den.

'Daniel!' he cried. 'Has your God saved you from the lions?'

He ordered Daniel to be thrown into the lions' den.

'Yes, your majesty!' shouted Daniel from the den. 'My God has saved me! He sent an angel to close the mouths of the hungry lions. I am unharmed.'

'Release Daniel from the den!' cried Darius, overjoyed to find Daniel alive. 'And punish those men who have tried to hurt him.'

Then Darius issued another decree.

'All the people in my kingdom must fear and respect Daniel's God. For he is the living God, whose kingdom will last for ever; he is the God who rescues and saves and performs signs and wonders; and he has the power to save, even from the mouths of lions!'

Daniel continued to love and worship God for the rest of his life.

Ezekiel was also exiled from Jerusalem. He was a priest. When Nebuchadnezzar attacked Jerusalem he had been taken captive and had settled with many other Jewish exiles on the banks of the Kebar River in Babylon.

One day God spoke to Ezekiel in a vision. First Ezekiel saw a storm cloud moving towards him, with lightning flashing around it in every direction. In the centre was a fire which glowed with intense heat, and within the fire, Ezekiel saw cherubim, four strange winged creatures which shot through the sky with lightning speed.

Then Ezekiel saw the four creatures moving on the ground, each with two crystal wheels, full of eyes, trailing fire. The sound of their wings was as loud as a marching army or the roar of rushing water.

Four strange winged creatures shot through the sky with lightning speed.

As Ezekiel watched, he heard a voice. The creatures lowered their wings and above a sapphire throne, Ezekiel saw something like the shape of a man. He glowed with brilliant fiery light, and shone with all the colours of the rainbow.

Ezekiel fell to the ground. He knew this was a vision of God in all his glory.

'Stand on your feet and I will speak to you,' said the voice. Then the Spirit of God helped Ezekiel to get up from his knees. 'I have chosen you as a messenger to my rebellious people, the Israelites. You must not be afraid, Ezekiel, but you must give them my message, even though they will not want to hear it. Now, open your mouth and eat what I shall give you.'

Ezekiel opened his mouth, and God gave him a scroll to eat, on which was written many words. It tasted as sweet as honey.

'Go now and speak to my people, and I will help you, even when they refuse to listen,' said God.

God spoke through Ezekiel in a very dramatic way - the people watched as the prophet acted out a drama. As people watched they understood the message that God had for them.

Ezekiel drew a picture of Jerusalem on a clay brick. Then he made armies, battering rams and ramps, and acted out an attack. He ate only wheat and barley, beans and lentils, millet and spelt; he drank only water, and rationed all of it, day after day so that he became thin and weak.

The people understood the message only too clearly: Jerusalem was being besieged by their enemies.

Ezekiel shaved off his hair and beard and divided it into three piles.

He took a third of the hair and burned it inside the model of the city of Jerusalem; he took another third and chopped it up around the outside of the model with his sword; the rest, apart from a few strands of hair, he scattered to the wind. Then Ezekiel tucked the few strands carefully inside his cloak.

Again God's message was clear: many of his people would die by fire or the sword in the siege of Jerusalem, others would be taken into exile and scattered. But there would still be a few, a remnant, who would survive and these few would one day return safely to their home in Jerusalem.

Scattered all around him were human bones.

Ezekiel continued to speak to the people through the events in his life for many years. Then, just as God's people in Babylon were ready to give up hope, Ezekiel had another vision.

God's Spirit took Ezekiel to the middle of a valley, where, scattered all around him were human bones, dry and lifeless. As Ezekiel walked through them, God asked him whether he thought the bones could ever live again.

'Lord, only you know that,' replied Ezekiel.

'Speak to these bones, Ezekiel,' said God.

So Ezekiel spoke to them.

'Dry bones, hear the word of the Lord! God says that he will put you together again and cover you with flesh. He will give you breath so that you will once more breathe and have life. Then you will know that you have a God who loves you.'

A rattling sound echoed through the valley, and one by one the bones moved and locked together, to form skeletons. Slowly the bones were held together with muscles and tendons, were covered with flesh and wrapped in new skin.

'Tell the wind to give these bodies breath!' said God.

Ezekiel spoke to the wind, and the lungs of the lifeless bodies filled so that they could breathe again and come to life. They stood up, and were so many that they formed a large army.

'This is what I will do for my people,' God told Ezekiel. 'I will breathe new life into them. I will take them back to the land of Israel, the land I promised would be their home. Then everyone will know that I am God.'

CHAPTER 20

THE QUESTION OF SUFFERING

THERE WAS ONCE A MAN NAMED JOB. HE HAD A LARGE AND HAPPY FAMILY AND MANY SERVANTS TO LOOK AFTER HIM. HE WAS VERY WEALTHY, AND OWNED THOUSANDS OF SHEEP AND CAMELS, AND HUNDREDS OF COWS AND DONKEYS.

Job was also a good man. He loved God and did all he could to obey him and live honestly.

One day Satan came into God's presence. Satan was God's enemy.

'Where have you been?' asked God.

'Roaming the earth,' replied Satan. 'Going here and there.'

'Have you seen Job?' asked God. 'He is a rare man - truly good and kind.'

'Of course he's good,' sneered Satan. 'You make it easy for him to be good. He has everything he could possibly want. But if all he has were

You may take away all that he loves.

to be taken away from him, no doubt he would not love you as much. He'd probably be as bad as the next man.'

206

'We will see,' said God. 'You may take away all that he loves, but do not harm Job.'

Satan went to work. He caused lightning to fall from the sky to burn up Job's sheep and servants. It was a terrible disaster. Raiders carried off Job's camels. Then a freak whirlwind caused the roof to fall in on Job's children. They were all killed.

Job cried out to God in his sadness and fell down to worship him.

'I had nothing when I was born and I shall take nothing with me to my grave. The Lord has given me all that I have and he has taken it all

> ## *I had nothing when I was born and I shall take nothing with me to my grave.*

away. Praise the name of God!'

Satan came again to God.

'Job may have no family and no material goods now – but he has still his health and strength. He would soon curse you if he became ill and was in pain,' said Satan slyly.

'We will see,' said God. 'You may take away his health and strength, but you must not let him die.'

Satan caused Job to be covered all over with painful sores.

'Curse God and die!' urged his wife. 'You cannot still love him!'

'No,' replied Job. 'We were happy to accept the good things that God gave us; we must also accept suffering when it comes.'

When Job's three friends heard what had happened, they came and sat with him. They felt very sorry for him. They had never seen him in such a bad state.

'Why was I born?' Job asked after some days. 'The worst that could

have happened has now happened!'

'Perhaps God is punishing you for some terrible sin,' said the first friend. 'Confess your sin and God may make you well.'

'But I can think of no such sin,' said Job.

'Curse God and die!' urged his wife.

'Well that must be it!' said his second friend. 'You cannot admit you have done something wrong!'

'I will ask God to tell me what I have done wrong,' replied Job.

'Maybe your sin is so huge God will make you suffer even more!' said the third friend.

'You are no help to me at all!' said Job to his friends. Job continued to pray in the hopes that God would answer him. Then God spoke.

'You want to know why you are suffering, Job? Let me ask you some questions.

'Where were you when I laid the foundations of the world? Have you ever called the morning into being or formed the stars into constellations? Have you given strength to a horse or clothed its neck with a flowing mane? Have you taught the hawk to fly or the eagle where to build his nest? You have asked me questions, but do you think you can understand the answers?'

Job realised how great and marvellous God was. He did not need to know why he was suffering. He knew that he could trust God whatever happened.

He knew that he could trust God whatever happened.

'I am sorry,' replied Job. 'There are things which are too wonderful for me to know.'

'Your friends were wrong,' said God. 'You did not suffer because you sinned. They must ask you to forgive them.'

Job forgave his friends. Then God blessed Job even more than he had before. Job enjoyed a long and happy life.

CHAPTER 21

TIME TO REBUILD A NATION

THE JEWISH EXILES HAD BEEN LIVING IN FOREIGN LANDS FOR MANY YEARS. THE PERSIANS HAD OVERTHROWN THE BABYLONIANS SO NOW THEY WERE RULED BY ANOTHER FOREIGN POWER.

It was time for God's promises to come true. The messages for his people, spoken by Isaiah, Jeremiah and Ezekiel were about to take place.

King Cyrus of Persia issued a decree to the Jewish people.

'I know that the Lord, the God of Heaven, has put me in charge of many people and many nations. He has told me to rebuild the temple in Jerusalem. Any one of you who wants to return to Jerusalem may now go and help with this work. Those who want to stay here can help in other ways, by making donations of gold or silver or livestock.'

God's people could hardly believe what was happening. After all the years of suffering they were being allowed to go home. Not only that, they were instructed to rebuild God's temple.

Preparations were made. Silver and gold were collected. The first group of excited people, led by

Zerubbabel, prepared to leave.

'I will give back to you all the things Nebuchadnezzar took from your temple,' said King Cyrus. 'They don't belong here.'

So God's people took back with them not only the riches they had been given, but also 5,400 pieces of gold and silver – in bowls and dishes and pans.

Over 50,000 people made the journey to Jerusalem along with horses and mules, camels and donkeys. They reached the lands that had once been their homes and stayed there for a few months before meeting together in Jerusalem.

Over 50,000 people made the journey to Jerusalem.

There they made plans for the rebuilding of the temple. Jeshua and Zerubbabel started to rebuild the altar. As soon as it was made, they started to offer sacrifices to God.

They celebrated the festivals as they had before they were captured and taken away, even though they were afraid of the peoples around them. They worshipped God even

before the foundation of the temple was laid.

Then they ordered the logs from Tyre and Sidon as Solomon had before them. They paid the masons and the carpenters to start to build the foundations, and when they were restored, the people met together to praise and thank God.

'God is good!' they sang. 'His love and goodness last for ever!'

But the Samaritans and others living in the land of Judah were not so happy. In the years that followed they made up bad stories about them, and wrote letters full of lies to the kings who were ruling at the time. After the death of King Cyrus, they questioned whether the Jews had any right to be there at all. They stopped the rebuilding work.

God spoke through the prophets, Haggai and Zechariah, to encourage the people.

'Keep on building!' they said. 'This is God's will for his people. Do not give up and he will bless us. Jerusalem will once more be a place where God is worshipped.'

King Darius of Persia supported them against their enemies.

'Do not stop the rebuilding work,' ordered King Darius. Then he warned their enemies that if they interfered any more, they would be punished. So the people continued to build the temple until it was finished.

When Xerxes had been king in Persia for three years, he prepared a wonderful banquet in Susa to which everyone important in the land was invited. When everyone was merry and enjoying themselves, Xerxes sent for his wife, Vashti, so he could show off her beauty. But Vashti refused to come.

Xerxes was humiliated in front of his guests. He was so angry that he decided never to see Vashti again, and instead sent to every province in his kingdom to find himself a new wife. He ordered that all the most beautiful women should come and take a year of beauty treatments, after which he would choose one of them to be his queen.

> ## He ordered that all the most beautiful women should come and take a year of beauty treatments.

Esther was one of the women chosen. Esther, who was very beautiful, was descended from the Jewish captives who had been taken from Jerusalem by the Babylonians. Her uncle Mordecai had looked after her when both her parents died.

'Don't tell them that you are Jewish,' her Uncle Mordecai warned when Esther was taken to the palace.

When Xerxes saw Esther, he loved her more than all the other beautiful women. He chose her to be his queen.

Mordecai worked as a palace official. One day he overheard two of King Xerxes' officers planning an attempt on the king's life.

Mordecai told Esther what he had heard, and Esther told the king. The two officers were executed and the incident was written down in Xerxes' palace records.

Some time later, King Xerxes chose to give great powers to a man called Haman, who was known in the palace. The king ordered that everyone should bow down to Haman and pay him respect. Everyone did this except Mordecai, Esther's uncle.

The king's attendants asked Mordecai why he would not bow down to Haman. They tried to persuade him. But still Mordecai refused. He would bow to no one except God.

He would bow to no one except God.

When Haman realised what was happening, he was very angry. He hated Mordecai. He wanted revenge not just against him, but on all the Jewish people, because he knew that they loved God. So he went to the king with a plot.

'Your majesty,' said Haman, 'there are people scattered throughout your kingdom who have different customs from us and do not obey your laws. I think you should issue a decree ordering that every one of them be destroyed. I will personally reward the men who carry out the decree.'

'Keep your money,' said King Xerxes. 'But do what you like with these people.'

So the matter was agreed. A date was confirmed for the deaths of every Jewish man, woman and child. The decree was posted up in Susa, and all the people wondered at how such a terrible thing could happen.

Mordecai tore his clothes and put on sackcloth and ashes when he heard about the decree. Jewish people all over Xerxes' kingdom were doing the same.

Mordecai sent a message to

Esther, asking her to beg the king for mercy.

'I cannot go to the king unless he sends for me,' Esther replied. 'Anyone who breaks this rule is put to death!'

'Even a queen will not escape this decree,' Mordecai replied. 'Perhaps God has made you queen in Persia so that you can save your people.'

'Pray for me then. Go without food for a while,' replied Esther. 'I will do the same. Then I will go to the king, even if I die because of it.'

I will go to the king, even if I die because of it.

The next day, Esther went to see the king. When he saw her, he was pleased she had come and was happy to talk to her. God had answered their prayers.

'What can I do for you, Queen Esther?' he asked. 'Ask anything – I will give you half my kingdom.'

Esther was waiting for the right moment.

'I have prepared a banquet for you and Haman. Please come,' she said.

The king agreed. When Haman received his invitation, he was delighted. But when he walked past Mordecai, who did not bow before him, Haman burned with anger.

'Build a gallows and ask the king to hang Mordecai on it tomorrow!' laughed his friends. So Haman went and ordered the gallows to be built and felt much happier.

That night, King Xerxes could not sleep.

'Read to me the history of my reign,' he said to one of his attendants.

The man read. When he came to the part when Mordecai had overheard the plot against the king and the men were executed, King Xerxes stopped his attendant with a question.

'How was Mordecai rewarded?' asked the king.

'He wasn't,' said the attendant. 'There is no mention of it here.'

'Who is in the court at the moment?' Xerxes asked.

Only Haman was there. He had arrived early to ask the king to agree to Mordecai's hanging.

'What do you think is a suitable reward for someone the king wishes to honour?' Xerxes asked Haman.

Haman smiled. He was sure the king was planning to honour him.

'Dress him in the king's robe,' said Haman. 'Let him ride one of the king's horses through the streets. Proclaim in a loud voice so that everyone can hear, "This is how the king rewards the man he is pleased with!"'

'Excellent!' said the king. 'Please do all this for Mordecai without delay.'

Haman felt sick. He couldn't admit to the king what he had come for. So he went from the palace and obeyed the king, but as soon as he could, he rushed home to tell his wife and friends what had happened.

'But this must put you in great danger,' they said. 'You cannot plot against someone the king has honoured!'

Before Haman had time to think of another plan, the king's servants arrived to take him to Esther's banquet.

'Well, my queen,' Xerxes said to Esther as the banquet began, 'what gift can I give to you? What special thing would you like so that I can show that I love you? Ask for anything and it is yours.'

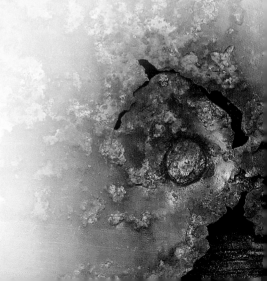

'Your majesty,' said Esther, 'the only gift I want is my life; please save my life and the lives of all my people! For there is a man who has plotted their destruction and we are all to be killed. If we were only to be sold as slaves, I would have said nothing, but our lives hang in the balance.'

'Who is this man? Who wants to destroy your people?' demanded the king.

'This man! This vile Haman!' said Esther, pointing at him.

Haman was terrified. The king and queen were staring at him. He could see the anger in the king's eyes. Xerxes stormed out of the palace in a rage while Haman begged the queen for mercy. But King Xerxes had already made up his mind.

'Haman has built a gallows on which to hang Mordecai,' said a servant.

'Take him! Hang him on his own gallows!' said the king. 'Get him out of my sight!' Haman was dragged from the room.

Then King Xerxes spoke to Esther.

'I cannot undo Haman's decree, for the law cannot be changed. But I can help the Jews fight their enemies and defend themselves,' he said.

Take him! Hang him on his own gallows!

Xerxes gave to Mordecai all the power that he had once given to Haman. He put a ring on his finger as a sign of his authority and a gold crown on his head. Mordecai left the palace wearing clothes of blue and white and a purple linen robe.

The Jews were safe. Every year after that they met to celebrate and remember how Queen Esther had saved them.

CHAPTER 22

THE PAST AND THE FUTURE

MORE THAN SIXTY YEARS
HAD PASSED SINCE THE
FIRST GROUP OF EXILES HAD
RETURNED TO JERUSALEM TO REBUILD
THE TEMPLE. NOW ANOTHER GROUP
FOLLOWED, WITH EZRA THE PRIEST AS
THEIR LEADER.

King Artaxerxes of Persia had
given Ezra permission to return.

'Return to Jerusalem with anyone
who wants to go. Take a copy of
God's Law, and my treasurers will
give you what money you need.
Teach the people God's laws and
report back to me,' he wrote.

Ezra was amazed. He called the
people to get ready.

'I have told the king that God will
protect us on our journey,' he said.
'We must fast and pray before we go
and ask God to help us.'

They journeyed safely to
Jerusalem, and met others who had
already returned and made Jerusalem
their home. Then some of the leaders
came to Ezra, embarrassed.

'Since we have returned, some of
our people have married wives who
do not believe in the living God.'

'What?' cried Ezra, falling to his
knees in despair. 'After all God has
done for us in bringing us back here?'
Then Ezra wept and prayed to God for
forgiveness of all the people.

'I am so sorry, Lord,' he prayed. 'We are your people and we should know the laws you have taught us. But we never learn. We make the same mistakes again and again. Please forgive us.'

Some of the people heard Ezra's prayer. They knew he was right. A large group of men, women and children joined him and wept and prayed with him.

'We have sinned,' they said. 'Forgive us and show us how we can obey you.'

A large group of men, women and children joined him and wept and prayed with him.

Meanwhile Nehemiah was still in exile, working as cup-bearer to King Artaxerxes.

One day he heard news from his brother, Hanani, that the walls of Jerusalem were still in ruins. Nehemiah wept in sorrow. He could not eat.

'Lord God, please listen to my prayer,' he said. 'I know that we have disobeyed you. I am sorry for all the wrong things we have done. I know that we were taken into exile because of our disobedience. But you also promised to return to Jerusalem those people who were obedient. Please let me go back to Jerusalem to help rebuild the walls.'

Four months passed. Then, as Nehemiah was serving the king, Artaxerxes noticed that something was wrong.

'Why do you look so sad, Nehemiah?' asked Artaxerxes.

Nehemiah knew that God was answering his prayer.

'I am sorry, my king, but I cannot help but be sad. I have heard that the walls surrounding the place where my ancestors are buried need to be rebuilt,' he said. 'Please let me go to Jerusalem.'

'When will you get back?' came the king's answer. 'How long will you be away?'

Nehemiah saw that the king had agreed to let him go and that God was on his side. He named a time.

'If you will let me go, will you also provide me with protection for my journey and the materials to rebuild the city gates and walls?'

God answered Nehemiah's prayer. Artaxerxes agreed to everything.

Nehemiah arrived safely in Jerusalem and set about inspecting the walls by night so that no one would know why he was there. All that remained were piles of rubble where there should be walls; and the gates were burned.

The next day he went to the city officials and told them his plans, and how King Artaxerxes had given him permission to rebuild the walls.

The people started work straight away. They organised themselves into groups, each working on different sections of the wall. But not everyone was happy. Two Samaritans, Sanballat and Tobiah, did not want God's people to succeed. At first they laughed and made fun of them.

'If a fox were to walk along the top of that wall, the whole thing would collapse!' they laughed. Then they tried to raise an army to come and attack them.

But Nehemiah kept on praying that God would help them. He told the workers to take weapons with them so they were prepared to defend themselves while carrying on the work. Even when Sanballat and Tobiah plotted to kill him, Nehemiah went on praying.

Even their enemies knew that God had helped them to succeed.

When the walls were completed, and the new gates were hung, all the people met together. The walls of Jerusalem had been rebuilt in fifty-two days. Even their enemies knew that God had helped them to succeed. They began to be afraid.

Some of the exiles who had returned were very wealthy. Others were poor. The wealthy lent large sums of money to the poor, but when the poor could not repay their debts, the wealthy men took away their fields. The poor people came to Nehemiah and told him what had happened and how they were being treated unfairly by their fellow Jews.

'Once our fields have gone we have no way of making any money,' cried the people to Nehemiah. 'Then we are forced to sell our children into slavery.'

Nehemiah was very angry. He called the people together.

'What you are doing is against God's Law,' he cried. 'We are all members of the same family. We

We are forced to sell our children into slavery.

shouldn't be hurting one another. What will our enemies say? Give back everything which does not belong to you.'

The people listened to Nehemiah. He was right. He was their leader, and they respected him. He worked as hard as any of them, and always used his position for the good of the people.

They had arranged a celebration when the walls were completed. Nehemiah called everyone together.

Ezra climbed a high wooden platform in the square before the water gate, carrying scrolls in his hands. He was a good teacher and knew God's Law well. Now he read the scrolls to the people. Everyone

listened. One by one, the people understood how disobedient they had been, and began to weep.

'Don't cry,' said Nehemiah. 'Today is a special day. Today we must be happy that we have heard and understood God's Law. Go and have something good to eat and drink, and share what you have with each other.'

Day after day the people listened to Ezra as he read God's Law. They remembered how God had looked after his people since they first left Egypt. They saw how they had disappointed God.

'We are sorry for all the things our ancestors did to make you angry,' they said to God. 'We are sorry for all our sins.'

When it was time to dedicate Jerusalem's new walls to God, the people came together with harps. Nehemiah gave instructions for the singers to form two choirs. Each choir processed around the top of the wall in opposite directions, while the people followed.

The people had wept in Babylon and been too sad to sing songs to God. But now they sang some new songs.

'Praise the Lord God! I will praise him all my life; I will sing to God for as long as I live!

'How happy are those who trust God, the maker of heaven and earth, the sea and all that lives in them. How happy are those who know that God will help them. God cares for the oppressed, and he gives food to the hungry. God sets the prisoners free and gives sight to the blind. God looks after those who are strangers in foreign lands and those who have lost parents, wives or husbands. Our God reigns for ever! Praise the Lord!'

God heals the broken hearted and binds up their wounds.

They met together in God's temple. Every man, woman and child

sang to God in their happiness. They knew that God had kept his promises.

'How good it is to sing praises to God! The Lord builds up Jerusalem; he gathers up the exiles and returns them to Israel. He heals the broken hearted and binds up their wounds.

'The Lord decides the number of the stars and calls to each of them by name. Our Lord is great and mighty, and his understanding is beyond measure. Sing to the Lord with thanksgiving! Make music to God upon the harp!

'The Lord loves those who come to him for help; those who put their trust in his unfailing love! Praise the Lord! Praise the Lord!'

Some time later, Nehemiah returned to work for King Artaxerxes, as he had agreed.

When Nehemiah left God's people in Jerusalem, they settled down to rebuild their lives. For a while they remembered how they had hated their time in exile and how much they wanted to come home. But time passed. Sometimes their lives were a struggle. Things were not as easy as they had hoped.

'People who don't worship God seem to live happily,' they said. 'Sometimes it seems pointless following God's laws; worshipping God all the time is boring.'

Malachi came with messages for the people.

'This is what God says: "I love you, just as I have always loved you from the beginning. Remember how a child obeys his father? Think about how a servant respects his master. I am your father; I am your master."

'The priests have stopped leading you as they should,' said Malachi. 'They have stopped obeying the laws God gave them. You've started marrying wives from the nations nearby, people who worship gods of wood and stone. You don't keep the Sabbath as a special day of rest and you don't trust God to provide for your needs.

'The time is coming when God himself will live among you! He will send a messenger to prepare the way.

The time is coming when God himself will live among you!

The one who is coming will be like a fire which makes gold and silver pure, removing all the impurities that spoil it. He will come to save us. Anyone who does what is good and right will be happy on that day.'

Nehemiah returned again to Jerusalem. He tried to help the people to put right the things which God had warned them about. But after Malachi, there were no more prophets in the land for 400 years.

CHAPTER 23

THE NATIVITY

ZECHARIAH WAS A PRIEST LIVING IN THE HILL COUNTRY OF JUDEA. HE WAS MARRIED TO ELIZABETH AND THEY HAD BOTH LOVED AND SERVED GOD ALL THEIR LIVES. BUT GOD HAD NOT BLESSED THEM WITH CHILDREN.

Zechariah had been chosen to burn the incense in the temple – almost a once in a lifetime experience as the priest was chosen by lot. Outside the temple, in the morning sunshine, people were praying. Inside the temple, where it was cool and quiet, Zechariah lit the incense.

Zechariah blinked hard as he began to realise that he was not alone. Standing on the right hand side of the altar was an angel.

'Don't be afraid,' said the angel. It was clear that Zechariah was

---

Standing on the right hand side of the altar was an angel.

---

terrified. 'God has heard your prayers. I am here to tell you that your wife will have a baby son – and not just a baby son but a child blessed by God in every way. Name him John.

God's Holy Spirit will help him so that he will be able to make people understand what God wants of them. Then they will be ready when he comes.'

'Can this be true?' asked Zechariah. 'Surely Elizabeth is now too old to have children.'

'My name is Gabriel,' said the angel, 'and I stand in the presence of God. I have brought God's message to you now and you don't believe me. When you leave here you will not be able to speak – and you will not speak again until you have seen for yourself that what I am telling you is true!'

Zechariah had been in the temple for longer than was usual. The people outside began to wonder what had happened. When he came out, he tried to tell them about the angel. But because he could not speak, he had to use gestures. Zechariah waved his arms about. The people could not understand him but they realised he must have had some sort of vision.

Some time later, Elizabeth found

she was expecting a baby... The angel Gabriel's work was not yet done - he had another surprise announcement to make.

Elizabeth, Zechariah's wife, had a young relative called Mary. Gabriel went to Nazareth in Galilee to visit her. Mary was not much more than a girl but she was engaged to be married to Joseph, the local carpenter. She was very surprised when the angel greeted her.

'Mary,' said Gabriel. 'I have come from God with some very special news for you. God has seen what kind of person you are. Now he has something very special for you to do.'

Mary was afraid. She didn't know what to think.

'There is no need to be afraid,'

This baby will be God's son, a king who will reign for ever!

said Gabriel. 'You will have a baby, a little son. Give him the same Jesus. This baby will be God's son, a king who will reign for ever!'

'But I am not even married,' said Mary. 'How can I have a baby?'

'The Holy Spirit will make this

The Holy Spirit will make this happen.

---

happen, Mary – nothing is impossible for God. Another woman in your family, Elizabeth, is now six months pregnant. Everyone said that she couldn't have children, but God has blessed her with a child in her old age.'

'I will do anything God wants me to,' said Mary.

Then Gabriel left Mary.

Mary thought about what the angel had told her. Would anyone believe her if she told them? But if Elizabeth was expecting a baby, perhaps she should go and visit her and talk to her about what had happened? Elizabeth lived in the hills. Mary prepared for her journey and went to stay with her.

When she reached Zechariah's house, Mary embraced Elizabeth.

Then the baby inside Elizabeth's belly jumped with joy.

'Mary!' Elizabeth said in surprise. 'Look how God has blessed you! And he will bless your baby too. You have been willing to do what God has asked of you – and you will be rewarded. But why am I so lucky to have you come to stay with me?'

'God is very great!' said Mary. 'I am no one, yet God has made me someone special by giving me this amazing thing to do. He has always been good to people who try to listen to him and follow his ways. He was good to Abraham and Isaac and Jacob and is good to us now. God always chooses people who feel they have nothing to offer – and he makes them great. But he also sends away people who think they are too good or important to need his help. God is good.'

Mary stayed in the hills with Elizabeth for three months before returning to her home in Nazareth.

Only a little while later it was time for Elizabeth's baby to be born. She had a little boy, just as the angel Gabriel had told her. Elizabeth was overjoyed, and her friends and neighbours shared in her happiness.

Eight days later, the baby boy was circumcised. They were ready to call him Zechariah after his father, but Elizabeth insisted he should be called John.

'What does Zechariah say?' they said. Then Zechariah asked for a writing tablet so he could tell them – he had not spoken since he met the angel.

'His name is John,' he wrote.

As soon as he had finished writing, he was able to speak once more. The first words he spoke were in praise of God who had blessed them with this special child.

Everyone was amazed. They couldn't stop talking about what had happened.

'God has not forgotten us, his people,' Zechariah said. 'He is sending his chosen one to save us from our enemies. And he has chosen this child, my child John, to be the one who will prepare the way. He will tell us about the one who is to come who will lead us into the way of peace.'

Mary was happy that Elizabeth had safely delivered her baby son; she was also happy to serve God and do all that he wanted of her. But Mary was enagaged to Joseph and Joseph was sad. He knew that Mary's baby was not his baby. But he cared about Mary. She had told him about the

He is sending his chosen one to save us from our enemies.

angel and what she had been told – but he wasn't sure... Yet he did not want her to face bringing up her baby alone. He didn't want people to be unkind to her. But should he marry her as they had planned?

Then one night Joseph dreamed a strange dream in which an angel appeared to him.

'You need not worry about marrying Mary,' the angel said. 'The Holy Spirit has caused the baby to grow inside her. She will have a baby boy and you must call him Jesus, because he will be the Saviour of the world.'

Joseph needed no further reassurance to marry Mary. Now

he was happy too. He did what the angel of the Lord had told him.

The months passed quickly and soon the time came for Mary's baby to be born. It looked as though this would not happen in Nazareth, but in Bethlehem.

The tiny part of the world where Mary and Joseph lived was now a part of the Roman Empire. The Roman emperor, Caesar Augustus, wanted to tax his people.

He ordered a census so that everyone had to go to the town of their ancestors to be counted. This meant that Joseph had to take Mary with him to Bethlehem, because he belonged to the family of King David.

Mary and Joseph made their way to the village of Bethlehem in Judea. The roads were full of people travelling, all obeying the commands of their Roman rulers. Bethlehem was bustling with people.

Men, women and children had all come to be registered there. By the time Mary and Joseph arrived, it was already difficult to find somewhere to stay.

Mary felt tired and weary; she was starting to feel the pains that meant her baby would soon be born.

Joseph went from house to house looking for a room because the inn was full. Eventually they found shelter where the animals were stabled.

That night, Mary gave birth to a baby boy, her first-born child. She wrapped him with strips of cloth and made a bed for him in a manger, because there was no room anywhere else.

While Jesus was being cradled by his mother Mary that night, shepherds were on the hills outside Bethlehem, looking after their flocks of sheep.

The soft flickering flames of their fire suddenly gave way to dazzling light as an angel appeared in the night sky. The shepherds were terrified.

An angel appeared in the night sky.

'Don't be afraid!' said the angel. 'I have come with good news! Tonight, in Bethlehem, a baby has been born who will be the Saviour of the world. You will find him wrapped in strips of cloth, lying in a manger.'

Then the sound of hundreds of angels, singing and praising God, filled their ears.

'Glory to God in the highest heaven!' the angels sang. 'And peace on earth.'

The shepherds wasted no time. They ran down the hillside, determined to find the baby who had been born that night.

They found the place where Mary and Joseph were staying, and knew that this baby, lying in the manger, was the baby the angels had spoken of. They paused to tell Mary and Joseph about the angels and the message they had been given – then they went from there to tell everyone what they had seen and heard so that no one could be in any doubt about who the baby was. But Mary, watching Jesus sleeping, thought about all she had heard that night.

When Jesus was just over a month old, Mary and Joseph prepared to take him to the temple in Jerusalem. They went to thank God for his safe birth and offer a sacrifice of two pigeons.

As they went into the temple courts, they met there a man called Simeon. Simeon had been waiting for the day when God would send his Messiah – the chosen one who would save his people. He believed that God had promised him that he would see this Saviour before he died.

When Simeon saw Mary and Joseph and the baby boy in their arms, he knew that the special day had arrived. He took Jesus from them and praised God.

'Lord, you can let me now die in peace, because I have seen with my own eyes the Saviour you have promised your people. This child will reveal your truth to all people on earth and be everything the Jewish nation have been waiting for.'

Mary and Joseph listened in some surprise to his words but before they had taken it all in, an elderly woman approached them. Anna was a prophetess who had lived in the temple, praying and worshipping God for most of her long life. She also knew that Jesus was God's chosen one. And thanked God for him.

Mary and Joseph made their offering. They wondered at all they had learned that day about their baby son.

Wise men living in the east had been studying the night skies when Jesus was born. They saw a strange new star shining brightly and wondered what it could mean.

They saw a strange new star shining brightly and wondered what it could mean.

Then they set out on a journey, following the star, because they thought it heralded the birth of a new king born to the Jewish nation, and wanted to worship him.

When they reached Jerusalem, they stopped at King Herod's palace.

'Where is the child born to be king of the Jewish people?' they asked. 'We have come to pay our respects, to welcome and worship him.'

Herod was disturbed by their arrival. He was not a good or a kind man; he was a jealous ruler who liked power rather too much. What king could there be apart from him? Quickly, Herod consulted the chief priests and teachers of the law. They told him what they knew from the ancient prophecies: the king would be born in Bethlehem.

Herod then talked to his eastern visitors and tried to find out exactly when they had first seen the star. This way he could know how old the baby might be.

Then he sent them on their way to Bethlehem.

'If you find the king,' he said, craftily, 'let me know. I would like to be able to worship him as well.'

The wise men continued their journey until they reached Bethlehem where the star seemed to stop over a house. They went inside, and found Mary with her young child.

The wise men knew they had found the right place. They worshipped Jesus, the new king.

Then they gave him the gifts they had brought – gold, frankincense and myrrh.

They stopped for the night before beginning their return journey, but they did not go back the way they had come. In the night they had dreamed that it was not safe to return to King Herod.

After the wise men had left, Joseph also had a strange dream. In it, he was warned by an angel.

'Wake up!' said the angel. 'Herod plans to kill Jesus. You must take your family and escape to Egypt!'

It was still night when Joseph woke Mary and took her and her child to safety.

Meanwhile Herod waited for the wise men to return. A day passed. Two days passed. Soon he realised that he had been tricked. The men from the east were not going to return. He was furious. Herod was a cruel man. He thought of another way to get rid of Jesus. He gave orders to kill all boys under two years old in the area – he had worked out how old Jesus must be from what the wise men had told him.

But Herod did not know that Jesus was safely in Egypt. Joseph kept him there until Herod had died. Then, when Jesus was a little boy, another

He gave orders to kill all boys under two years old.

angel came to Joseph in a dream and told him it was safe to return. Joseph travelled to Nazareth and they made their home there. Jesus grew up strong and healthy and wise.

Jesus worked alongside Joseph, learning the trade of a carpenter in the area of Galilee.

Each year they went to Jerusalem with everyone else to celebrate the

Passover festival. So when Jesus was twelve, Mary and Joseph expected their journey to be as it had been before. Jesus travelled with Mary and Joseph and a group of other people from Nazareth. Then, at the end of the festival, they made their way home.

Mary and Joseph had been walking for some time when they realised that Jesus was missing. They assumed he was with friends or relatives; but it became clear that they all thought he was with someone else. They began to panic. Where could he be?

They returned to Jerusalem where it was always busy and anyone could get lost. They questioned the market traders, they asked other children if they had seen him. At the end of three days, Mary was desperate. Then they went to the temple.

Surrounded by experts and teachers of the law, there was Mary's son. Jesus was listening to them and asking questions. Mary watched as he

spoke and saw that the elders were surprised by his answers.

But Mary's anxiety got the better of her.

'Where have you been?' asked Mary. 'We have been so worried! We have been searching everywhere for you.'

'I have been here in my Father's house' Jesus replied. 'Did you not guess?'

Jesus was a good son. He went back home with them. And as he grew older, Mary remembered all the special things that had happened to him.

CHAPTER 24

PREPARING THE WAY

PEOPLE WERE CROWDED TOGETHER ON THE RIVERBANK. THEY HAD ALL COME TO LISTEN TO JOHN. He was a strange man. He didn't dress like anyone else – he looked wild in his clothes of camel's hair; he ate strange things – locusts and wild honey. But when he spoke, it was difficult not to hear the things he said.

He ate locusts.

Elizabeth's son, John, had become a man. He had gone to live alone in the desert and here he learned about the job that God wanted him to do. When he was ready, he started to tell people how God wanted them to live.

'Stop doing things that you know are wrong. Listen to God – and obey him,' John told them. 'Be baptised, and show that you are sorry. Change your ways. Live as people who know that God has forgiven them.'

Somehow they knew that what John said was true. They knew that God spoke through him and they needed to do the things he said.

The people came to the River Jordan and John baptised them.

'It is not enough that you have

Abraham as your ancestor,' he said.
'You must show that you love God
by the way you live. If you have two
coats, give one away to someone
in need. If you have plenty of food,
share it with someone who is hungry.
If you are a tax collector, live honestly
and fairly – don't cheat people. If you
are a soldier, don't bully people but
do your job remembering that other
people are human too.'

'Who is this man?' the people
whispered. 'Is this God's Saviour? Is
John the one God has promised us?'

But John heard them.

'I baptise you with water,' he
said. 'But soon someone will come
who will baptise you with God's own
Spirit! I am no one compared to this
man.'

Then one day, Jesus himself came
to the River Jordan. He was now a
man of about thirty and had been a
carpenter for many years.

Jesus stepped forward as John
was calling people to be baptised.

John knew straightaway who

Jesus was. He also knew he was not
worthy to baptise Jesus!

But Jesus persuaded him. He told
John it was what God wanted. As
Jesus came out of the water, God's
Spirit came down from heaven like
a dove and rested on Jesus. A voice
from heaven said:

'This is my Son. I love him very
much. I am pleased with him.'

After his baptism, Jesus was led
by God's Spirit into the desert. Jesus
went without food for forty days and
at the end of this time, he was weak
and very hungry.

Then God's enemy, the devil,
tried to test Jesus.

'You need food,' he said craftily.
'If you are God's Son, you can make
this stone turn into bread.'

If you are God's Son, you can make this stone turn into bread.

But Jesus knew that the devil
could not be trusted.

'Life is much more than food,'
replied Jesus, quoting God's law.
'Man needs to know God's purposes
to live well.'

Then the devil led Jesus to a very high place and showed him all the kingdoms of the world.

'Look!' whispered the devil. 'Wouldn't you like all this? I will give it to you, all of it, if you will only worship me.'

'God has said that we must worship him alone,' replied Jesus. 'Power and possessions cannot satisfy.'

Then the devil took Jesus to Jerusalem. They stood on the highest part of the temple.

The devil left, and Jesus was alone.

'God has promised to send his angels to protect you,' continued the devil. 'Throw yourself off the temple so we can see how powerful he is!'

'God's law says that we must not put him to the test,' Jesus replied.

The devil had tried to tempt Jesus to break God's laws three times; but Jesus would not give in. The devil left, and Jesus was alone.

CHAPTER 25

LIVING GOD'S WAY

JESUS RETURNED TO THE AREA AROUND LAKE GALILEE AND BEGAN TO TRAVEL FROM PLACE TO PLACE. HE MET ORDINARY PEOPLE LIVING ORDINARY LIVES — MEN AND WOMEN, OLD AND YOUNG, RICH AND POOR, FISHERMEN AND TAX COLLECTORS, FARMERS AND WEAVERS. HE LISTENED TO THEIR PROBLEMS AND HELPED THEM UNDERSTAND HOW GOD COULD HELP THEM. HE ALSO CHALLENGED THEM ABOUT WHAT WAS IMPORTANT IN THEIR LIVES.

'Stop doing things that are wrong; live your lives the way God wants you to. Love God and learn to love the people around you as much as you love yourself.'

Jesus watched Simon and Andrew. The sun was glinting on the water as they cast their nets into Lake Galilee.

You can catch people for God instead of fish.

'Come and follow me!' Jesus called to the two brothers. 'You can catch people for God instead of fish.'

Simon and Andrew knew who Jesus was. They had listened to him many times. They dropped their nets and joined Jesus straight away.

Further along the lakeside, they saw James and his brother John mending their nets. Their father Zebedee was in the boat with them.

'Come and follow me!' called Jesus.

James and John got out of the boat and went with him too.

These four fishermen became Jesus' first disciples. Jesus went with them to their homes in Capernaum. There Jesus taught in the synagogue.

One day, there was a wedding in the village of Cana. Jesus' mother, Mary, had been invited. Jesus and some of his disciples went too.

While everyone was celebrating and enjoying themselves, the wine ran out. Mary went to Jesus and told him what had happened.

'I know what you want me to do,' Jesus said, 'but it's not yet the right time.'

Mary smiled at Jesus. She knew her son was special. She also knew he would find a way to help in some way.

'Do whatever he asks,' she whispered to the servants.

'Fill these six jars with water,' Jesus said. The jars were used for washing; they were very large and heavy, each holding many gallons of water.

The disciples saw what Jesus had done and were amazed.

The servants went back and forth until all six jars were filled to the top with cool, sparkling water. Then Jesus asked them to pour some out into a cup and offer it to the man in charge of the feast. The servants looked at each other nervously but did as Jesus asked. As soon as they poured it, they saw that the water they knew they had put there had somehow changed into wine.

The man in charge of the feast tasted it and then went to speak to the bridegroom.

'This wine is wonderful,' he said. 'Most people serve the cheap wine last when no one notices. But I congratulate you – you have saved the best till the end.'

The disciples saw what Jesus had done and were amazed. They began to realise that he was no ordinary man. This was a miracle.

News about Jesus was spreading. Many people throughout Galilee heard Jesus talk about the way God loved and cared for everyone. This was a different kind of teaching – they were not used to this from the religious leaders. But Jesus also had the power to heal. People came to him in pain and he made them well.

Now it was time for Jesus to visit nearby Nazareth, where he had grown up. He went as usual to the synagogue on the Sabbath day, and stood up, ready to read from the Scriptures. Someone handed him the scroll containing the words of the prophet Isaiah.

He has chosen me to free those who are in chains.

'God's Spirit is with me,' read Jesus. 'He has chosen me to bring good news to the poor, to free those who are in chains, give sight to the blind, to help those who are suffering and to tell everyone that God's blessing has come.'

Jesus rolled up the scroll and sat down.

'Those words were written hundreds of years ago. Today, here in this place, you have seen it come true.'

The people stared at him. They began to whisper among themselves.

'But this is Joseph's boy,' they said. 'We know him; we know his mother. We knew Joseph. He's no one special.'

'I know what you think,' replied Jesus. 'And because you cannot believe that I am anyone other than Joseph's son, you will see no miracles here.'

The people of Nazareth were

angry. They would not accept what he was saying and drove him away.

They would not accept what he was saying and drove him away.

It didn't matter. It was different in Capernaum. Here crowds of people gathered to hear Jesus speak about God wherever he went. They were hungry for the truth. They wanted to know that God loved them.

Four men were particularly keen to find Jesus. They were carrying their friend, a man who was lying on a mat because he was paralysed. The man could not walk. Perhaps Jesus would heal him as he had healed others.

When they reached the house where Jesus was speaking, the four friends found it was too crowded; people were packed all around him; they were spilling out of the doorway.

Outside the house, steps led up to the flat roof. The men climbed up carefully, carrying the man on the mat between them. They were desperate for Jesus to help their friend. They laid down the mat and began to dig

through the mud and branches that made up the roof. Soon there was a ragged hole. They kept digging with their hands until the hole was large enough to lower the man and his mat down in front of Jesus and the amazed crowd, who had been showered with bits of the roofing material while this had been going on.

Jesus saw how certain the four friends were that he could help them. He smiled at the man on the mat and spoke kindly to him.

'Go,' he said, 'your sins are forgiven.'

Jesus had been talking to some of the religious leaders – the priests and teachers of religious law. They were shocked. Surely only God could forgive sins? they thought. Jesus may have interesting things to say – but this was too much! But Jesus knew

But Jesus knew what they were thinking as clearly as if they were speaking.

what they were thinking as clearly as if they were speaking aloud to the room.

'Which is easier,' Jesus asked them, 'to forgive this man's sins or to make him walk? Nothing is impossible for God.' Then he looked again at the paralysed man.

'Stand up, take your mat, and go home,' he said.

The man began to get to his feet. Everyone in the room moved back in amazement. Then he stood up and waved to his friends looking down from the open roof. They laughed out loud and slapped each other on the back!

What had Jesus done? Everyone was amazed! They praised God for the miracle they had seen there in that room.

Soon there was almost no one in Capernaum who hadn't heard of the things Jesus had said and done. So when Matthew saw Jesus walking beside Lake Galilee, teaching the crowds of people who followed him, he knew who he was, and he knew what people were saying about him.

Jesus also knew Matthew. He knew that he was a tax collector and that he had set up his booth so that, day by day, he could collect money for the Romans. But Jesus saw more than that. Everyone knew that much about Matthew.

'Come, follow me,' Jesus said to him one day.

Matthew stopped what he was doing straightaway. He didn't need to be asked twice. He joined the others who were following Jesus. He was not ashamed to be seen with Jesus; he walked with them, happy to be part of their group.

Later that day, Matthew invited Jesus back to his house for dinner with many of his friends. The religious leaders were there again, watching, shaking their heads and criticising

Why does Jesus mix with such terrible people?

everything Jesus did.

'What is he doing? Why does Jesus mix with such terrible people?' they asked the other disciples. 'There are tax collectors here – and many people who we do not see in the synagogue every week. He should keep away from such bad people.'

But Jesus heard them.

'No,' Jesus said. 'You are wrong. Healthy people don't need a doctor.

I am here with the people who most need to hear God's message of love and forgiveness.'

The people who heard Jesus speak told others about him. Soon there were people following Jesus wherever he went.

One day Jesus walked up the hillside overlooking the Sea of Galilee. He sat down and began to talk to the people about the way God wanted

---

Soon there were people following Jesus wherever he went.

---

them to live their lives.

'The people who are happy are not the proud ones who think highly of themselves, but those who know how much they need God's help and forgiveness,' Jesus said. 'If you follow God's ways, you will be like a little salt in the cooking pot, making the whole meal taste good; or like a lamp shining brightly in a dark place, bringing light so that everyone can see.'

Then Jesus began to talk about God's Law. It was the Law the

Pharisees knew all about, but Jesus spoke about it in a way that no one had understood before.

'If someone hurts you, don't try to get your own back,' said Jesus. 'Instead, be kind to those who hurt you. Go out of your way to help everyone. God's Law says that we must love not only those who are our friends, family and neighbours, but also our enemies as well. It's easy to love people who already love us – anyone can do that. God wants us to be different. God is perfect. We must try to be like him.'

Jesus went on to teach the people how they should talk to God in prayer.

'Be careful,' said Jesus, 'not to pray with empty, meaningless words so that others will notice you or think you are holy or clever. Make sure your prayers are honest conversations between you and God. That's what matters. God sees everything. He knows what you want to tell him before you begin to speak. So talk to God simply and quietly, like a child might share things with his father.'

Then Jesus gave his disciples a pattern to use when they prayed.

'Our Father in heaven, hallowed be your name, your kingdom come, your will be done, on earth as it is in heaven. Give us today our daily bread. And forgive us our debts, as we also have forgiven our debtors. And lead us not into temptation, but deliver us from the evil one.

'Begin by speaking to God as if you are talking to someone who loves you and wants the best for you – God is like the very best father you could have but you cannot see him,' explained Jesus. 'God is holy, so ask that God's name be treated as something holy, remembering who he is and what he has done. Ask that God's kingdom will arrive quickly

Ask that God's kingdom will arrive quickly here on earth.

here on earth so that there will be no more cruelty or injustice, slavery or poverty but instead love and kindness, justice, freedom and plenty. Ask God for the things that you need for today, like the food you need to eat. Then ask for God's forgiveness, and at the same time, forgive anyone who may have hurt you. And ask God for help to keep you from doing anything wrong.'

Jesus looked at the people around him. Some were poor; others were sad or anxious; some could not walk or see.

You will not live a day longer by worrying about your life.

'Don't worry about the things that make up your everyday lives,' Jesus said. 'Don't worry about what you will eat or drink, or what clothes you're going to wear. Look around you at the wild birds. They don't have huge cupboards full of food – they rely on God to feed them. God takes care of them; but he cares about you even more than the birds. You will not live a day longer by worrying about your life. As for worrying about clothes, look at the beautiful flowers that grow wild in the fields. They do not work to get rich, but God has made them beautiful.

'If you put God first in your life and do things that are good and kind, God will make sure that you have everything you need — and much more besides.'

Put God first in your life and do things that are good and kind.

As people listened to what Jesus had to say, the people divided into groups. Many were eager to hear more. They wanted to know how to please God. Others were suspicious or angry at this way of teaching and the way Jesus spoke as if he knew God as his friend, as if he were part of his family. It was different from the teaching of the religious teachers, the scribes and Pharisees. So Jesus told a story.

'If you listen to me, and then act on what I say, you will be like the wise man who built his house on a rock. Before he started work, the man made sure that his house had firm foundations. Then when the rain battered against the house, and the wind blew around it, it did not collapse. It remained firm and solid.

'But if you take no notice of what I have said, you will be like the foolish man who built his house on the shifting sand. When the wind blew and the rain beat against his house, it had no foundations and so it fell down. The walls and roof, the door and all his belongings were swept away leaving him with nothing.

'Don't be like the foolish man, regretting his mistake when it is too late to change things. Be like the wise man; listen well and act on what you hear.'

CHAPTER 26

THE MAN AND HIS MESSAGE

WHEN JESUS RETURNED TO LAKE GALILEE, HE TALKED TO THE CROWDS OF PEOPLE ON THE SHORE WHILE HE SAT IN A BOAT ON THE WATER. JESUS TAUGHT THE PEOPLE USING PARABLES. THEY WERE STORIES ABOUT THINGS THEY SAW AROUND THEM EVERY DAY BUT THEY HAD A SPECIAL MEANING.

'A farmer went out to sow some seed,' began Jesus. 'He took handfuls of seed, and cast them from side to side as he walked along.

'Some seed fell on the path. Birds came and quickly gobbled it up.

'Some seed fell on soil that was full of stones. The seed grew quite quickly at first, but it did not last long. Its roots had not stretched down deep into the soil so when the

The seed was choked by the thorns and withered.

sun beat down upon it, the plants shrivelled up and died.

'Some seed landed among thorns. As it grew up, it was choked by the thorns and withered so it could not produce fruit.

'But some seed fell on good,

243

rich soil. There it began to grow, strong and healthy, until eventually it produced a good harvest.

'Now, listen well, and try to understand the message of this story.'

Later, when the disciples were alone with Jesus, they asked him what the story about the farmer and the seed meant. Jesus explained it to them.

'The farmer who sows the seed is like God. He plants his message of truth in those who hear it. Some people who hear the message are like the seed on the path. They hear the message about God, but quickly forget about him. Some people are like the stony soil. They start by obeying God, but when things get difficult or people criticise them for their faith, they give up. Some are like the seed that fell among thorns. They try to follow God, but quickly become distracted by money or the worries of their daily lives and their faith is choked. But others are like the good, rich soil. They hear God's message of truth and grow up like strong healthy plants, living fruitful lives that God can use. They don't let the cares of the world distract them but they

share their faith with others.'

Jesus told other stories to explain what God's kingdom is like.

'Imagine that there is some treasure hidden in a field. One day, a man accidentally finds the treasure. The man buries it again quickly, then goes back home. He is so keen to buy the field so he can own the treasure that he sells everything he owns: his home, his furniture, his cooking pots – even his donkey – so that he can buy the field. Then the treasure belongs to him, and he has everything he could possibly want. Nothing could be worth more than that.'

The people around Jesus listened. Some of them understood what he was saying. God's kingdom was more valuable than anything they could own on earth - it was worth doing anything to be part of it: it was like the treasure in the field.

Then Jesus told another story.

'God's kingdom is like a man who buys and sells pearls. One day he finds a pearl which is more valuable than any other. It is also extremely beautiful. What does the man do? He goes home and sells all his possessions so that he can buy that beautiful pearl and have it for himself.'

Many people heard about the amazing things Jesus did and the incredible things he said. Among them was Nicodemus, a Pharisee, a member of the important religious council, the Sanhedrin. Nicodemus was eager to hear what Jesus had to say but he was also afraid of what others might think. He knew that Jesus was already making enemies among the religious leaders.

So Nicodemus visited Jesus at night.

'Teacher,' said Nicodemus respectfully, 'I have seen you do many amazing things. God has clearly blessed you.'

Jesus looked at Nicodemus. He knew that Nicodemus longed to know more about God.

You must believe in the Saviour God has sent into the world.

'To see God's kingdom, you need to start all over again,' said Jesus. 'You need to be born again.'

'But that's impossible,' said Nicodemus. 'No one can do that!'

'Your mother cannot give birth to you again,' said Jesus. 'But God can give you a completely new start, a new life with God by the power of his Holy Spirit.'

'Tell me how I can do this,' asked Nicodemus.

'You must believe in the Saviour God has sent into the world. God has love enough for all the people he has made, but many of them love the darkness rather than light. They want to hide the evil things they do and are afraid that the light will show up their sins,' Jesus answered. 'God has sent his Son so that all who do bad things can be forgiven. Once they are forgiven, they can have eternal life. They need only put their trust in God's Son to know that forgiveness. Anyone who believes in God's Son will not die, but live for ever!'

Nicodemus was a very different person from the woman he met in a village in Samaria called Sychar.

His friends had gone to buy food in the village and left him sitting by the well – the well that Jacob had drunk from many generations before. It was midday and the sun beat down on Jesus. He was tired and thirsty.

The Samaritan woman walked towards the well. Although it was the time of day when people would usually be sheltering in the shade, she had brought her jar to fill with water.

'Please, will you give me a drink?' Jesus asked her.

The woman looked at him suspiciously.

'You're a Jew, aren't you?' she said. 'And I'm a Samaritan. Don't you know our people are enemies? Why would you ask me for a drink?'

But Jesus was not discouraged by her rude tone.

'If you knew who I am, you would be asking *me* for water!' said Jesus. 'I would not give you water from this well, but God's living water, so that you would never be thirsty again!'

'Give me that water!' replied the woman. 'It would save me having to come here every day.'

'Go and tell your husband what I have said, and come back to me.'

'I have no husband,' the woman replied.

'That's true,' said Jesus. 'But you have been married five times, and now you live with someone who is not your husband.'

The woman looked around, amazed. Had someone been talking about her to this stranger? How could Jesus know these things about her? She forgot about her water pot, and ran back to the town.

'Quickly!' she said to everyone she met. 'Come and meet a very special man. He knows all about me! Could he be the Saviour God has promised us?'

Come and meet a very special man. Could he be the Saviour God has promised us?

While Jesus continued to challenge the way people thought, John, who had baptised him and prepared the way for him, was having a difficult time.

John's message was a hard one. By speaking the truth, and telling people to stop doing the things that went against God's laws, John made enemies.

One of these was Herodias, the woman married to King Herod. She had been married before to Herod's brother, Philip, who was still living. This was forbidden by Jewish law.

Herod had put John in prison to please his wife, but he was afraid to punish John further because Herod knew he was a man of God. He knew it would cause a riot among the people.

Then, on his birthday, Herod held a party. Herodias' beautiful daughter got up and danced to the music. Herod was entranced. He told her she could ask anything of him, and she could have it.

The girl went to her mother to see what she should ask for; and Herod regretted it immediately. Herodias' daughter asked for the head of John the Baptist on a plate.

Herod knew that all his guests had heard his promise. He could not go back on his word and refuse her request. So it was that John was executed – and his head brought to Herod.

John's work was over. Some of his friends buried his body. Then they made sure Jesus knew what had happened.

She asked for the head of John the Baptist on a plate.

Jesus was very sad at the news of John's death. He wanted to be alone to think, to grieve and to pray. But wherever he went, people followed him.

One day Jesus took his closest friends, Peter, James and John, to a high mountain.

While they were there something strange happened to Jesus. As they watched, Jesus' face and clothing became like a bright shining light. Then two men appeared, standing beside Jesus and talking to him. They recognised the men as Moses and Elijah. Peter could not keep quiet.

'Let us build three shelters, one for each of you,' he called out. But before Peter could finish speaking, a bright cloud covered them and they heard a voice speaking from heaven.

'This is my Son,' said the voice. 'I love him. I am pleased with him.

Listen to what he says.'

At the sound of God's voice, Jesus' friends were terrified. They fell to the ground.

While they were lying there, Jesus came and touched them.

'Don't be frightened,' he said. 'And don't tell anyone what you saw till you have seen God's Son risen from the dead.'

When Peter, James and John looked up, Jesus was there, but he was alone with them. The two other men had gone.

One day a man came to Jesus to see how he would answer questions about God's laws. He had heard that people followed Jesus because what he said about God was different from what the other teachers taught.

'Teacher,' he said, 'what must I do to live with God for ever?'

What must I do to live with God for ever?

'What does God's Law say?' Jesus asked the man.

'Love God with all your heart, your soul, your strength and your mind. Love your neighbour as you love yourself,' replied the man.

'Then you know the answer,' said Jesus. 'Do it and you will live with God for ever.'

Love God with all your heart, your soul, your strength and your mind.

'But tell me who to love. Who is my neighbour?' asked the man.

'I will tell you a story,' said Jesus. 'There was once a man who was walking on the lonely road from Jerusalem to Jericho. He was attacked by some robbers who stole his money and took his clothes. They left him half dead by the side of the road.

Later on, a priest came along the same road. He saw the injured man, but decided not to stop and help him. Instead he walked past on the other side.

Some time later, a Levite came along the road. He also saw the wounded man, but did not stop to help.

Finally, a Samaritan came along the road. As soon as he saw the man lying there, he stopped to see how badly hurt he was. Then he gave him something to drink and cleaned and bandaged his wounds. He helped the wounded man on to his own donkey, and took him to an inn. He gave the innkeeper some money, and asked him to look after the injured man till he was well again. "When I return I will repay you anything more you have spent helping him get well," he said.'

Then Jesus asked the man who was listening to the story:

'Who was a good neighbour to the wounded man?'

'The one who helped him,' came the answer.

'Then you must do the same,' said Jesus.

Jesus had friends in the little village of Bethany, a man called Lazarus, and his two sisters. When he passed through the village with his disciples on the way to Jerusalem, Martha made them welcome and invited them in to eat.

While the men sat and relaxed, Martha made herself busy in the kitchen, preparing the food and clearing up. She wanted everything to be just right for her visitors. But her sister Mary sat on the floor in the other room, listening to Jesus as he talked.

Martha was hot and flustered. Mary was doing nothing to help her. Martha was cross.

'Lord,' she said to Jesus, 'Mary is just sitting there, doing nothing, while I am having to do all the work. Tell her to help me!'

'Martha,' Jesus answered, 'there is always something that has to be done. Sometimes it's good to stop and listen and spend time with people. Mary has chosen to do that now. Let her stay here.'

Jesus had many friends and made new ones every day. But he also made enemies. Many of the Pharisees and teachers of the law criticised him because he spent time with ordinary people, many of whom they thought were sinners, doing things that were wrong.

'If you owned 100 sheep,' Jesus said to them, 'and one of them was lost, what would you do? Leave it to die and be content with the ninety-nine sheep safe in the sheep pen? No, you would go in search of the one that was lost. You would look everywhere until it was found, then you would be happier over that one lost sheep than all the others. So it is with God. He cares about all the sheep, and will not be happy till he has saved the one who has wandered away from the right path.'

'I am like a good shepherd,' Jesus also said. 'I know all my sheep by name and care about them; they know my voice and know that when they come to me I will lead them to good pasture. I will give my sheep everything they need and much more besides.

'Like a good shepherd, I love my sheep and will let no harm come to them. When someone who is not a real shepherd looks after the sheep, he runs away if a wolf comes and attacks the flock. He doesn't really care about them. But I am willing to die for my sheep.

'I am the good shepherd. I know my sheep and my sheep know me. I have other sheep not in the same

---

I will lay down my life for the sheep.

---

sheepfold. One day there will be one great flock, all led by one shepherd. I will lay down my life for the sheep; no one will take my life from me. Then I will take up my life again.'

'Whatever is he talking about!' some of the people said. 'Is Jesus mad?'

Jesus often told stories about God's love. One became known as the story of the prodigal son or the loving father.

'There was once a man with two sons. One day, the younger son said to his father, "Let me have my share of everything I will inherit when you die. I'd like to travel and enjoy myself now." So the father divided everything that he had between his two sons.

'The younger son took his money and went far away. He used all his money enjoying himself and making lots of friends but after a time, he had spent it all.

'Then there was a terrible famine in the land. There was nothing to eat. The younger son took the only job he could find, feeding pigs. He was so hungry, he could have eaten the pigs' food. Then the young man realised how silly he was.

'"The people who work for my father have far more than I have now. I should go home and ask if dad will give me a job on his farm. I'll tell him I am sorry for being so selfish."

'But the boy's father had been watching and waiting, hoping every day that his son would come back. When he saw his son in the distance, he ran to meet him. He threw his arms around him and hugged him.

'"I have let you down and done things I am ashamed of," the boy said. "I'm so sorry. I don't deserve to be treated as your son. Let me work for you instead." But his father shook his head.

'"Fetch the best clothes for my son," the father called to one of his

I thought my son was dead but he is alive.

servants. "Find new sandals and a ring for his finger. Prepare the best food! I thought my son was dead but he is alive. He was lost, but now he's found. Let's have a party! Let's celebrate!"'

Once Jesus had a reputation for being wise and knowing so much about God's ways, people asked him all sorts of questions. Jesus would use their concerns to help them see what really mattered in life.

One day a man in the crowd listening to Jesus shouted out to him.

'Teacher, tell my brother to share his inheritance with me!'

'I am not here to settle family arguments,' Jesus replied. 'But I can warn you about greed. Make sure you don't fall into the trap of thinking that your life is made up of the things you own. Life is worth so much more than that!

'Let me tell you a story. Once there was a rich farmer. His land produced an excellent harvest. He had so many crops he couldn't store them all. So he thought he would pull down his barns and build new, bigger barns. Then he could store everything he owned and rest and enjoy life. He could eat all he wanted, drink all he wanted and be happy.

'But that night God said to him: "Tonight will be your last. It is your time to die. You have stored up many things on earth but now you must leave them all behind."

Tonight will be your last. It is your time to die.

'What good was all the rich farmer's money to him after his death?' asked Jesus after the story was ended. 'None at all. This is what happens when people live their lives for themselves alone, thinking only of how many possessions they have. Live your lives for others, thinking of their needs before your own. God will look after you, and you will store treasure in heaven, where no moth can eat it and no thief steal it away.'

The disciples heard Jesus teach day after day. Sometimes they also had questions for Jesus.

'How many times should I forgive someone if they wrong me?' Peter once asked. 'Will seven times be enough?'

'No,' Jesus had replied, 'not seven times but seventy times seven! Really there is no limit. You must always be ready to forgive.

'Imagine there is a king who wants to settle accounts with his servants. The first man came before him owing £10,000. But he could not pay any of it. The king was ready to sell the man, his wife and his children into slavery and sell everything he owned so the debt could be paid. But the man begged him to let him have more time to pay. The king was more kind than the servant could have imagined. He cancelled the debt completely.

'The servant left the king, unable to believe how lucky he was – until he bumped into a man he knew who owed him £10.00. He grabbed the man by the neck and shouted at him.

'"Give me back what you owe me now!" he said.

'The man begged him to be patient – he needed more time to pay. But the servant would not listen. He had the man thrown into prison until he could pay back his debt. The other servants who had seen what had happened felt the servant had been

---

How many times should I forgive someone if they wrong me?

---

wrong and acted unfairly. They went and told the king.

'Then the king called back the servant.

'"What you have done is wicked. I forgave you a huge debt; I cancelled it because you begged me to. How then could you not show the same kindness to the man who owed you a much smaller sum? I will give you time to think about this: you must go to prison and stay there until you can pay me back all you owe."

'This,' said Jesus, 'is why you must forgive others from your heart whatever they have done. You need God's forgiveness for all you have done wrong.'

People asked Jesus how best to pray to God many times. Jesus once told this story.

'Two men went to the temple to pray. One was a Pharisee; the other a tax collector.

'"Thank you, God, for making me what I am,' said the Pharisee in a loud voice. Everyone could see him and hear him praying. "I don't steal or break any of your laws. I am much better than this man here, one of the hated tax collectors! I give you a tenth of all I have and pray on an empty stomach twice a week to show you how good I am."

'The Pharisee was very pleased with himself. But the tax collector bowed his head and mumbled his prayers in his shame.

'"God, please forgive me and be kind to me, for I am a sinner, and I deserve nothing from you."

'God heard the prayers of both men,' said Jesus. 'But only the prayers of the tax collector were acceptable to him.'

The people who came to Jesus were not just blind or deaf; not all of them were ill and in need of his healing touch. Some came to Jesus just for his blessing.

When some parents brought their babies and small children to Jesus to be blessed, the disciples tried to send them away.

'Jesus is too busy,' they said. 'Take the children home.'

Jesus got down to the level of a small child and smiled.

'Come here,' he called to one. 'Let them all come.'

Jesus welcomed them all. Then Jesus spoke to the disciples.

'God's kingdom belongs to people like this. Learn from them.

They trust me and love me without question. No one can be part of God's kingdom without such simple trust. Don't ever send the children away.'

The poor came to Jesus but also the rich. A young man who had great wealth came to him and fell to his knees.

'Good teacher: tell me please – how can I live for ever?'

'You must keep God's laws,' replied Jesus.

'I have done this since I was a boy,' said the man.

Jesus smiled kindly at the man. He saw what the problem was.

'There is one more thing you can do,' said Jesus. 'Sell everything you

Give your money to the poor, and follow me.

have, give your money to the poor, and follow me.'

The rich man suddenly looked sad. He got up, and walked away. He was very wealthy. He could not do what Jesus asked – his money would always mean more to him than God.

Jesus looked at his friends.

'It is very hard for a rich man to enter God's kingdom,' he said. 'It is easier for a camel to go through the eye of a needle.'

Jesus often told stories about what God's kingdom was like.

'There was once a man who owned a vineyard. He had many rows of vines, and plenty of work to be done. He went down to the marketplace early in the morning to hire some workers.

'He agreed to pay them a silver coin each as fair payment for the day and the men came to work for him.

'At nine o'clock in the morning the owner went again to the marketplace. He found there were more men there looking for work and so he hired them too.

'At midday the owner went a third time and hired yet more workers. He went again at three o'clock and then at five o'clock. Each time he found more men who were looking for work and he hired them.

'When evening came and the day's work was ended, the men all came to be paid. The owner told his foreman to start paying the men who were hired last first of all, and to end with those who had been in his vineyard all day.

'Each of the men was paid a silver coin – the same amount whether he had been there a few hours or all day.

'"But this is not fair!" grumbled one of the men who had started early in the morning. "I have been here all day and worked in the hot sun – but have no more for my trouble than those who came a short while ago!" Other agreed with him. They were so unhappy they complained to the owner.

'"But what is your problem?" the owner asked. "I have been fair to you; I paid you what we agreed. You had what you expected at the end of the day. The only difference is that you have seen that I was generous to the other men here. The vineyard is mine and I chose to give to all who came here the same reward. Surely I have the right to share all I have in the way I choose?"

'This is the way God is,' said Jesus. 'He will not just be fair, he will be generous. Those who come last will still be rewarded.'

Those who come last will still be rewarded.

Jesus talked to his disciples about how to love and serve God and other people. But he also told them about a time in the future when God would send his angels to the whole earth to gather together all the people who loved him.

'No one knows when that time will come,' said Jesus, 'except God himself. People will be working right up to that time; they will be marrying and having children. When it happens, one person will be taken to be with God and another will be left behind. Make sure you are one of those who loves God. Be ready for that day to come.

'Let me tell you a story about ten bridesmaids,' said Jesus. 'Each one had a little oil lamp so she could welcome the bridegroom to the house that night. Five of the bridesmaids were prepared. They had brought some spare oil. But the other five were not prepared. Hours passed and the bridegroom did not come. The bridesmaids grew tired with waiting and fell asleep.

'Then in the middle of the night, they heard a noise. "The bridegroom is coming! Wake up!" someone shouted.

'The bridesmaids picked up their lamps. The five who had brought the spare oil could light them; but the lamps of the others had gone out and they had to go and get some more.

'While they were away, the bridegroom arrived. The other five bridesmaids held up their lamps and walked with him into the wedding feast. Then the door was shut. The other five were too late; they missed the wedding feast completely.

'At the end of time the King will sit on his throne surrounded by angels. He will divide all the people of the earth into two groups.

'"Come to me and enjoy all the good things I have prepared for you," the King will say to one group. "For you lived the way God wanted you to live. When I was hungry, you shared your food with me. When I was thirsty, you gave me a drink. You welcomed me into your home when you didn't know me and gave me clothes when I had none. You cared for me when I was ill and even came to visit me in prison."

'Then those people will say to the King, "But when did we ever do these things? When did we see you hungry and feed you, thirsty and give you a drink? When did we clothe you, or welcome you in our homes, look after you in illness or visit you in prison?"

'The King will answer, "Whenever you helped someone in need, you did this for me."

'The King will turn to the other group and he will send them away. "You gave me no food when I was hungry; you let me die of thirst. You shut your door against me and wouldn't let me in. You saw that I needed clothes but you wouldn't help me and when I was ill and in prison, you were too busy to take care of me."

'"But when did we do these things?" the other group will say desperately. "When did we ever see you in need – hungry or thirsty, in need of a home or clothes, ill or in prison?"

Whenever you helped someone in need, you did this for me.

'The King will reply, "Whenever you saw someone in need and you walked by without helping them, you refused to help me."'

CHAPTER 27
MAN OF MIRACLES

THE CROWD STAYED WITH JESUS AS HE WALKED BACK TO CAPERNAUM. BUT THE PEOPLE FELL BACK WHEN THEY SAW A ROMAN CENTURION RUSHING TOWARDS HIM.

'Will you help me?' the soldier asked Jesus. 'One of my servants is very ill. He is in terrible pain and cannot move at all.'

'Shall I come to your house?' said Jesus. 'Then I will heal him.'

There were many Roman soldiers in the area around Lake Galilee but some recognised the centurion. He was known as a good man. He had come to love God while living among them. He had even built the local people a synagogue. But they were all surprised at what he said next.

'Lord, I don't deserve to have you under my roof. I know that if you only say that my servant is healed, he will be healed. In my work, I know about power and authority. Those above me expect me to obey any orders they give me; in turn, I tell people below me to come and go, and they obey me without question. You don't need to come to see my servant for him to be well.'

Jesus was amazed at the centurion.

'I have not found anyone here with such faith, even among God's own people,' he said. 'Go home now and you will find that your servant is well again.'

The centurion went home. His servant had recovered, just as he knew he would.

Some time later, Jesus and his disciples visited the town of Nain. Although it was some twenty miles away, a large crowd followed them there.

As they approached the gates of the town, another group of people was making its way to the little cemetery on the hillside outside.

Jesus watched as the procession went by, and saw that they were carrying the body of a young man on a stretcher. The dead man's mother was weeping as she followed behind; he was her only son, and her husband had already died. She was now quite alone.

Jesus was moved by the woman's sadness. He went to comfort her.

'There's no need to cry,' Jesus said to her. 'Come, look.'

Then Jesus went up to the stretcher and touched it. The men carrying it stopped and waited.

'Young man,' Jesus said to the dead man lying there, still and cold, 'sit up!'

As soon as Jesus spoke, the young man stirred and sat up on the stretcher. He began talking straight away! His mother could barely believe her eyes. Her tears changed from tears of sadness to tears of joy at the miracle that had happened. Jesus helped him get up and watched as the young man hugged his mother.

Everyone around was amazed. They slapped the man on the back and laughed out loud that the funeral had turned into a celebration. But some among them remembered the stories of Elisha who had lived nearby. He had also brought a boy back from the dead and had restored him to his mother in much the same way.

The funeral had turned into a celebration.

'Praise God!' they said. 'God has sent another prophet to help his people!'

After this, the news spread all over the country about what Jesus had done.

Jesus went from village to village, and from town to town, telling people he met about how much God loved them. He spent time with people, listening to their worries and healing people who were ill.

It was evening, and Jesus was tired after teaching the crowds of people all day.

'Let's cross to the other side of the lake,' Jesus said to his friends. So they prepared the boat and set sail across the waters of Lake Galilee.

Jesus went to the stern of the boat and lay down, a cushion under his head. In a short time he had fallen asleep.

At first the boat bobbed up and down gently and rhythmically. Jesus' friends thought about all they had seen and heard during the day as they made progress across the lake. But then, as so often happened on that stretch of water, the wind suddenly changed direction. The waves began to slosh over the side and the boat lurched dangerously up and down. They were caught in a storm as it passed over the lake.

The men held tight to the sides or clung to the mast of the boat. Even the fishermen among them knew they were in danger. They felt sure they were going to drown. But despite the noise and panic, Jesus was still fast asleep.

'Be calm!' Jesus said. The wind dropped and the sea was still.

'Master, help us!' they shouted, waking him. 'Don't you care if we die?'

Jesus stood up. He quickly saw what they were afraid of and spoke to the wind and to the waves.

'Be calm!' Jesus said. The wind dropped and the sea was still.

Then Jesus turned to look at his frightened disciples.

'There was no need to be afraid,' he said. 'Didn't you trust me?'

Jesus' friends were amazed. They could hardly believe what had happened.

'Who is he?' they asked one another. 'Even the wind and the waves do what he says!'

When Jesus arrived in

Capernaum, the crowds came out to greet him.

But Jairus, the leader of the synagogue, hurried to speak to Jesus. Everybody knew him. They watched as the important man knelt at Jesus' feet.

'Please help us,' he cried. 'My daughter is dying. She is only twelve years old. Will you come quickly?'

Jesus followed Jairus at once and they made their way through the crowds to his home.

But while they were on their way, Jesus stopped suddenly.

'Who touched me?' he asked those around him.

'Master,' Peter said, 'there are crowds all around, pressing close to you. Any one of these people could have touched you.'

But Jesus knew that someone in the crowd had needed his help.

'I felt power go from me,' Jesus said. 'Someone touched me and now they are healed.'

Then a woman stepped forward. She saw that she could not hide from Jesus.

'It was me; I touched your cloak,' she said, falling to her knees. 'I have been suffering for many years. No

doctor has been able to help me. I didn't want to stop you or bother you but I thought that if only I could touch the hem of your cloak, it would be enough, and I would be well again.'

'I felt power go from me,' Jesus said.

Jesus spoke gently to the woman.

'There's no need to be afraid any more,' he said. 'Your faith has healed you.'

Just then, someone came quickly through the crowd. He had come from Jairus' house with bad news.

'Sir,' he said, 'it's too late. Don't bother Jesus any more. Your daughter has died.'

Jesus looked at Jairus. He was close to tears.

'Don't be afraid by this news. Keep on believing; trust me and your daughter will be well.'

Jesus knew which house belonged to Jairus, because mourners were already weeping and wailing outside.

'Stop crying,' said Jesus firmly. 'The little girl isn't dead; she's only asleep.'

Jesus went inside with the girl's anxious father and mother, and with Peter, James and John. Then Jesus took the little girl's hand in his.

'Get up, little girl,' he said.

The girl's eyes opened immediately, and the colour came back into her cheeks. She sat up.

'She is hungry,' smiled Jesus. 'Give her something to eat.'

They wept tears of joy.

Jairus and his wife were astonished by what they had seen. But their little girl had been given back to them. They wept tears of joy.

Another time Jesus went by boat into the hills on the far side of Lake Galilee. When he found people waiting for him even there, he could not turn them away. He healed those who were ill till late in the day.

Then Jesus looked at how many

had come. There were more than 5,000 men, plus the women and children. Jesus turned to Philip, who came from nearby Bethsaida.

'Do you know where we could buy bread for all these people?' Jesus asked.

'It would cost far too much to buy bread for this number!' answered Philip.

Then Andrew, another of Jesus' friends, noticed a boy in the crowd who had with him a picnic lunch of five small barley rolls and two little fish. He brought the boy to Jesus.

'This boy has some food he will share,' he said, 'but it won't go very far!'

Jesus took the food he was offered.

'Ask the people to sit down,' he said to his friends.

The people sat down on the grass and watched as Jesus took the food and asked God to bless it. Then he began to break the bread and fish into pieces, and passed it to his friends, who then shared it again with the people.

The people shared the food among themselves and ate until

they were no longer hungry. Then Jesus' friends went among the people picking up anything that was left over. They collected twelve baskets full of leftover pieces.

Over 5000 people ate that day and had more than enough to eat. It was a miracle.

In the evening Jesus said goodbye to the crowd, and told his disciples to go back across the lake without him.

Jesus went further into the hills to pray. He needed to spend time talking to God, his Father.

It was a windy night and the disciples worked hard in the boat, being buffeted against the waves. Just before dawn, they saw a figure out on the water. They didn't realise it was Jesus, and at first they were alarmed.

'Don't be afraid!' Jesus said to them, as he walked across the water. 'It's me.'

Peter heard Jesus' voice.

'If it's really you,' he shouted, 'tell me to come to you on the water.'

'Come on then,' said Jesus.

Peter stepped out of the boat in the darkness, on to the choppy waves. He walked towards Jesus until a gust of wind blew around him and he looked down at the water. Then Peter panicked.

'Don't be afraid!' Jesus said to them, as he walked across the water. 'It's me.'

'Lord, save me!' he called out to Jesus as he began to sink.

Jesus reached out and took Peter's hand.

'Why didn't you trust me?' he asked, as he helped Peter back into the boat. The wind dropped and the sea became calm.

The other disciples who had seen what happened knelt before Jesus.

'You really must be God's Son,' they said.

On another occasion, Jesus was travelling through the region of the Decapolis when a group of people came out to meet him. They brought to him a deaf man who could hardly talk.

'Please help him,' they said. 'Make him well so that he can hear us.'

Jesus took the man away from his friends and all those who were there. When they were a little apart, Jesus put his fingers in the man's ears, then put some of his own saliva on the man's tongue. He prayed for the man, asking for God's help.

'Open up!' Jesus said.

Suddenly the man could hear the birds singing and the waves lapping and the voice of Jesus close to him. Then the man realised he could talk! Now he couldn't stop talking! His friends and the others in the crowd were amazed and excited.

Jesus tried to keep them from telling anyone else about it – but they wouldn't listen. They could talk of nothing else – of how Jesus had given speech and hearing to a deaf and mute man.

Once, when Jesus passed through a village on the border of Samaria and Galilee, he saw ten men standing together in a huddle. They were dressed in rags and had covered their faces and their damaged limbs. Jesus knew why they were there. They had the skin disease called leprosy that made them outcasts.

They needed his help but were afraid to come too close.

They called to Jesus from a distance.

'Jesus! Please heal us!'

Jesus went towards them. He wanted to help them.

'Go to the priest,' Jesus told them. 'Show him your skin.'

The ten men turned to walk away but as they did so, they realised that they had been healed. Their skin was healthy. The leprosy had gone!

One of the men was from Samaria. He turned back to Jesus, praising God, and knelt at Jesus' feet.

'Thank you, Master! Thank you!' he said.

Jesus looked at the man on his knees and he looked into the distance at those who were still walking away.

'Were there not ten men who needed help?' said Jesus. 'Are you the only one who came back to thank God? Go home now. You are well because you believed that God could heal you.'

Jesus was travelling when his friend Lazarus became very ill. Mary and Martha, Lazarus' sisters, were very anxious and sent a message to Jesus, asking him for help.

Jesus received the message with sadness but he knew exactly what he had to do. Instead of leaving immediately, he told those around him that he would go a little later. That way people would see something that would teach them greater things about God. So it was two days later when Jesus told his disciples that they should set out for Bethany.

'But they tried to kill you when you were last there, Master! Surely you should stay away?' one asked.

Jesus explained that there was a right time for everything. This was the right time for going to help Lazarus.

'Our friend has died; we need to go to restore him to life.'

Thomas looked at the other disciples.

'Come on,' he said. 'Let us die with him if that's what's needed.'

By the time Jesus had arrived in Bethany, Lazarus was dead and had been buried for four days. There were many friends there, mourning his death and weeping with his sisters.

'If you had been here earlier, Lord, Lazarus would still be alive!' said Martha, going to meet him. 'But even now I know that God will give you whatever you ask for.'

'Lazarus will live again,' said Jesus. 'I am the resurrection and the life. If you believe in me you will live for ever. Do you believe that, Martha?'

'If you believe in me you will live for ever,' said Jesus.

'Yes, I do!' said Martha. 'I know you are God's Son, his chosen Saviour.' Then she ran to fetch her sister.

When Mary saw Jesus she fell at his feet, weeping. Jesus knew how sad she was, and he cried with her. Then they took Jesus to the place where Lazarus was buried.

'Open the tomb!' he ordered.

'But he's been dead for days!' cried Martha.

'Trust me, Martha,' said Jesus to her. Then Jesus prayed to God before calling to his friend, Lazarus.

Everyone was stunned when Lazarus walked out of the tomb, still dressed in his grave clothes. Mary

and Martha were overjoyed to have
their brother back. Many of their
friends knew from that moment that
they should put their faith in Jesus
because they had seen the miracle
that had happened – a man was dead
but now he was alive.

Bartimaeus was begging at the
side of the road when Jesus and his
friends went to Jericho. Bartimaeus
was blind. He could see nothing, but
there was nothing wrong with his
ears. He heard the crowd who were
following Jesus. He knew something
unusual was happening.

'Who's passing by?' he shouted
out. 'What's happening?'

'It's Jesus,' someone answered
him. 'The teacher from Nazareth is
here in Jericho!'

Bartimaeus had heard all about
Jesus. He knew that he had made a
paralysed man walk and helped a deaf
man hear.

Bartimaeus knew Jesus could help
him too.

'Help me!' he shouted out. 'Jesus,
have pity on me!'

'Be quiet!' said someone else in
the crowd.

'Stop shouting!' said another.

But Bartimaeus would not stop.
He shouted even louder.

'Jesus! Help me!'

Jesus heard Bartimaeus and
stopped.

'Tell him to come to me,' he said.

'It's OK!' someone told
Bartimaeus. 'Jesus has heard you.
He's asking for you!'

Bartimaeus threw off his cloak
and jumped to his feet. He felt his
way through the crowd, until he
came to Jesus.

'How can I help you?' asked
Jesus.

'I want to see again,' said
Bartimaeus.

'Then you shall see,' replied
Jesus. 'Go now. You believed I could
make you well. You can have what
you asked for.'

Bartimaeus was blind no longer;
he could see! He didn't return to
his place on the roadside to beg;
Bartimaeus joined the crowd of
people following Jesus.

Further up the road, a crowd
was gathering to hear Jesus speak.
Zacchaeus, the tax collector, was
among them. He was trying to see
over the heads of the people – he

was not very tall – but because he cheated people when he collected their taxes, he was also unpopular. He wanted desperately to see Jesus but no one would let him through to the front.

Then Zacchaeus saw the overhanging branches of a fig tree up ahead. He had an idea. Zacchaeus went on ahead of the crowd, and climbed the tree so that he could see Jesus coming down the road.

When Jesus reached the tree he stopped.

'Zacchaeus!' said Jesus, looking up at him. 'Come down! I want to come to your house today.'

Zacchaeus couldn't believe what he was hearing. He couldn't wait to get down the tree again.

'You are welcome to stay with me, Jesus!' he said.

But the people in the crowd were cross.

'Why would Jesus stay with that cheat?' said one.

'Why would he even speak to him?' another said.

They muttered to each other, saying unkind things about Zacchaeus.

This is why I am here – to save people who need help.

Zacchaeus knew what the people were saying. He wanted to put it right.

'Jesus!' he said in a loud voice. 'I'm going to give half of all I own to the poor. And if I have cheated anyone, I will pay them back four times the amount.'

Jesus smiled at Zacchaeus.

'Today is a wonderful day,' he said. 'This is why I am here – to save people who need help to live the way God intended.'

CHAPTER 28
AN END AND A BEGINNING

THE PASSOVER FESTIVAL WAS APPROACHING. LAZARUS INVITED JESUS TO HIS HOME IN BETHANY. Lazarus and the disciples sat with Jesus at the table while Martha served the food. Mary went to wash Jesus' feet – but instead of using water, as she would for any other guest, Mary poured out some expensive perfume. Then she wiped Jesus' feet with her long hair.

The room was filled with the beautiful smell of the perfume. Judas Iscariot watched and shook his head.

'What a waste!' he said. 'That perfume could have been sold and the money given to the poor.'

Judas wasn't being completely honest. He looked after the money that was given to support Jesus, but he often stole from the amount they collected to help others and spent it on himself.

Jesus was sad at Judas' reaction.

'No,' he said, 'leave Mary alone. What she has done has prepared me for my burial. There will always be people in need of your help, but this was a kind and caring thing to do. I will not be here with you for much longer.'

Jesus and his friends went on to Jerusalem by way of Bethphage on the Mount of Olives. Jesus asked two of his disciples to go ahead and bring back a young donkey which would be waiting for them.

'If anyone asks what you are doing, tell them that I need it – they will not stop you.'

The two friends did as Jesus asked. They found the young donkey, and brought it to Jesus. They put a cloak on the back of the animal, which had never yet been ridden. Then Jesus sat on its back, and started to ride towards Jerusalem.

A large crowd had gathered along the sides of the road. Some people spread their cloaks on the ground for the donkey to walk on. Some cut huge palm branches from the trees and spread them over the road while others waved them above their heads.

Everyone was excited and shouting.

'Hosanna!' they cried. 'God bless the King!'

There were some Pharisees there watching and they spoke to Jesus.

'What nonsense is this!' they said to him. 'Stop these people shouting these things. Make them be quiet!'

But Jesus knew that this would be the last time he received such a

welcome. The next crowd would be shouting something very different.

Once inside the city, Jesus went into the temple courtyard. He saw the money-changers and dove-sellers busy making money for themselves. He was angry.

Jesus took hold of one table after another and overturned them. Money scattered everywhere.

'This is God's house!' he said. 'It is a place for people to pray and worship God, but you have made it into a dishonest marketplace, a hideout for thieves and robbers!'

> **Jesus took hold of one table after another and overturned them. Money scattered everywhere.**

Every day Jesus taught in the temple, surrounded by crowds of people, not wanting to miss anything he said. Others came to him to be healed, the blind people, the deaf, those who couldn't walk, or suffered from various illnesses – anyone who needed Jesus came, and he healed them.

The chief priests and the Pharisees watched Jesus. They hated what he was saying. They hated what he was doing. They hated Jesus. But because the people loved Jesus, there was nothing they could do without causing a riot.

Little children danced around the temple courts singing:

'Hosanna! Praise Jesus! God has come to save us!'

The Pharisees and the Sadducees kept asking Jesus questions to see if they could find some fault with him.

'Tell me, which is the most important of all the commandments?' asked one of the teachers of the law.

'The most important of all is this,' said Jesus. 'The Lord our God is the only Lord. Love the Lord your God with all your heart, with all your soul, with all your mind and with all your strength. The second is this: Love your neighbour as yourself.'

'You are right,' said the teacher. 'To do these things is better than to offer sacrifices to God.'

Jesus looked at the man. He was pleased with the wisdom of his answer.

'If you understand this much, you are close to God's kingdom,' Jesus said to him. Then no one else dared to ask him anything else.

You are close to God's kingdom.

While he was in the temple, Jesus saw some rich men putting money into the temple treasury boxes. As he watched, a poor widow came and slipped two small copper coins into the box.

Jesus turned to the people around him.

'That woman has given far more than anyone else,' he said. 'The men gave large gifts but they were not generous – their gifts were small compared to what they own. They could well afford to give them; it didn't cost them much. But that woman gave everything she had to God.'

The chief priests and the elders met together secretly.

'We can't let this go on any longer,' they said. 'We must find a way to destroy Jesus.'

'But the people are on his side,' said one. 'Passover is only two days away and Jerusalem is too busy. If we have Jesus arrested now, there will be trouble!'

Meanwhile Judas Iscariot was also plotting. He went looking for some of the chief priests.

'What will you give me if I betray Jesus?' he asked.

What will you give me if I betray Jesus?

'Thirty silver coins,' they answered. This was the opportunity they needed – someone who could help them trap Jesus when he was not surrounded by crowds of people.

Judas took their money. Now all he had to do was wait for the right moment.

The people in Jerusalem were getting ready for the Passover feast. Lambs were being killed as part of the final preparations.

Jesus sent Peter and John to make arrangements for them.

'Where would you like to celebrate Passover?' they asked.

'You'll meet a man carrying a water jar as you go into the city,' Jesus told them. 'Follow him into the house where we'll celebrate the feast. Find the owner and ask him which room he has prepared for the Teacher and his disciples. He will show you a large furnished room upstairs. Then you can get everything ready.'

The two men went into the city and saw the man with the water jar. They went into the house with him and the owner took them to the upstairs room. It seemed that everything had been planned. Peter and John started to get things ready for the special feast.

The night before Passover, Jesus and his disciples met in the upstairs room to have supper together.

Jesus knew what the next twenty-four hours would mean for him. He knew that his time with his friends was drawing to an end. He had grown very attached to his disciples – this band of men from different backgrounds – but there was still so much he wanted to teach them.

Jesus wrapped a towel around his waist and filled a basin with water. Then he knelt down in front of each of his friends in turn and washed their feet. He took the towel from his waist and dried them carefully. Normally a servant would wash the dust from their feet before they sat down to a meal. Jesus knew how strange it would seem to his friends that he was doing it now.

'I won't let you wash my feet,' said Peter, as Jesus prepared to do just that.

'Peter, if I don't wash your feet, you cannot be my friend.'

'Then don't just wash my feet – wash all of me!' said Peter. It was always Peter's way, to speak out emotionally.

'There's no need,' said Jesus. 'Only your feet are dirty.' His thoughts turned to Judas. 'Although that's not true of everyone here,' he added.

When Jesus had finished, he returned to the table with his disciples.

'Do you understand what I have just done?' Jesus asked them. 'I am your teacher, but I have just done the job of a servant. I want you to treat each other with that same love and respect. Don't behave as if you

Do you understand what I have just done?

are greater or better than each other, but serve one another. Follow my example.'

Jesus ate with his friends but they could see that he was thoughtful – and even unhappy. He was thinking carefully about what he would say next.

'One of you here is going to betray me,' he said.

The disciples looked at him in amazement. Then they looked at one another in disbelief.

One of you here is going to betray me.

'Ask him who it is,' mouthed Peter to John, who was next to Jesus.

John whispered to him, 'Who is it, Lord?'

'I will dip some bread in the sauce and give it to him,' Jesus told John. Then Jesus gave the bread to Judas.

'Go now,' Jesus said to Judas. 'Do what you have to do.'

Judas took the bread, stood up and made his way out of the room quietly into the darkness.

Then Jesus held the loaf of unleavened bread and thanked God for it. He broke it into pieces and shared it with his friends.

'Eat this. It is my body, which is given for you,' he said. 'Remember me whenever you eat bread together.'

Then Jesus picked up a cup of red wine. 'Drink this. This wine is my blood, shed for you so that your sins may be forgiven.'

Jesus' friends ate and drank with him, but they did not understand what Jesus was telling them until after he had died.

After supper, Jesus and his disciples walked to a nearby olive grove where Jesus wanted to pray.

'All of you will run away and leave me tonight,' Jesus said to them. 'But after I am raised from the dead, I will go to Galilee. I will meet you there.'

'I will never leave you,' said Peter hotly, 'even if all the others do!'

'Peter,' Jesus replied sadly, 'before the cock crows at first light, you will have denied three times that you even know me.'

'I would die first!' said Peter bravely – and all the other disciples agreed with him.

When they arrived at a garden called Gethsemane, Jesus told them to wait for him while he went to pray. He asked Peter, James and John to go further but he wanted to be alone when he talked to God in prayer. They saw that he was very sad.

'My Father,' Jesus said, 'don't make me go through all the pain and suffering ahead of me! Take it away if that's possible. But let me do what you want me to – not what I want.'

After a while, Jesus got up and walked back to his waiting friends, but he found they had all fallen asleep.

'Can't you even stay awake with me for one hour?' he asked. 'I know you want to help me, but you have no strength.'

Then Jesus went again to pray.

'Father, if I must go through this suffering, then I am ready to obey you. Please help me to be brave.'

When he went to his friends a second time, they were once more sleeping. Jesus prayed for a third time, alone in the darkness of the night, and when he returned to his disciples, they were asleep. They could not keep their eyes open.

'Wake up!' said Jesus. 'It is time. Here is the man who has betrayed me.'

The quiet of the dark olive grove gave way to the sound of people, a large crowd with clubs and swords in their hands. Leading them all was Judas Iscariot.

Judas walked straight up to Jesus, and kissed him as if he were greeting a friend.

It was the signal the crowd needed. They closed in around Jesus and rough hands held him so he could not move.

One of them lashed out with a sword.

The disciples were afraid. One of them lashed out with a sword and cut off the ear of the High Priest's servant.

'Put down that sword!' said Jesus, touching the man's ear and healing him. 'There's no need for violence. If I wanted help, I could ask God to send angels to rescue me!' Then he spoke to the men holding him. 'But why do you men need to use force to take me away? You could have come any day when I was teaching the people.'

They marched Jesus away to see Caiaphas, the High Priest. His friends ran away, leaving him alone. It seemed as if Jesus had known about all this beforehand. Only Peter followed some distance away.

There was a crowd seated around a fire in the courtyard of the High Priest's house. Peter went in the darkness to sit with them.

Inside the house, the elders and teachers of the law had gathered to await Jesus' arrival. They talked among themselves trying to find some reason to put him to death. They needed some crime to accuse him of – but they could find none. Finally the High Priest asked Jesus if

---

They talked among themselves trying to find some reason to put him to death.

---

he were the Christ, the Son of God, whom everyone had been waiting for – the one the prophets said God would send them.

'I am,' said Jesus, 'and I will soon be seated at God's right hand.'

'That's it! Blasphemy!' shouted Caiaphas. 'You have committed the sin of blasphemy and should be put to death!'

They had the reason they needed to ask the Romans for his execution.

Outside, a servant girl had been watching Peter in the flickering firelight.

'I know you!' she said. 'You're one of Jesus' friends!'

'No, I'm not!' said Peter, getting to his feet. 'I don't know what you mean!'

Some time later a man noticed Peter there.

'I'm sure you were with Jesus,' he said.

'You're mistaken!' Peter replied angrily. 'I'm not his friend.'

Just before dawn, another man accused Peter.

'You come from Galilee too!' he said. 'I can tell by your accent! You must know Jesus!'

'No! I don't know what you're talking about!' Peter answered.

At that moment, a cock crowed. It was dawn, and Peter suddenly remembered what Jesus had said to him.

Peter felt hot tears of shame running down his face.

Pontius Pilate, the Roman governor, stared thoughtfully at the man in front of him, bound and with his head bowed.

'You know that the chief priests want you dead,' Pilate said to Jesus. 'Have you nothing to say? Help yourself!'

The chief priests want you dead.

Jesus stood silently. Pilate was anxious. He could find nothing under Roman law that would justify Jesus being punished by death, but he could see that the leaders of the people wanted some excuse for trouble. He decided to ask the crowd outside, who were waiting for his verdict.

'You know it is the custom at Passover to release a prisoner,' he said. 'Shall I release Barabbas, or Jesus, whom some believe is the Messiah, the chosen one?'

The chief priests and the elders had made sure their supporters were in the crowd.

'Barabbas!' they shouted. 'Set Barabbas free!'

'Then what shall I do with Jesus from Nazareth?' asked Pilate. 'He has done nothing wrong! Shall I have him whipped and then set him free?'

'Crucify him!' the men in the crowd shouted.

'But why?' asked Pilate. 'I can find no crime to punish him for!'

'Crucify him!' they shouted even more loudly. Pilate looked down at their angry faces as they began to shout and wave their fists. He shook his head sadly and called for water. Then he washed his hands in front of the crowd.

'This man's death is nothing to do with me,' he told them.

But Pilate had Jesus taken away by soldiers while he released Barabbas, the murderer.

The Roman soldiers took away Jesus' clothes and dressed him in the scarlet cloak of a Roman soldier.

He released Barabbas, the murderer.

They twisted together branches of sharp thorns into a crown and forced it down on his head so that blood trickled down his face. They put a stick in his right hand and knelt in front of him, laughing.

'Look! Here is the King of the Jews!' they sneered, spitting in his face. Then they took away the stick and beat him again and again.

When they were bored with making fun of Jesus, the soldiers gave him back his own clothes. They pushed him before them on the way to his crucifixion.

Jesus was bruised and bleeding; he was exhausted from the beating. As he tried to carry the wooden bar on which he would be crucified, he stumbled and fell.

'You! Here!' they said to a man in the crowd. 'Carry this!'

The man, Simon from Cyrene, took the long piece of wood from Jesus and put it on his shoulder. He followed Jesus to the place of execution outside the city walls.

The route was lined with people. Some shouted and jeered; others watched sadly; yet more wept and cried to see Jesus taken away to Golgotha, the Place of the Skull.

Two other men were led out to be crucified that day, both of them thieves. Jesus was nailed to the wooden bar and hoisted up between them.

'Forgive them, Father!' said Jesus. 'They don't know what they are doing!'

'Forgive them, Father!' said Jesus.

The crowds watched and waited. The soldiers jeered.

'You saved other people, but you can't help yourself!' they said.

Some of the soldiers gambled for Jesus' clothes. Others made a sign to hang over his head.

'This is the King of the Jews,' it read.

One of the thieves who hung beside Jesus shouted to him.

'If you really are God's Son, then save us all!'

'Be quiet!' said the other thief. 'We deserve our punishment but this man has done nothing wrong.' Then he spoke to Jesus. 'Remember me,' he said.

'Today you will be with me in paradise,' Jesus replied.

was already dead and checked first with the guards. They put a sword in his side to make sure and blood and water gushed out. Then, with Pilate's permission, Joseph went with

---

They put a sword in his side and blood and water gushed out.

John, one of Jesus' disciples, was standing near the foot of the cross. A group of women, including Jesus' own mother, was also there.

'Dear mother,' Jesus said to Mary, 'treat this man as your son. John,' he then said to his friend, 'treat this woman as if she were your mother. Take care of each other.'

At midday the sky turned black. Then at around three o'clock in the afternoon, Jesus called out loud:

'It is finished!' and breathed his last breath.

Joseph of Arimathea was a member of the Jewish Council, the Sanhedrin. Like Nicodemus, he was a secret follower of Jesus, and neither man had been among those who plotted to kill him.

As it was almost the Sabbath, Joseph went to Pontius Pilate and asked if Jesus' body could be taken down from the cross and buried.

Pilate was surprised that Jesus

Nicodemus and took Jesus' broken body from the cross. There were wounds in his hands and feet and in his side.

The men wrapped Jesus in strips of linen with myrrh and aloes, and placed his body in the newly-made tomb that Joseph had prepared for his own burial. Then they rolled a great stone door across the entrance to seal it, watched by Mary Magdalene and her friends.

The women wanted to anoint Jesus' body with spices. They hadn't been able to do it on Friday night or on Saturday because it was not allowed on the Sabbath day. So they went early on Sunday morning so they could be there at sunrise.

When they arrived in the garden, they saw that the huge stone door that had been in front of the tomb had been rolled away. The tomb was empty.

Mary Magdalene ran back to find Peter and John.

'They've taken Jesus away!' she cried. 'I don't know where his body is!'

Peter and John ran to the tomb to see if there could be any mistake. They saw the linen cloths but they were empty – Jesus was not there. The two men ran home, leaving Mary alone in the garden.

Mary was still weeping when she went to look inside the tomb again. But this time she saw two angels, sitting where Jesus' body should have been.

'Why are you crying?' asked one of the angels.

'They have taken my master away,' Mary sobbed. 'I don't know where they have put him!'

Mary turned as she heard someone else behind her. She thought it was the gardener.

'Who are you looking for?' the man asked.

'Please, just tell me where his body is,' she said.

The man answered with just one word.

'Mary!' he said. Mary knew straight away who the man was. It was Jesus!

'Master!' she said, overjoyed to see him.

'Don't touch me,' he said to her gently, 'but go and tell the others what you have seen.'

I have seen Jesus!' she said. 'He's no longer dead. He's alive!'

Mary ran all the way.

'I have seen Jesus!' she said. 'He's no longer dead. He's alive!'

Later that same day, two of Jesus'

followers were walking along the road from Jerusalem to the village of Emmaus. They were talking together about all the events of the last few days.

As they walked, another man came alongside them.

'What are you talking about?' he asked them.

Cleopas looked at the stranger, surprised.

'Surely you must have heard what has happened?' he said. 'We were talking about Jesus of Nazareth. We thought he was the Saviour God had promised to us. But, three days ago, our chief priests and elders had him executed. Then today we have heard that his tomb is empty – they say he has risen from the dead!'

The stranger then began to explain all that the prophets had told the people about God's Saviour, about how he had to suffer and die.

It was almost dark when they reached Emmaus.

'Come,' said Cleopas to the stranger. 'Stay here with us and have something to eat.'

As they sat down to share a meal together, the stranger picked up the bread, thanked God for it and broke it.

Suddenly the two friends knew who the stranger was. They had been walking and talking with Jesus! But as soon as they recognised him, Jesus disappeared. They left everything and rushed back to Jerusalem to tell the others that Jesus was alive and they had seen him.

When they arrived with their news, they found that the other disciples were together behind locked doors, talking about Jesus.

'Jesus is alive!' they said. 'He appeared today and spoke to Peter!'

'We've seen him too!' Cleopas told them. 'He walked with us to Emmaus and told us how he had to suffer and die before he could be raised. We didn't recognise him – until he broke the bread!'

At that moment, Jesus stood with them in the room.

'Peace be with you,' he said. At first they were afraid, but Jesus held out his hands and showed them the wounds where the nails had been.

'It really is you!' cried his disciples. 'You're alive!'

Then, because he said he was hungry, they gave him some cooked fish, which he ate in front of them.

Jesus reminded the disciples what they must do next.

'Start in Jerusalem,' he said. 'Tell people that I died and rose from the dead. Tell them they must repent of their sins and that now they can be forgiven. Then go out to all nations and tell them too!'

I don't believe it!' said Thomas. 'I won't believe that Jesus is alive, unless I see him for myself.'

Thomas had not been there when Jesus appeared to his disciples in the upstairs room.

'I don't believe it!' said Thomas. 'I won't believe that Jesus is alive, unless I see him for myself and touch his wounds.'

A week later, Thomas and the others met together. As before, the doors were locked to protect them

from Jesus' enemies. And, as before, Jesus appeared as if from nowhere and stood among them.

'Peace be with you,' he said. Then he turned to Thomas. 'Look at my hands, Thomas. Touch them. Look at the place where the sword cut my side. Touch that too. Now stop doubting and believe!'

Thomas sank to his knees. He knew that this was no ghost. Jesus was real and he was alive.

'My Lord and my God,' he said.

For a few weeks after Jesus' death, the disciples did not know what to do. One evening Peter was back at Lake Galilee and he decided to go fishing with some of his friends. He still could not forget that he had let Jesus down so badly, and denied even knowing him.

They fished all night, but caught nothing. As dawn came, they sailed back to the shore.

A man was standing watching them.

'Have you caught anything?' he called out.

'No!' they replied.

'Try throwing your nets on the right side of the boat.'

The fishermen did as the man

suggested. Immediately, they felt the tug of the net as it filled with fish.

Peter looked at the man on the beach.

'It's Jesus!' he shouted. He jumped into the water and waded ashore.

Jesus had made a small fire and had some bread warming there.

'Bring some of the fish you have caught,' he said. So the disciples dragged the net on to the shore and sat with Jesus on the beach.

'Come,' said Jesus. 'Let's have breakfast together.'

When breakfast was over, Jesus took Peter to one side to talk to him alone.

'Peter,' he said, 'do you really love me?'

'You know I do,' said Peter.

'Then take care of my lambs,' Jesus replied.

A few minutes later, Jesus spoke again.

'Peter,' he said, 'do you truly love me?'

'Yes!' said Peter. 'You know I do!'

'Then take care of my sheep,' said Jesus.

After a little while, Jesus spoke for a third time.

'Peter,' he said, 'do you love me?'

Peter was hurt. He remembered how he had disowned Jesus, how he had let him down. But he loved Jesus so much.

'You know everything,' he said to Jesus. 'You know that I love you.'

'I have a special job for you to do,' said Jesus. 'When I have gone away, I want you to look after my followers.'

After Jesus rose from the dead, his disciples saw him many times and in different places. Jesus taught them more about God. They had no doubt that he was the same man they had known before his crucifixion. They knew that now he was alive.

After Jesus rose from the dead, his disciples saw him many times.

'Stay in Jerusalem,' he told them. 'Wait there, because I will send the Holy Spirit to you. Then go and tell people everywhere about me. Teach them everything I have done and said. I promise that I will always be there to help you.'

The apostles had often heard

Jesus talk about the Holy Spirit, and how he would come to be with them after Jesus had gone.

About six weeks after Jesus rose from the dead, the apostles were with him on the Mount of Olives.

'When the Holy Spirit comes, you will have power,' Jesus said. 'The whole world will hear about me, because you will tell them. You will be my messengers.'

Then Jesus was covered by a cloud and seemed to rise up and disappear while they stood and stared.

Jesus had gone.

'What are you looking for?' asked two angels, standing among them. 'Jesus has gone back to heaven, but one day he will return.'

The eleven friends returned to Jerusalem. They usually met to pray with some of the other believers. Now they called everyone together. There were about 120 people there.

'My friends,' Peter said to them, 'we have lost a member of our group. Judas was with us from the beginning; he was chosen to learn with us and work with us. But he led the authorities to Jesus and betrayed him. Now he is dead.'

All the people there knew that Judas Iscariot had realised that he had done a terrible thing by betraying Jesus. Judas had taken his own life and been buried in the field that God had told the prophet Jeremiah to buy.

When the Holy Spirit comes, you will have power.

'We must find someone to replace Judas. The person must be one who has seen all we have seen, and been with us from the start.'

Two men were suggested from the group. Then they all prayed, asking God to help them to choose the right person. Matthias then became the twelfth man, now known as apostles rather than disciples. They were not just those who followed and learned from their master; they had been sent out with his authority to speak and act in the name of Jesus.

Chapter 29

MEN WHO CHANGED THE WORLD

JERUSALEM WAS FULL OF VISITORS FROM ALL OVER THE WORLD. THEY HAD COME FOR THE FESTIVAL OF PENTECOST.

The believers were all together in one room when, suddenly, a sound like a strong wind blew through the house, filling it with noise. Something like flames seemed to burn in the air and touch each person there. It was the Holy Spirit, the helper Jesus has promised to send to them. As the Holy Spirit touched them, they all began to speak in other languages.

The noise from the house attracted a crowd.

'What's happening?' some of the people outside said. 'I can understand what these men are saying. They are speaking in my language, talking about God. How is this possible?'

'They're drunk!' laughed others.

'No, we're not!' said Peter, coming out to speak to the crowd. 'It's only nine o'clock in the morning.'

Then Peter, the man who had been too afraid to say he was a friend of Jesus, stood up to teach all those who would listen about what had happened there recently.

First, Peter reminded them of

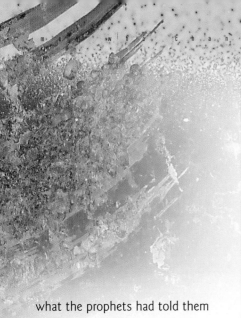

what the prophets had told them would happen. Then he told them that his friend Jesus, God's chosen one, the Messiah, had been arrested and beaten and then put to death. The crowd was horrified.

'What shall we do?' they asked.

That day 3,000 people became followers of Jesus.

'You must turn away from your sins and be baptised,' Peter told them. 'Then you can be forgiven, and you will receive the Holy Spirit and know his strength and power and comfort as we have.'

That day 3,000 people became followers of Jesus. The apostles found they were able to perform many miracles in the name of Jesus. They met together with the other believers to worship God, to pray and to share what they had with each other.

One afternoon, as Peter and John went to the temple to pray, they passed a man begging at one of the temple gates. He held out his hands.

'Have you anything to spare?' he asked them, hopefully.

Peter stopped and looked at him. The man had not been able to walk in more than forty years. He was carried there, to where he sat, day after day, hoping to be given enough money so he could feed himself.

'I have no silver or gold,' said Peter, taking the man by his hands, 'but I can give you something much more. In the name of Jesus, stand up and walk!'

The man stood up with Peter's help. But, once on his feet, he took some steps – then jumped in the air with joy.

'Praise God!' he shouted. 'I am healed! I can walk!'

Peter and John carried on towards the temple, smiling, but the man would not let them go.

The people all around stared, amazed.

'Isn't that the beggar who sat by the gate?' they asked each other. 'How is it that he can walk?'

Peter gave the people the answer they needed: it was faith in Jesus that had enabled them to help the beggar. He told them that the same Jesus whom they had crucified had risen from death. Now Jesus was waiting in heaven until the time when there would be a new heaven and earth.

The people listened eagerly to all he had to say – until the temple guards and Sadducees came to see what was happening. Once they heard that Peter was telling everyone that Jesus had risen from death, they stopped him and put both Peter and John in prison. The Sadducees taught that there was no resurrection of the dead!

But many who were there believed what Peter had said and joined the growing number of people who now called themselves Christians.

The next morning, Peter and John stood before the High Priest and the other elders.

'How did you do this?' they demanded. 'How was the man healed?'

Peter was telling everyone that Jesus had risen from death.

The Holy Spirit gave Peter power to answer him.

'He was healed in the name of Jesus,' he said. 'Jesus is the man you crucified and God brought back to life. God has given us Jesus so that we might be saved.'

The High Priest and elders could not understand what had happened – either that the man had been healed or that Peter, an uneducated fisherman, could speak to them with such authority. But they would not be convinced that what Peter said was true.

They had no real reason to keep them in prison so they had to let Peter and John go, but they warned them not to talk about Jesus any more.

'We can do nothing else!' Peter and John replied. 'We cannot keep these things a secret! Which would you do? Obey God or obey men?'

When Peter and John returned to their friends, they prayed together, asking for God's help not to be afraid to speak boldly about Jesus whatever happened to them. Then they were filled with the Holy Spirit and went out as God's messengers.

Wherever the apostles went, people brought out their friends or family to meet them. The streets were lined with those who were ill, lying on their mats or beds. The people in the nearby villages heard what was happening in Jerusalem and crowds of people in need of help were brought to them.

The High Priest and the Sadducees saw how many were being healed day by day; they saw how many new believers there were and they were very angry. They arrested all the apostles and locked them up in the public jail.

During the night an angel came to the prison, opened the gates and led out the men.

'Go to the temple,' the angel said. 'Tell everyone about the new life God has given you.'

The next morning the High Priest and the elders met to decide what to do with the prisoners. But when they sent for them, the news of their disappearance came back.

'The prison doors are still locked, the guards are on duty – but the men we arrested are no longer in the prison!'

A man then came to them from the temple.

During the night an angel came to the prison.

'I have seen your prisoners,' he said. 'They are not hiding but in the temple, teaching the people.'

The captain of the temple guard was sent to bring them back without causing a riot.

'We told you not to talk about Jesus any more!' the High Priest said to them. 'You not only disobeyed us, you are also blaming us for his death!'

'We obeyed God,' replied Peter. 'Our sins have been forgiven; we must share this news with everyone.'

The Sanhedrin were so angry that they wanted the apostles executed, but one man, Gamaliel, asked for the men to be taken out of the room so he could speak to the Sanhedrin privately.

'Leave these men alone,' he said. 'Every now and then someone rises up and tries to lead the people. After a while, people forget about them; their followers disappear. Perhaps this will be the same. But if it comes from God – if it is what they say it is, nothing we can do will stop it.'

The Sanhedrin decided to listen to Gamaliel. They had the apostles beaten and set free, with a warning to abandon their work. But as soon as the apostles left, they continued to teach the people about Jesus.

Now that there were so many believers, the apostles needed help to share out all they had so that no one was in need. Seven wise men were chosen, Stephen among them.

Stephen had been blessed by God with a number of special gifts and had healed many of the people. One day, some of Stephen's enemies, jealous of his wisdom and power,

accused him of blasphemy in an attempt to get rid of him.

Stephen knew that blasphemy was a serious crime, but he listened calmly to the lies spoken against him before the Sanhedrin. His face shone like the face of an angel.

When it was his turn to speak in his defence, Stephen told them all about God's plan to save his people from the time of Abraham. His closing words made them cover their ears in their anger.

They pelted Stephen with stones until he fell to his knees.

'You are as stubborn as our ancestors! God has tried to speak to you but you have rejected him. God has sent Jesus to you but you had him killed. Now you reject the gift of the Holy Spirit!'

They marched Stephen outside the city and cast down their cloaks at the feet of a man called Saul. Then they pelted Stephen with stones until he fell to his knees.

'Lord Jesus,' said Stephen, 'forgive

them for this sin and receive my spirit!' Then Stephen died.

Saul watched with interest. He was pleased that Stephen was no longer a threat.

Stephen's friends went to collect his body and buried him. His friends were shocked at what had happened to him and were very sad at his death. But there was little enough time to think about it. That very day, Saul and the authorities set about destroying the Christian believers. Saul went from house to house, dragging out from their homes any who believed – men and women – and locking them up in prison.

The Christians were scattered. Some hid from their persecutors; others moved away from Jerusalem.

People who were ill or paralysed came and were healed.

But wherever they went, they told people about the good news of Jesus. They could not be stopped.

Philip, another of the seven men who had been chosen to help the apostles, went to Samaria. He shared all he knew of Jesus with the people there and many came to hear him speak. People who were ill or paralysed came and were healed by him and many more were baptised in Jesus' name.

Philip was still in Samaria when an angel spoke to him.

'Get ready to travel south on the desert road to Gaza,' the angel told him.

Philip went and, as he travelled along the road, he was passed by a man seated in a carriage. The man was the treasurer of Queen Candace of Ethiopia. He had been to Jerusalem to worship God and was now reading the words of the prophet Isaiah.

The Holy Spirit prompted Philip to go over to the man's carriage and walk along beside it. The Ethiopian was looking puzzled.

'Can I help you?' offered Philip.

'I need someone to explain these words to me,' the man replied. Then he invited Philip into the carriage to travel with him.

'"Like a sheep that goes to be slaughtered, like a lamb that goes to have its wool cut off, he was silent and did not complain,"' he read aloud. '"He was treated unjustly, his life was ended before its time." Who is the prophet speaking about?' the man asked.

So Philip told him. Philip explained that Isaiah knew about the Saviour God would send to his people, who would be taken and killed and would die in the place of all sinners.

'He is talking about Jesus, who died so that all who believe can be forgiven,' said Philip.

The Ethiopian treasurer now understood and believed; he wanted to be baptised.

'Here is a river,' the Ethiopian said. 'Will you baptise me?'

Both men went into the water and Philip baptised him. The man continued his journey home happy, ready to tell them about Jesus too, but he never saw Philip again.

Saul continued to look for all Christian believers, to stop them preaching about Jesus. He hated them and wanted to destroy them all.

'I want to go to Damascus,' Saul told the High Priest. 'I need letters of introduction to the synagogues so I

A bright light from the sky suddenly dazzled him.

can find and arrest any Christians I find there.'

Saul set out along the road with some companions. When the city was finally in sight, a bright light from the sky suddenly dazzled him. Saul fell to the ground and heard a voice coming from nowhere.

'Saul, Saul, why are you persecuting me?'

'Who are you?' asked Saul, terrified.

'I am Jesus,' said the voice. 'Get up and go to Damascus, and you will be told what to do next.'

Saul got to his feet but found that he could not see. His companions were as confused as he was – they had also heard the voice but seen no one. They led him by the hand into the city of Damascus. Saul's sight did not return for three days. He ate nothing during that time but spent his time praying.

Meanwhile, Jesus spoke to a Christian believer in Damascus called Ananias.

'Ananias, I want you to go to Straight Street and call on Judas. There is a man there from Tarsus called Saul. He is blind and is praying. He has seen you in a vision, restoring his sight.'

'But, Lord, I know of this man! He hates all Christians and has come here to destroy us!' Ananias replied.

'I know all this and I have chosen him to suffer for my sake,' said Jesus. 'He will tell my people and the Gentiles and even kings about me.'

So Ananias went to find Saul. He placed his hands on him so that he was healed of his blindness.

'Brother,' said Ananias, 'Jesus himself has sent me here so that you will see again and be filled with the Holy Spirit.'

Saul was able to see again! He was baptised and given something to eat. Then he stayed with the believers for a few days.

Saul went to the synagogue and preached.

'Jesus is the Son of God,' he said. 'Jesus is the Messiah!'

The people who heard him were amazed.

'Isn't this the man who killed Christians in Jerusalem?' they asked. 'We thought he had come here to do the same – yet now he speaks like one of them!'

Soon the Jews were plotting to kill Saul. They put guards on the city gates so he could not escape. But Saul now had new friends. One night they lowered him in a basket down through a gap in the city walls.

Saul went back to Jerusalem and tried to find the believers so he could join them. But they were afraid of him – he had been imprisoning and murdering their friends only a short while before.

Barnabas spoke up for Saul.

He went with him to the apostles and explained to them what had happened to Saul on the road to Damascus, and how he had preached the good news about Jesus in the synagogues there.

'I have seen Jesus for myself,' Saul told them, 'and Jesus has spoken to me.'

Saul then went into Jerusalem. Because he spoke Greek, he preached to the Greek-speaking Jews there until they too wanted to kill him. Then the apostles helped him escape to Caesarea and sent him back to Tarsus, his home town.

Meanwhile, Peter travelled to many places, teaching and encouraging any Christian believers he found.

Once he went to Lydda, about twenty-five miles north-west of Jerusalem, where he met a man called Aeneas who had been paralysed for eight years.

'You are healed in the name of Jesus Christ,' Peter said to him. 'You can get up and make your bed.'

Aeneas was able to get up and walk from that moment. Many people in Lydda saw how amazing God's healing power was and put their trust

in him because of it.

The news of what Peter had done reached Joppa nearer the coast. The Christians in Joppa were very sad because their friend, Tabitha, had just died. Tabitha had been a good friend to everyone who was poor or in any kind of need. So the believers asked Peter to come and visit them.

Peter walked the twelve miles to Joppa and went to the place where Tabitha's body lay. All her friends were there, weeping and talking at once and making him look at all the beautiful clothes that Tabitha had made while she was alive. Peter sent everyone out of the room, then prayed for a while in the silence. Then he turned to Tabitha's lifeless body and spoke.

'Tabitha, get up!'

She opened her eyes and sat up. Peter let the women come back into the room. He saw how happy they all were that Tabitha was alive again.

Everyone soon heard what had happened and many more people became Christians because of it. Peter then stayed in Joppa for a while at the house of a tanner called Simon.

The headquarters of the Roman forces occupying Judea were about thirty miles north of Joppa in the city of Caesarea. Cornelius was a Roman centurion in the Italian regiment stationed there.

He saw an angel who called to him by name.

Cornelius loved God and prayed to him regularly. He was also kind and generous to the poor, but he did not know about Jesus.

Cornelius was praying at the normal time of 3 o'clock in the afternoon when he saw an angel who called to him by name.

'What do you want from me?' Cornelius asked the angel.

'God has heard your prayers and seen how well you have treated those in need around you,' the angel replied. 'God wants you to invite a man called Peter here. You will need to send someone to Simon's home to find him. Simon is a tanner and his house is by the sea in Joppa.'

When the angel had gone, Cornelius called two of his servants and one of his soldiers who also believed in God. He told them what he had seen and then sent them to Joppa to find Peter.

While the men were travelling to Joppa, Peter was praying on the rooftop of Simon's house. He was hungry and a meal was being prepared for him. Then Peter saw a vision of a large sheet being lowered

Then Peter saw a vision.

down by its four corners in front of him. The sheet was full of creatures that were good and safe to eat, but also those that were forbidden according to Jewish law.

'Here is food for you, Peter. Take what you need. Prepare it and eat,' said God's voice.

'But I can't!' said Peter. 'Some of these animals are unclean and forbidden.'

'You don't need to call them unclean any longer. I have made them clean,' said God. The sheet came and went three times in Peter's vision before the sheet disappeared.

Peter did not have long to sit and think about what the vision might mean.

'Three men are at the gate looking for you,' the Holy Spirit said to him. 'I have sent them. Don't be afraid to go with them.'

Peter went downstairs and met the three men who had just arrived and were asking for him.

'I am Peter,' he greeted them. 'Why are you here?'

When the men explained about the angel who had spoken to Cornelius, Peter invited them in to stay until the next morning. He was beginning to understand the meaning of his vision.

Peter travelled to Caesarea the next day with some of the other believers. When they arrived at Cornelius' house, they found that he had invited all his family and friends to hear what Peter had to say.

'You know that Jewish law forbids a Jew to come into a Gentile's house. I am here because God has shown me that he does not have favourites; God accepts anyone who comes to him and wants to do what is right, no matter where they are from, no matter what their background is.' Then Peter told them everything he knew about Jesus.

While Peter was speaking, the Holy Spirit blessed all the people there. Cornelius and all the people there believed that Jesus had died and risen so that their sins could be forgiven; they praised God and spoke in other languages. So Peter arranged for all of them to be baptised.

The believers who were with Peter were amazed. They all saw that what Peter had said was true: God's invitation was to everyone, whoever they are.

Now King Herod started to persecute the believers. First he arrested them; then he executed James, John's brother, who had been one of Jesus' first followers; then he put Peter in prison.

The night before Peter's trial, there were soldiers outside the prison cell and there were soldiers on either side of Peter as he sat in chains. All his friends in Jerusalem prayed for Peter's safe release.

Then, while Peter was asleep, his prison cell was filled with bright light as an angel woke him. The chains fell from his wrists and the prison gates opened as the angel led Peter past the guards.

Once in the street, the angel disappeared and Peter, who had thought it was all a dream, went to the house where everyone was praying. Peter knocked at the door and Rhoda, the servant girl, recognised his voice. She ran to the others and told them he was outside.

At first no one believed her but Peter kept on knocking. When they opened the door and found that he was there, they could hardly believe it! God had answered their prayers.

The chains fell from his wrists and the prison gates opened.

Peter told his friends to explain what had happened to him to the other believers and then he went away so that Herod would not find him.

Herod was furious when he found that Peter was gone, and he had the guards executed. But no one could tell him how it had happened.

CHAPTER 30

GOOD NEWS TRAVELS FAST

Antioch in Syria was full of Christians. After Stephen's death, some of the believers had gone there to escape persecution and they had told people there about Jesus.

Barnabas was sent there to encourage them and he brought Saul to join him from Tarsus. Then one day the believers heard the Holy Spirit telling them that Saul and Barnabas had been chosen to take the message about Jesus to the people on the island of Cyprus in the Mediterranean Sea. John Mark went with them.

They travelled over the island, teaching in the synagogues. When they reached Paphos, they met a sorcerer called Elymas, who worked for the Roman governor, Sergius Paulus. The governor sent for Saul and Barnabas because he wanted to hear about God, but Elymas did not want them to talk to his master.

'You mustn't listen to them!' Elymas told the governor.

Saul, who was also known now as Paul, looked straight at Elymas.

'You are full of tricks and deceit,' Paul said. 'You are an enemy of

God and all his work. To stop you interfering in God's work you will lose your sight.'

From that moment Elymas went blind. He could do nothing without someone to lead him. Sergius Paulus saw what had happened and was amazed. He believed in the power of Jesus.

Then John Mark went back to Jerusalem while Paul and Barnabas sailed to Galatia.

In Lystra, a man sat listening to Paul as he talked about Jesus. The man had never been able to walk but began to believe that Jesus could heal him. Paul saw that the man had faith.

'Stand up and walk!' said Paul, looking straight at him.

There was an uproar as the crowd watched the man get up and walk among them.

'Here are Zeus and Hermes! The gods are here among us!' the crowd cried out. Then one of the Greek priests came with garlands and tried to prepare sacrifices for Paul and Barnabas.

'Stop this!' Paul shouted. 'We are here to tell you not to worship worthless things. You should worship the living God who made heaven and earth! We are only God's messengers, human, as you are!'

Still the crowd would not listen until some Jews joined them. They persuaded the crowd that Paul and Barnabas had come to deceive them. The mood of the crowd changed. Soon there were angry voices and they stoned Paul in an angry attack.

The mood of the crowd changed. They stoned Paul in an angry attack.

Paul collapsed and lay motionless on the ground until the men dragged his body outside the city. They thought he was dead – but Paul's friends came to his aid. He returned to the city but left Lystra with Barnabas the next day.

Many good things happened in those days after the Holy Spirit came, amazing miracles occurring almost every day. But with so many people coming to believe in Jesus, disagreements began to arise about how best to follow him. Paul and

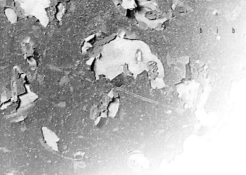

Barnabas argued with some in Antioch who said that the Gentile Christians had to be circumcised as Moses had taught.

The matter was so important that Paul and Barnabas were sent to Jerusalem to discuss it with the leaders there.

'The Holy Spirit knows what goes on inside everyone,' Paul said. 'He came to Gentiles and blessed them just as he came to us and to other Jewish believers. We are all saved because of God's grace alone. It does not matter whether or nor we have been circumcised in the Jewish way.'

Eventually the leaders there agreed what should be taught to everyone. They gave a letter to Paul and Barnabas to take to the believers in Antioch.

'Paul and Barnabas come with our love and recommendation. They have risked their lives already in teaching people about Jesus,' the

letter said. 'Now we are agreed that there is no need for circumcision when Gentiles become Christians. There are other rules we think are more useful such as avoiding food sacrificed to idols and learning to live faithfully with your wives or husbands.'

Paul and Barnabas took the letter and stayed for a while in Antioch, teaching the people there.

When the time came to move on, Barnabas wanted to take John Mark with them but Paul did not. The two men agreed to work in different places. Barnabas went with John Mark to Cyprus; Paul went with Silas to Syria and Cilicia.

Paul wrote to the Christians in Galatia about how they should worship God:

'You are children of God because of your faith. There is no difference between the Jewish believer and the Gentile believer; between the believer who is a slave and the believer who is a free person; between the male believer and the female believer. Once you are a Christian, you are all the same. You are all equally descendants of Abraham and will receive all the blessings that God promised him. God has given you the Holy Spirit as proof of that – the Spirit that cries out to God and knows that he is your loving Father.

'You are all free – free to love and serve God as equals. This freedom

You are all free – free to love and serve God as equals.

is not so that you can behave badly but so that you can love each other as Jesus showed us how to love others. Don't become a slave to your human nature to do what everyone else does; instead let your lives be controlled by the Holy Spirit so that the qualities of love, joy, peace, patience, kindness, goodness, faithfulness, humility and self-control can be seen among you and all Christian people.'

Paul and Silas met Timothy, the son of a Jewish Christian mother and a Greek father, among the Christians in Lystra. Paul invited Timothy to join them.

Everywhere they went they encouraged those who already

believed. They told others about Jesus so that more and more people became followers. Soon they were also joined by a doctor named Luke.

During this time Paul had a vision in which he saw a man from Macedonia asking for help. The friends decided to go there on the next stage of their journey.

They stayed in Philippi for several days. On the Sabbath they went outside the city to the river where the Jews met to pray. Paul sat down and began to speak about Jesus to some women who had gathered there.

Lydia was a businesswoman, a trader in expensive purple cloth. She already worshipped God, but as she listened to Paul and heard what he said about Jesus, she understood and believed that Jesus was God's Son.

After she and her family had been baptised, she invited Paul and his friends to stay as guests in her home.

There was a slave girl in Philippi who earned money for her owners by telling fortunes. Wherever Paul and his friends went, the girl followed them.

'These men are servants of the Most High God,' she told anyone who would listen. 'They can tell you how to be saved!'

Paul knew that the girl had an evil spirit in her and he wanted to help her.

'In the name of Jesus, come out of her!' he ordered.

The girl was healed immediately; and all her supernatural powers left her. When her owners realised what had happened, they were very angry. Now she was worth nothing to them!

The girl's owners took Paul and Silas to the marketplace and reported Paul and Silas as troublemakers. The crowd supported them and the magistrates ordered that they be beaten and thrown in prison – and to be guarded carefully.

The jailer made sure Paul and Silas had their feet fastened in the stocks in an inner cell. There would be no escape for them.

It was night. The prisoners were in darkness. But Paul and Silas were awake. They were not afraid. Instead they prayed and sang songs to God, listened to by the other prisoners.

Suddenly, every door in the prison burst open and the prisoners' chains came loose. A violent earthquake had shaken the foundations of the prison.

The jailer had been sleeping. When the earthquake woke him and he saw the prison doors open, his first thought was that his prisoners had escaped. He drew his sword to kill himself in a panic.

'It's all right! Don't harm yourself! We're all here!' shouted Paul. 'No one has escaped!'

The jailer stopped and brought lights so he could see. Then he fell to the ground in front of Paul and Silas.

'Tell me how I can be saved,' he asked.

'Believe in Jesus,' said Paul, 'and you and your family will be saved.' Then Paul and Silas told the jailer all about Jesus' death and resurrection and how the sins of all believers could be forgiven.

The jailer washed and treated the wounds the men had received from their beatings and asked to be baptised. Then he took Paul and Silas to his home and prepared a meal for them.

Every door in the prison burst open and the prisoners' chains came loose.

In the morning the jailer received a message that the men could be released, but Paul was angry. He told the officers who had come that they were Roman citizens and could not be treated so unjustly, to be beaten and imprisoned and released as if nothing had happened.

The magistrates had not realised they were Roman citizens and were frightened. They came to the prison anxiously and led them out, hoping there would be no more trouble. Then Paul and Silas went to Lydia's house for a while where they met with their friends before leaving Philippi.

Trouble seemed to follow Paul. When he talked about Jesus in Thessalonica, he caused a riot amongst some of the Jews. His friends encouraged him to go on alone until they could join him.

While he waited for them, Paul walked the streets of Athens, which was full of beautiful buildings, but he was very anxious when he saw how many idols the Greeks there worshipped.

In the synagogue Paul talked to the Jews; and in the market place he talked to the Gentiles; soon he was taken to the council of the Areopagus where the Athenians discussed all the latest ideas.

'Tell us about your ideas,' they invited him. 'These are new to us. We have never heard anything like them.'

Paul was pleased to explain his message to them.

'Men of Athens,' he started, 'I can see that you are a very religious people. As I walked around your city I saw many objects of your worship. I even saw an altar to an unknown god. Now you worship him as unknown, but I can tell you all about this God because I know who he is. The living God who made the earth and everything in it is so great he does not need to live in a temple made by the people he created, and he does not need anything from us. Rather, God himself gives us life and provides everything that we need. God made us so that we would seek him and find him, and he gave us his Son, Jesus, who rose from the dead, so that our sins could be forgiven.'

The people listened. Some wanted him to come back and tell them more; some sneered at his message and thought it nonsense; but some – Dionysius and Damaris among them – believed him and became followers of Jesus.

Paul went from Athens to Corinth where he met a tentmaker named Aquila and his wife Priscilla. They were among the Jews who had been ordered by Emperor Claudius to leave Rome. Paul stayed and worked with them, cutting and sewing goats' hair cloth to make tents.

Week by week, Paul went to the synagogue to preach and explain that Jesus was the one they had been waiting for, but few would listen and most were angry with Paul. So Paul spent most of his time in Corinth with Gentiles, who became believers and were baptised.

When Paul left Corinth for Ephesus, he took Priscilla and Aquila with him. He left them there while he sailed to Antioch. Priscilla and Aquila then welcomed Apollos, an Alexandrian Jew, into their home. Apollos was a believer and preached in the synagogue, but Priscilla and Aquila were able to encourage him and teach him more because of the time they had spent with Paul.

When Paul returned to Ephesus, he met twelve believers who had never heard of the Holy Spirit, even though they had been baptised. Paul explained to them about Jesus and when he put his hands on them, they were filled with the Holy Spirit.

For the next two years, Paul preached in the synagogue, read the Scriptures and talked in public places, so that as many people as possible could hear about Jesus. God worked

The believers also saw the power of God changing them and making them more like Jesus.

through Paul so that many sick people were cured just by touching cloths that Paul had touched. The believers also saw the power of God changing them and making them more like Jesus.

Then one day Demetrius, the silversmith, called together all the other craftsmen who, like him, made items to help people worship the god Artemis.

'This man Paul could stop us earning any money,' Demetrius said. 'He goes around telling people that there are no man-made gods, and lots of people, in Ephesus and beyond, believe him. We could lose our jobs and the great goddess Artemis will be forgotten.'

'Artemis is great!' the craftsmen chanted, walking through the city. Soon there was a riot and the crowd seized two of Paul's friends and dragged them to the theatre. Eventually an official stopped the riot.

'Ephesians!' he shouted. 'Our city is well known as the home of the great goddess Artemis. But these men have done nothing wrong. Demetrius must go through the courts if he has a complaint. You must let these men go before something happens that everyone will regret.'

The crowd dispersed and Paul's friends were released. But Paul decided it was time to move on.

Paul wrote to the Christians in Corinth while he was in Ephesus.

He had heard that some of the new Christians were jealous of each other and were arguing among themselves. Paul wanted to show

There was a riot and the crowd seized two of Paul's friends.

them how important it was for them to care about each other and work together peacefully:

'Christ is like one body that is made of many different parts. We were all baptised so that we are part of that body and we were all given the Holy Spirit.

'Each part of the body has its own special place; each part is important. If each part works and does its job well, the whole body works well, but if any part fails to do its job, the whole body suffers.

'So it's no good if the foot decides it cannot be a part of the body because it is not a hand; and it's no good if the ear decides it cannot be a part of the body because it is not an eye. If the whole body were an eye, it could not hear; if the whole body were an ear, it could not smell.

'In just the same way, one part of the body cannot decide that another part is not important or doesn't belong in the body. The eye cannot tell the hand that it is not needed; the head cannot tell the feet that they are not needed.

'Every one of you is part of the body of Christ. God has given each one gifts to use for the good of everyone else. We all need each other. We suffer together and we are happy together. God has given us each other so that his work can be done.'

Paul tried to explain in the same letter to the Corinthian Christians how God wanted them to behave so that others would know they loved him:

'I may be able to speak many languages; I may even be able to speak the language of angels; but if I cannot love, then all I do is make a loud and horrible noise!

'I may be able to prophesy the future and explain things that others find difficult; I may understand what others cannot know and have enough faith to move mountains – but if I have no love, I am nothing.

'Love is patient and kind. Love is not jealous, or conceited or proud. Love is not rude or selfish or bad tempered. Love doesn't get angry easily and it doesn't bear grudges.

If I have no love, I am nothing.

Love is generous and kind and forgiving. Love is only happy with the truth. Love always protects, always hopes and does not give up. Love never fails.'

While Paul was in Macedonia he wrote again to the Christians in Corinth:

'Let me tell you about some of the things I have done. Let me boast a little about what has happened to me since I first heard Jesus call me to follow him.

'I have worked harder than anyone, been in prison more often, been flogged more severely and been near death more times than I can count. On five occasions the Jews gave me thirty-nine lashes and I was close to death; on three occasions the Romans beat me with rods. Once I was stoned and three times I was shipwrecked. I have moved from place to place, unable to rest and live what most people call a normal life. I have been in danger from floods and from robbers, lived in fear of my fellow Jews and in fear of Gentiles. I have known danger in cities, danger in the countryside and danger at sea. I have sometimes not known whom I could trust. I have worked so hard I thought I could not survive it. I have often gone without sleep or food or water and known what it is to be hungry and thirsty. I have suffered cold and been without shelter or enough clothing.

'To stop me from becoming proud, God also gave me a thorn in the flesh. When I asked God to take it away, he told me that his grace was enough for all my needs. When I am weak, then I ask for his help and strength and he gives it. So –

whatever hardships or difficulties I endure, however weak I feel, I can be happy in them, because I know that it is then that God can make me strong.'

Everything in creation is waiting for that day when God will make all things perfect.

Paul was in Corinth when he wrote a long letter to the new Christians in Rome:

'I believe that anything we suffer now will seem as nothing compared with all the good things that wait for us in the future. Everything in creation is waiting for that day when God will make all things perfect. We are looking forward to that day too, when we will be changed and made perfect.

'We know that in everything God works for the good of the people who love him. And if God is on our side, who can fight against us? Who can separate us from God's love? Can trouble come between us and God? Can hardship or persecution, hunger or poverty, danger or death? No! Jesus loves us, and nothing can separate us from his love: whether we live or die, are in danger or trouble – not even angels or devils can separate us from God's love. Nothing that has ever been made can do that.

Paul travelled for a while, sometimes changing his plans suddenly when he was warned of plots against his life.

Then, staying briefly in Troas, Paul met one evening with some fellow Christians in an upstairs room. Paul knew that he would be leaving the next day, so he ate with them and they talked long into the night. He felt there was so much to tell them.

A young man called Eutychus was there with them, sitting on the windowsill listening to Paul. The room was lit by oil lamps and Paul talked on and on. Around midnight Eutychus became so sleepy that he lost his balance and fell out of the window. He died as he hit the ground.

Paul was overcome at the tragic accident. He rushed downstairs and threw his arms around Eutychus. As he did so, a miracle occurred – and Paul restored the dead man to life.

'It's all right!' Paul said to the other believers. 'He's alive!'

He lost his balance and fell out of the window.

The young man's friends had been very shocked. Now they were very relieved that Paul had been able to save Eutychus.

Paul went back upstairs and had something to eat. Then he continued talking about Jesus till dawn.

Paul knew that it was time he returned to Jerusalem. He also knew that it would be dangerous. The Holy Spirit had warned him that prison and hardships awaited him there.

After some time at sea, Paul landed at the port of Caesarea, and stayed for a few days with Philip, the evangelist, and his family. It was while he was there that a Christian called Agabus came to see Paul.

God had given Agabus the gift of prophecy. He took Paul's belt and tied up his own hands and feet with it so that he could not move.

'This is what the Holy Spirit says will happen to the owner of this belt when he goes to Jerusalem,' prophesied Agabus. 'The Jews in Jerusalem will capture him and give him to the Gentiles.'

All his friends were very anxious for Paul's safety. They begged him not to go on any further when they heard this. But Paul would not listen.

'You mustn't cry for me,' he said. 'I am prepared to die in Jerusalem for Jesus, if that's what lies ahead. But I must go.'

The believers knew that they could not stop him. Paul was determined.

'God's will be done,' they said, as they prepared to let him leave for Jerusalem.

Once in Jerusalem, Paul met his friends and told them about the thousands of people who had become believers in the places where he had travelled. They were as happy as Paul was about this and they praised God. But then they warned him that this very good news would cause problems for him. It would make him very unpopular with the Jewish leaders.

They were right. When Paul went to the temple, he was recognised.

'Look!' a group of men shouted. 'This is the man who tells people to ignore our Jewish customs!'

People rushed into the temple from all directions. They seized him and, dragging him outside the temple area, started to beat him to death. There was such an uproar that Roman troops were sent to stop the riot. As soon as the soldiers rushed into the crowd, the men attacking him stood back.

They started to beat him to death.

'Arrest this man and bind him in chains,' the Roman commander ordered. Then he asked the crowd what Paul had done.

Everyone in the crowd started shouting at once, but the commander could make no sense of what they were saying. It was chaos.

'Take him to the barracks,' the commander ordered. But the crowd became so noisy and violent at this that the soldiers had to carry Paul over the heads of the crowd.

Before they took him away, Paul asked the commander if he could speak to the crowd. He then turned to address them. He tried to explain how God had changed him from the person he was and then given him the task of speaking to the Gentiles about Jesus. But this was too much for the crowd.

'Get rid of this man!' they shouted. 'We've had enough of him. Put him to death!'

Paul was taken away. The orders were to flog him with the scourge – a cruel instrument of torture. But as they were preparing him, Paul asked whether it was legal to flog a Roman citizen who had not been found guilty of any crime.

The centurion stopped immediately. He told his commander that Paul was a Roman citizen. Suddenly everything changed. The commander questioned Paul himself and when he found that it was true, he released him.

A plot was then uncovered against Paul – forty Jewish men met secretly and sworn they would not eat or drink until Paul was dead...

'Prepare 200 soldiers, 70 horsemen and 200 spearmen,' the commander ordered. 'Nothing will happen to harm this man. He will be taken safely on horseback to Caesarea tonight!'

The commander sent a letter to Governor Felix explaining what had happened. He asked him to judge the case when Paul's accusers arrived there.

Five days later, Ananias, the High Priest, plus some elders and a lawyer called Tertullus arrived in Caesarea.

'This man is a troublemaker,' Tertullus said to Felix. 'Talk to him yourself; he will not deny that trouble follows him wherever he goes!'

Felix gestured to Paul to speak and defend himself.

The orders were to flog him with the scourge – a cruel instrument of torture.

'I had only been in Jerusalem for twelve days before I was taken prisoner,' Paul said. 'I have been guilty of nothing. I caused no riot or disturbance. I did not go around with a crowd causing trouble. But I am a

Christian, a follower of what is called here 'the Way', and I know that I have offended some people because I believe that there is life after death.'

Felix had heard of 'the Way' and adjourned the case. He kept Paul under guard but made sure his friends

Two years later, Paul was still in prison.

were allowed to see him and make him comfortable. Felix and his wife Drusilla even met Paul and listened to him as he talked about Jesus.

Felix waited. He hoped that Paul would offer him a bribe to release him. But he was wrong. So it was that two years later, Paul was still in prison.

Then a new governor took over. When Porcius Festus arrived, Paul's enemies tried to set a date for a new trial in Jerusalem. They planned to find a way to kill Paul on the journey there.

Festus refused. Instead he went with the Jewish elders to Caesarea and the new trial began. Still nothing could be proved.

'I have broken no Jewish law; I have not broken Caesar's law either,' insisted Paul. 'I am a Roman citizen and I have the right to appeal to Caesar.'

Festus talked with his council.

'You have appealed to Caesar,' he said. 'We have wasted enough time here. Now Paul, we are sending you to Rome! You have your wish.'

Paul was finally on his way.

A centurion called Julius took charge of Paul. He was put on a ship with his friend Luke and some other prisoners and they set sail for Italy. They sailed from port to port, but it was nearly the time of the autumn storms and the winds were against them. They made slow progress.

When they reached the island of Crete, Paul tried to warn Julius that lives could be lost in such bad conditions. Julius would not listen. They continued the journey.

Soon they were hit by a strong hurricane-force wind. The sailors struggled to keep the ship under control but they suffered so much damage they had to throw some of the cargo overboard. Then dense clouds made navigation impossible; the sailors could not see the planets and stars they needed to guide them. The ship was driven aimlessly by wind and waves.

Day after day the storm raged. The passengers were tossed up and down. No one ate. Everyone believed they would die – everyone except Paul.

An angel appeared to Paul one night and told him not to be afraid.

'You must go to Rome to stand trial,' said the angel. 'God will save the lives of all who sail with you.'

So Paul told the rest of the ship's passengers what the angel had said. The ship may well be lost – but they

would all be saved. He urged them all to eat and to save their strength.

There were 276 people on board the ship. When daylight came, they saw land but the ship had run aground and started to break up. The soldiers thought the prisoners would try to escape and made ready to kill them first – but Julius prevented them. Instead, everyone made their way to land, either by swimming or by clinging to pieces of the wreckage and drifting in to shore.

The soldiers thought the prisoners would try to escape and made ready to kill them first.

Rain was falling heavily and it was cold but the people who lived on the island rushed to the beach to help them. Paul and the shipwrecked men had landed on the island of Malta.

Soon they were huddled around an open fire. As Paul gathered some wood to add to the fire, a snake slithered out. It sank its fangs into his hand. The islanders who saw the snake whispered among themselves.

'This man has escaped from the sea only to be killed by a snake bite! He must be a murderer!'

But Paul shook off the snake and did not seem to be in pain. They watched and waited but Paul did not become ill or die.

'This man cannot be a murderer,' they said. 'Perhaps he is a god!'

The chief official in Malta was a man named Publius. He invited everyone to his home and made them welcome for three days.

During this time, Paul found that Publius' father was ill. He lay in bed, hot and feverish and suffering from dysentery. Paul went and prayed with him and God healed him. After that, many people on the island came to Paul with their illnesses and went away well.

When it was safe to resume their journey by sea once more, the people on the island made sure that they had all the supplies they needed. They sailed on an Alexandrian ship to Rome.

Paul arrived safely in Italy. He was placed under house arrest in Rome but was otherwise allowed to live freely.

First he called together the leaders of the Jewish population there. He explained to them why he

It sank its fangs into his hand.

had been sent there and tried again to help them see that Jesus was the one they had been waiting for. Some among them believed him; others were not convinced.

Paul now knew that his job was to reach the Gentiles in Rome with his message. For two years he welcomed people to his rented house and taught them all he knew about Jesus. Many believed what he had to say and were baptised.

Paul also wrote many letters to the Christians he had met over the years, helping them in their Christian faith and teaching them when they came to him with problems.

Paul knew that God had brought him to Rome for a purpose. He was there to preach the good news of Jesus – and he did, to anyone who would listen.

Chapter 31

ADVICE FOR NEW BELIEVERS

WHILE HE WAS A PRISONER IN ROME, PAUL WROTE TO THE CHRISTIANS IN EPHESUS:

'Since you are God's children, you must try to be like him. That means you should live your lives controlled by love, not hate, just as Jesus himself did. Jesus even gave up his life because he loved us.

'Don't be afraid to stand up against what is wrong. Be brave! Remember that God will look after you and give you power. Just as a soldier wears armour to keep him safe, you can wear God's armour:

wear truth like a belt around your waist; cover your heart with the breastplate of goodness; wear trainers so you can be ready to tell other people about the good news of Jesus when the opportunity arises; carry faith as your shield against doubt or attacks from others; accept as a

Carry faith as your shield against doubt.

helmet the salvation which Jesus bought with his life on the cross; and use God's word as your sword.'

One day a slave called Onesimus visited Paul in his house in Rome. Onesimus had run away from his master, but when he listened to all that Paul told him about Jesus, he became a Christian and asked to help Paul in his work.

Onesimus went with Tychicus to take a letter from Paul and his friend Timothy to the Christians in Colossae. Here is some of what it said:

'God is invisible – but Jesus shows us what God is like because he came to us in the form of a man.

'Once you were far away from God; you were his enemies because of the bad things you thought and said and did. Now, because Jesus took punishment for our sin when he was crucified, God has made you his friends.'

Onesimus still belonged to his master, Philemon, who was a leader in the church at Colossae. Onesimus had become a good friend while Paul was a prisoner, but he knew he could not let Onesimus stay in Rome. Paul therefore wrote a letter for Onesimus to take back with him:

'My dear friend Philemon, I have heard so much about your love for God and for other people. Now I need to ask you to do something for me. I am sending Onesimus back to you. But while he was away, he has become a Christian. Now he is not only your slave but your brother.

'Please welcome him back as you would welcome me into your home. If he owes you anything, I will pay it back. I hope to be able to visit you soon. Please get the guestroom ready for me!'

What is the purpose of our lives? Why are we here?

The Christians at Philippi also received a letter from Paul:

'What is the purpose of our lives? Why are we here? For me, it is to do what Jesus wants me to do. Yet if I die, that too is good, because then I will be with Jesus always. I cannot choose which is better: to live or to die!

'Make sure you live in a way that pleases God and shows other people that you belong to him. Don't be selfish or conceited, but be humble and think of others as better than yourself. Put other people first. Think about how Jesus treated other people and try to be like him.

'Jesus was the Son of God; he had the nature of God himself – yet he didn't behave as though he was above anyone or more important than the people he had come to serve. Instead he came to earth as a man and then acted as a servant. He allowed himself to be betrayed and humiliated, beaten and then unjustly executed as if he were a criminal. Jesus did not think about himself, but obeyed God. So God has given him the highest position in heaven and earth. One day, when people hear the name of Jesus, the whole world will bow down and call him Lord.

'So, there is nothing I want more than to know Jesus and share in his sufferings, even if it means that I die, because then I will also know his resurrection and eternal life. This is my aim in life: to follow Jesus to the end.'

Paul was not the only apostle to write letters to encourage other Christians. Peter wrote two letters:

'Some of you are suffering and going through difficult times because you are now Christians. Be happy that you are sharing in what Jesus suffered for you, but tell God all about your troubles because he cares about you.

'The time will come when everyone will know that God is king. But remember that God is outside time. For him one day is like a thousand years. It may be tomorrow; it may be after we have died. God is patient; he wants everyone to repent and know him; God wants no one to die without knowing about his love.

'When the final day comes, no one will expect it. The earth as we know it will be destroyed. There will be no warning. We must therefore live our lives so that we will not be ashamed when it happens. We must be ready for God to come in glory, and we can look forward to a new heaven and a new earth.'

Another long letter was written to help Jewish Christians.

'God's word is living and active, sharper than any sword, helping us to judge between right and wrong. We can hide nothing from God. But we do not need to be afraid, because we have a special high priest, Jesus, God's Son, who understands our human nature and sympathises with our weaknesses, though he himself did nothing wrong. We can always come to God with confidence and know that we will receive his mercy and that God will help us in our need.

'We are saved by God because we have faith. Faith is being sure of what we hope for, certain of what we do not see. We are part of a huge number of others who had faith before us – among them Abel, Enoch and Noah; Abraham, Isaac, Jacob and Joseph; Moses and the people with Joshua including Rahab;

Don't just talk about God's love! Show what it means by sharing.

all the faithful prophets and kings of Israel. So, with them, we must set out on the race God has set before us, throwing off all the sins that get in our way, and looking at Jesus, focusing on him as our finishing line. Be strong and don't get discouraged.'

John wrote at least three letters to the Christians in new churches.

'God is like light; there is no dark side to him. We must live in that light and not try to hide things from him. He wants us to be honest and confess our sins, not pretend we haven't sinned when we know we have. And if we do confess our sins and tell God we are sorry, then he will forgive us.

'Loving God means loving other people. It is wrong to hate someone. Hatred is a sin – and we need to confess that sin. God's love is so great that he calls us his children! Let's behave as if we are his children and love the other members of his family.

'We know what real love is by looking at Jesus. He gave up his life for us. We should be prepared to do that for someone else. If we have enough to eat and drink and a home to live in – and we know people who are starving or in any kind of need and we ignore them – then how can we say God's love is in us? Don't just talk about God's love! Show what it means by sharing what you have with people in need.

'We love other people because God first loved us. God is love. Now we must show that love to the people of the world by loving them in practical ways.'

CHAPTER 32
A VISION OF THE FUTURE

WHEN JOHN WAS AN OLD MAN, HE WAS SENT TO LIVE IN EXILE ON THE ISLAND OF PATMOS.

One day, when John was praying, the Holy Spirit revealed strange things to him. He gave John messages for the new churches in Ephesus, Smyrna, Pergamum, Thyatira, Sardis, Philadelphia and Laodicea. John wrote them down on a scroll so that the new Christians would be guided by them.

When John looked to see who was giving him the messages, he was amazed to see Jesus, not as he remembered him from when they worked together in Galilee, but shining like the sun, God in all his glory.

I was dead, but look, I am alive now and I will live for ever and ever.

The sight was so awesome that John fell at Jesus' feet. Then Jesus touched John's head gently and spoke:

'You don't need to be afraid, John,' he said. 'I am the first and the last, the Living One. I was dead, but look, I am alive now and I will live for ever and ever.'

John wrote down all that Jesus told him to say to the people in the seven churches. Then he looked up and saw a door opening into heaven.

'Come here!' said the voice that John had first heard. 'I will show you what will happen in the future.'

John no longer felt as if his feet were on the ground, but he saw everything clearly. He saw a magnificent throne surrounded by an emerald green rainbow with someone sitting on it, who seemed to shine like colourful precious stones. There were twenty-four other thrones and on each one there was someone dressed in white, wearing a golden crown.

The throne in the middle was God's throne. It flashed with light and John heard a sound like thunder. In front of it was a sparkling crystal sea.

Around the throne were four strange creatures, covered with eyes. They were like a lion, an ox, a man and an eagle, yet they each had six wings.

'Holy, holy, holy God, who was, and is, and is to come,' they sang. The sound of the music was heavenly.

The twenty-four people fell down before God and worshipped him.

Around the throne were four strange creatures, covered with eyes.

'You are worthy to receive glory and honour and power. You created everything, and everything lives and breathes because of you,' they said.

Then John saw thousands upon thousands of people from all over the world, dressed in white, and holding palm branches in their hands. They stood before God's throne, which was surrounded by angels and the four strange creatures, all worshipping him.

A man came from one of the thrones.

'These people are those who have suffered,' he told John. 'They have been saved because of the blood shed by Jesus, who is the Lamb of God.'

Later, John saw that the earth had gone, and that there was a new heaven and a new earth. He saw a wonderful new city.

'Now God will live among his people. They will know no more pain or suffering or death, no more sadness or weeping. God will wipe every tear from their eyes. From

They will know no more pain or suffering or death, no more sadness or weeping.

now on, everything will be made new! I am the first and the last, the beginning and the end. Anyone who comes to me will drink and never be thirsty again. I will be his God and he will be my child.'

Then an angel showed John the beautiful new city, with the water of life flowing in a sparkling river over which grew the tree of life. Its fruit brought healing and freedom to people of every race and colour and nation.

John could see that God's throne would remain in the city for ever and that God's people would always be with him. There would be no more darkness or night, for God himself would be their light.

Then Jesus spoke: 'I am coming soon! I am the first and the last, the beginning and the end. Anyone who wants to can come to me and they will be forgiven; and those who are forgiven will be happy. They will live in the city of God and enjoy life. Anyone who wants to can come and drink freely from the water of life. I am coming soon!'

MEHDI'S STORY

Julia Paillier

Mehdi's Story
Text copyright © Julia Paillier 2007
Illustrations copyright © Jacques Paillier 2007
Edited by Catherine White

First published and distributed in 2007 by Gatehouse Media Limited

Printed by Wallace Printers, Houghton

ISBN: 978-1-84231-029-8

British Library Cataloguing-in-Publication Data:
A catalogue record for this book is available from the British Library

A CD-ROM of tutor resources, mapped to the
ESOL Core Curriculum, is available
to support this publication.

Mehdi's Story Tutor Resources CD-ROM
ISBN: 978-1-84231-030-4

Gatehouse Media Limited provides an opportunity for writers to express their
thoughts and feelings on aspects of their lives. The views expressed are not
necessarily those of the publishers.

Author's Note

Mehdi's Story is about a young asylum seeker who wants to go to Canada, but finds himself in London without friends or family. It is suitable for beginner ESOL learners who may have basic literacy needs.

My thanks to Jacques Paillier for the line drawings. Thanks also to the young ESOL learners at Lewisham College who inspired *Mehdi's Story*.

Julia Paillier
ESOL Tutor

Chapter 1

I come from Afghanistan.
I have a mother,
a father
and a sister.

One day, the army come
to my house.
They take my father.

My mother says, "Go Mehdi.
Go to Canada.
Your aunty is in Canada."

A man says, "Come Mehdi.
I can take you to Canada."

It is night.

The man says, "Bye Mehdi.

This is Canada."

"Where is my aunty?"
A woman laughs,
"You are not in Canada.
You are in London.
You are in England."

Chapter 2

I say, "How can I get to Canada?"
The woman shakes her head.
She does not understand.

I walk for many hours.

The streets are noisy.

There are many cars.

There are many people.

I am tired.

I am cold and hungry.

I sleep.

"Wake up. Wake Up."

I see a bright light.

I see a man and a woman.

They are police.

"Afghanistan," I say.

"Afghanistan."

They take me
to the police station.
They give me a blanket.
They give me a hot drink and food.

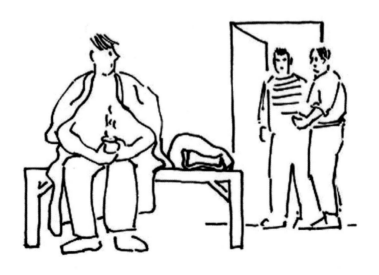

They bring another man.

He speaks Pashto.

I tell him about my father.

I say, "I want to leave Afghanistan."

He looks at the police.

"Mehdi is an asylum seeker,"

he says.

Chapter 3

I have a room.

The room is in Peckham.

Peckham is very noisy.

I can't sleep.

I have a social worker.
His name is Tom.
Tom is nice,
but he is very busy.

I have a solicitor in London.
The solicitor is very busy.

I don't have any friends.

There is a boy from Afghanistan
in the hostel.

The boy's name is Jamal.

He is tall and good-looking.

He has a girlfriend.

Tom says, "Go to college.
Learn English.
You need English
to live and work in the UK."

I go to college.
I like my class.
I am happy.
I have friends.

One day, Jamal says,
"Where are you going?"
I say, "I am going to college."
Jamal laughs.
His gold chain is bright in the sun.

I see Jamal on the bus.

Jamal shouts, "College boy!"

He laughs.

Jamal comes to my room.

He says, "Come with me tomorrow.

Don't go to college.

I can get you a job.

Don't tell your social worker."

I can't sleep.

I like my college.

I want to learn.

I like Jamal.

I want to work.

I need money.

I don't know what to do.

Gatehouse Books®

Gatehouse Books are written for older teenagers and adults who are developing their basic reading and writing or English language skills.

The format of our books is clear and uncluttered. The language is familiar and the text is often line-broken, so that each line ends at a natural pause.

Gatehouse Books are widely used within Adult Basic Education throughout the English speaking world. They are also a valuable resource within the Prison Education Service and Probation Services, Social Services and secondary schools - both in basic skills and ESOL teaching situations.

Catalogue available

Gatehouse Media Limited
PO Box 965
Warrington
WA4 9DE

Tel/Fax: 01925 267778
E-mail: info@gatehousebooks.com
Website: www.gatehousebooks.com